TRUE *Brew*

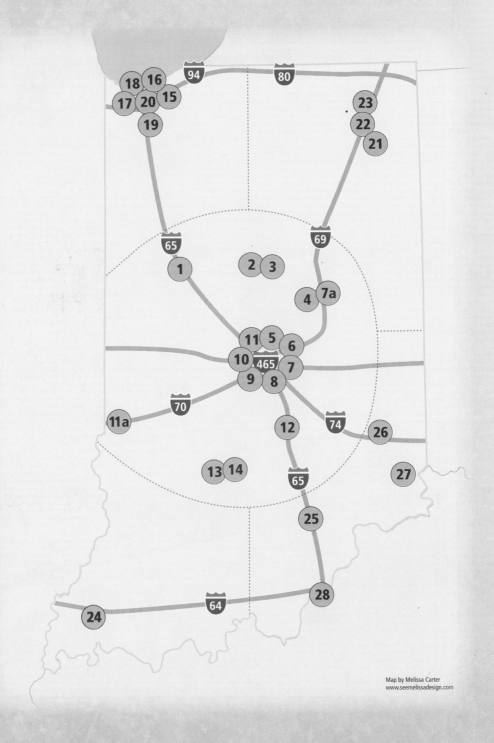

TRUE
Brew

A GUIDE to CRAFT BEER in INDIANA

RITA T. KOHN

Photographs by KRIS ARNOLD

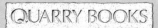 *an imprint of*   INDIANA UNIVERSITY PRESS
Bloomington & Indianapolis

This book is a publication of

Quarry Books

an imprint of

Indiana University Press
601 North Morton Street
Bloomington, Indiana 47404-3797 USA

www.iupress.indiana.edu

Telephone orders   800-842-6796
Fax orders   812-855-7931
Orders by e-mail   iuporder@indiana.edu

∞ The paper used in this publication
meets the minimum requirements of the
American National Standard for Information
Sciences—Permanence of Paper for Printed
Library Materials, ANSI Z39.48-1992.

Printed in China

Library of Congress Cataloging-in-Publication Data

Kohn, Rita T.
  True brew : a guide to craft beer in Indiana /
Rita Kohn ; photographs by Kris Arnold.
     p.   cm.
  Includes index.
  ISBN 978-0-253-22214-5 (pbk. : alk.
paper) 1. Brewing—Indiana. 2. Brewing
industry—Indiana. I. Title.
  TP573.U6K64 2010
  663'.4209772—dc22

                                        2009041896

1   2   3   4   5   15   14   13   12   11   10

To

Michael Jackson, who set the standard

Bill Friday, who inspired

John Hill, who acted

"We Make It, We Drink It, We Sell What's Left"

CRAFT BREWERS CREDO

Contents

Photographs

Foreword

A Belgian shoe manufacturer in the early 1950s sends his oldest son to the Belgian colony of Congo to prospect for new markets. The son comes back saying: "Dad, there is absolutely no market there. People don't wear shoes." Not happy with this result, the dad sends his youngest son to Congo. He comes back with a glow in his eyes, jumping in the air saying: "Dad, this is fantastic. There's an enormous market over there for us because people don't wear shoes!"

This story popped up in my mind so many times when new prospects told me: "We cannot sell specialty beer here. People don't drink that stuff." But the first craft brewers of Indiana, especially John Hill, the godfather of them all, the late Lauren Hansen and her husband, Tom, of BonVivant Libations, and Jim Schembre, the founder of World Class Beverages, had the same attitude as the youngest son in the shoe story. They had vision. They had passion. They dared to go the "other way." They BELIEVED that quality trumps quantity, that hard work and long hours pay off, that perseverance is the key to success. Such people are the true entrepreneurs, the driving force of this great country.

When my wife, Claudine, and I moved from Flanders in Belgium to California and started the Global Beer Network from scratch in 1994 to import the best Belgian beers to the United States, we arrived with the same passion and the same drive. It was the right time. Homebrewers were experimenting in every village and town. Passionate risk-takers were opening brewpubs. A few microbreweries were posting double-digit growth year after year. The five big breweries were competing against each other with the same yellow watery stuff. Their biggest invention at the time: light beer with even less taste.

What invigorated us, and the beer entrepreneurs of Indiana and other states, was the rediscovery by a small section of the public of taste, flavor, aroma, and age-old tradition in the healthiest beverage ever created by mankind: beer. Our Belgian beers, brewed for centuries, have all these qualities. To name only a few of these beers: Piraat, the historic triple IPA, the unique Scotch de Silly ale, the Wittekerke genuine Belgian Wheat beer, the hoppy Poperings Hommel ale, the superb Ename Triple Abbey ale, the Brugse Zot blond ale, the Troubadour mild stout, etc. They are all well-known Belgian icons. In concert with some fine English, Scottish, and German beers, the exceptionally wide range of Belgian beer styles lifted the horizon of the American craft brewers, gave them another perspective on beer, and launched them into experimenting to create great beer on their own.

Together with the beer entrepreneurs of Indiana and every other state, we spread the gospel of quality and excitement. We brought the treasure of rich flavors and satisfying tastes, all in combination with forgotten history and colorful tradition. We were the messiahs of the "new" beer, which was at the same time the beer that was brewed for centuries by mothers, by bakers, by monks and by nuns in their abbeys and monasteries, and by the hundreds of independent family breweries in Europe.

This great effort over the last twenty years is an ongoing game changer in the beer industry. Big breweries came around and are now brewing more tasty beers. Not one beer distributor can survive without a large selection of crafts and imports. Shelf space at every retailer must offer a wide selection of unique beers. The days are gone when restaurants and pubs only offered a maximum of five yellow and bland tasting beers with maybe one dark beer in the mix. The beer selection then was as boring and ridiculous as going to a fictitious ice cream parlor where five times the same va-

nilla flavor is offered plus only one chocolate flavor. If restaurants today don't have a wide range of beer styles, crafts and imports, they will not attract the young, the trendsetters, those ready to spend money on quality.

What an honor it was for both of us to have played a part in this exciting beer revolution. Make no mistake: the United States is today the best country in the whole world to enjoy good beer! What an unbelievably rich choice of excellent beer we have here! First: creative and passionate American brewers are turning out consistently quality brews. Second: the best beers from all over the world are imported and available to the American beer drinker. Beer as a beverage category offers the widest palate in flavor, taste, aroma, and history. No other category comes close. Beer is the best beverage to combine with your next dinner and lunch. Cheers to all the daring brewers in Indiana and to all the distributors and retailers proud to offer the best beers of the world to their clientele. Many more years! *Gezondheid,* as we say in Belgium.

Johnny Fincioen and Claudine Van
    Massenhove
Founders, Global Beer Network
Santa Barbara, California
June 27, 2009
www.globalbeer.com

Preface: Learning Our Story Is a Journey

Craft beer is a phenomenon across the United States, yet the public perception is that Indiana is off the map. For a state with a legacy as a major producer prior to Prohibition, that was a hard swallow for a Hoosier-state-based beer writer and a photo-journalist gearing up to honor the seventy-fifth anniversary of the repeal of Prohibition.

Indiana has a 200-year tradition of brewing practiced by people whose beer heritage was part of their cultural, social, and economic life as homebrewers and commercial brewers. It was part of everyday life as attested to by no less a luminary than nineteenth-century banker Calvin Fletcher, who migrated to Indianapolis in 1821 from Vermont. Fletcher became a leading citizen, practiced law, was active in a wide array of civic duties, held public office, and acquired extensive farm holdings, which he oversaw as a "husbandman." An avid diarist, Fletcher noted daily incidents including:

Monday, June 16, 1862
"On my return I turned off on the ledges to a place where I got some Petridge [partridge berry?] or winter greenbush for beer. Susan is to make some."
[Vol. VII 1861–1862, p. 446]

Wednesday, June 18, 1862
"On my return it began raining. I stopped on the ledges and got some Spruce to make beer having got heretofore Partridge Bush or winter green for this purpose. Susan made beer."
[Vol. VII 1861–1862, p. 448]

Tuesday, July 22, 1863
"I returned home. Wm. went and got a half barrel of Beer promised by Mr. Colgan. At 2 both haying parties The one under Mr. Colgan and the other under my charge met to finish. We did so at 6. All hands came to the stack sat down and enjoyed the Beer. It was not strong. [List of names of twenty-eight workers] We drank toasts etc. and I feel grateful we had brot this harvest to a close."
[Vol. VIII 1863–1864, p. 185]
[Calvin Fletcher Diaries are housed at the William Henry Smith Memorial Library of the Indiana Historical Society in Indianapolis]

"Feeling in the present" with Fletcher's diaries put us on the path of learning the stories of contemporary brewers. *NUVO Newsweekly* with Brewers of Indiana Guild convened the first Indiana Craft Beer Roundtable at the Indiana State Fairgrounds on March 15, 2008, to mark the eighteenth anniversary of both *NUVO* as a weekly newspaper with a distinctive voice for social justice and the arts and culture of greater Indianapolis and of Broad Ripple Brewpub as Indiana's first brewpub with its distinctive neighborhood ambiance leadership for growing the craft beer category.

The Roundtable's two-hour spirited conversation elicited spirited audience participation that continued with readers' comments following publication of the Roundtable's transcription in the April 9–16, 2009, edition of *NUVO Newsweekly*. Audience members and *NUVO* readers wanted more about Indiana's craft brewers "in their own voices." So we traveled to Indiana's five geographic sections—Central, Northwest, Northeast, Southwest, Southeast—to visit brewers at work in brewpubs, breweries, and in their homes to record their stories. We chronicled craft beer festivals whose individual and collective missions are to raise funds for philanthropic causes, educate our palates, and build a culture of responsible use. In the process of listening and documenting, we learned about communities and their intersections with brewing—past, present, and future. We found interconnections driving this fledgling industry and heard the trajectory of challenges and opportunities for growth. We witnessed the distinctive, vibrant aspect of craft brewing in Indiana rooted in the camaraderie between all brewers and warm relationships between homebrewers and professional brewers.

When we started in spring 2008, there were twenty-four Indiana-based brewpubs and breweries listed in the Brewers of Indiana Guild brochure. When we concluded interviews a year later, there were twenty-seven. One had closed, but four had opened, and just after the manuscript was completed we learned a fifth anticipated a September 2009 opening. Chris Johnson, a former brewer at Lafayette

Brewing Company, and Brett VanderPlaats announced People's Brewing Company in Lafayette is starting with draught accounts of their flagship German Pilsner, American Amber, and American IPA supplemented by seasonal lagers and ales. A bottling operation will follow. PBC brings back the name of a Terre Haute–based pre-Prohibition brewery.

Ensuring continued, responsible, community-centered growth of the craft beer category throughout Indiana is the basic mission of the Brewers of Indiana Guild, which was organized to provide a unifying voice for the microbreweries and brewpubs of Indiana. BIG, together with the regionally based homebrew clubs, promotes public awareness and appreciation for the quality and variety of beer produced in Indiana while endeavoring to bring benefits to the community through philanthropy, sponsorships of arts and crafts and organizations, economic development, academic research, and educational programs. Sustainability is a collective as well as an individual pursuit. Members of BIG and homebrew clubs along with suppliers and distributors utilize homegrown and locally produced products. There is a pattern for reclaiming and restoring buildings and neighborhoods, conserving energy, and pursuing alternative sources of energy.

The current craft brewing industry in Indiana reflects a balance between the neighborhood brewpub and a microbrewery that reflects the intent of the first and second established brewing operations in Indiana. John Hill founded Broad Ripple Brewpub to be solely a localized entity. Tom Schmidt opened Mishawaka Brewing Company to brew for both his brewpub and a bottling line for statewide distribution. This counters the prevailing post-Prohibition intent that centered on eliminating the neighborhood brewpub in favor of bottling. Consolidation of operations led to macrobreweries, which in turn led to Indiana's decline as a beer-producing presence. *True Brew* brings forward the newest story of a valiant, vigorous return to Indiana's original roots, one brewpub, brewery, and homebrewer at a time.

True Brew does not strive to be all-inclusive, encyclopedic, or definitive as history but rather to be representative of the people involved in the various facets of the craft category—homebrew supply stores and homebrewers, legal aspects involving the state of Indiana, beer judging and competitions, distributors and point of sale stores, restaurants that bring in their company beer brewed elsewhere, homebrew clubs, brewpubs, breweries, and brewers. In every case it was the distinctive voice of the individual we sought to convey to you, the reader. To that end, oral history recordings were transcribed verbatim and verified by each interviewee prior to inclusion. Photographs represent the individuals at work and the products they share. Throughout, it's a dynamic introduction to the people, their passion, and their purpose during one particular year, spring 2008–spring 2009. For the most current events concerning Indiana craft beer, log on to www.brewersofindianaguild.com.

Part 1 opens with Bob Ostrander's brisk history of brewing—worldwide and down home—followed by the gathering of brewers for Indiana's first-ever roundtable, where we feel the energy of the current industry. Homebrewer Paul Edwards describes the interface with state legislators and the importance of the Indiana State Fair Brewers' Cup Craft Beer Competition at the beginning of Indiana's presence in the category. Through Joan Easley and Anita Johnson, we learn of the core importance of homebrew supply stores to reinvigorate craft beer in Indiana. We learn too of the individuals who "made the difference"; names that we'll continue to hear throughout the book.

Part 2 shares the stories of homebrewers and professional brewers within five regions. We invite you to follow our journey and visit each brewpub and brewery within each region by branching off from the major highways that have come to define the regions: Central (a hub encompassing I-65, I-69, I-74, I-70); Northwest (a trajectory off I-65, I-90, I-94, I-80); Northeast (a cluster off I-69, I-469); Southwest (stops off I-64, I-164); and Southeast (splits off I-74 and I-65, I-265).

Part 3 brings us back to the beginning and the challenge put forth by Jim Schembre at the Indiana Craft Beer Roundtable: "It's important to have a local brew with a local personality. You have to put your story on the bottle. You have to put a face on the name of the beer, clearly define your difference." Jim Schembre's point is carried forward by Penn Jensen, Andy Klotz, Cari Crowe, and Mat Gerdenich, as they each put forward how "Indiana can get a bigger share of the market."

True Brew started with questions: "What is happening in Indiana seventy-five years after the repeal of Prohibition? Who is making beer? Where are they making it? Why? How is it getting from the brewer to us? When will Indiana craft beer be "on the map"?

Circuitously, *True Brew* brings us to our collective, connective beginnings with Calvin Fletcher reportedly active in the Indiana Temperance Society. He not only fits the profile of today's craft brewer in utilizing local ingredients and as an advocate for consuming with a keen sense of responsible use, but he equally echoes the spirit of beer's earliest history as payment for work well done.

At the completion of the work we set out to accomplish, we too can report, "All hands came to the stack sat down and enjoyed the Beer. . . . We drank toasts etc. and [we] feel grateful we had brot this harvest to a close."

Rita Kohn
Kris Arnold
Indianapolis
June 2009

Acknowledgments

The people whose stories and photographs appear in this book have our sincerest appreciation. They gave of their time and opened their hearts. They entrusted us with their life stories. We cherish the gift and return a small portion through sharing of royalties toward the Brewers of Indiana Guild scholarship fund.

Bob Mack, whose boundless enthusiasm for and knowledge about the craft beer industry inspired us to undertake this book, initially helped outline its parameters as a contemporary view of the craft category in Indiana. Bob introduced us to Johnny Fincioen and the Global Beer Network tour of Belgian breweries. Bob stepped back from full partnership when work and family required the time and attention he would have given to the book.

NUVO Newsweekly, Brewers of Indiana Guild, and Indiana State Fair sponsorship of the Roundtable helped make viable this project to collect the oral histories of Indiana craft brewers. We are grateful to Ted Miller, president of BIG, for helping to organize the Roundtable and for continuing to assist in countless ways. Our colleagues at *NUVO,* including Kevin McKinney, Jim Poyser, Amy Crook, Sarah Meyer, Melissa Carter, and the entire production team became enthusiastic partners.

Bob Ostrander has been a constant source of verification in addition to providing the overview history of brewing. Paul Edwards particularly helped us understand the influence of homebrewers and Bill Friday's abiding role. Tom Stillabower has been unflagging in cheering us on. Jef Versele of Brewery Van Steenberge immediately embraced the idea of first-person stories as a way of bringing Indiana's craft brewing story to a global audience. His hospitality is warmly recalled.

Linda Oblack at Indiana University Press believed in this project from the outset. She has played an integral role in making this book a reality and a visual treat. Peter Froehlich assisted in essential tasks, including a marathon weekend to meet deadlines.

Thanks go to Michael Naish for his assistance and companionship as we made the journey to photograph brewpubs and breweries across northern Indiana, traversing back and forth until we ended at Dark Lords Day.

Gray Bowman rescued and nurtured the manuscript through all sorts of computer glitches.

Our families have put up with absences with good grace as we traveled throughout the state and labored at computers.

Andy Hein earns our abiding gratitude for his devotion to the project and his input to make this book exciting.

Throughout, Anita Johnson and her staff at Great Fermentations, and the members of the Brewers of Indiana Guild and of home-brew clubs have been stalwart supporters, as have been the members of the distribution and retail industry. The Hoosier Beer Geeks have been a delightful source of encouragement. *True Brew* reflects their passion and mirrors their humanity.

We remain grateful to each other for the collegiality and friendship throughout these intense two years. Collectively, we've had a wonderful experience.

Rita Kohn
Kris Arnold

1

The Background

A History of Brewing: From Iraq to Indiana in 120 Centuries
Bob Ostrander

THE MEDITERRANEAN

Twelve thousand years ago, give or take a couple of months, beer was first brewed by a woman in Mesopotamia (now Iraq). It was probably just bread that got wet and fermented, and it was no doubt pretty horrible stuff, but it was interesting enough to make more. It isn't far-fetched to claim the people of the time liked their brew well enough to stop hunting and gathering and settle in one place in order to tend crops.

In fact, barley may have been one of our ancestors' first cultivated crops. Wild barley is brittle, and when ripe, the seeds fall to the ground. By replanting the ripe grain that remained on the stalk ancient man made the job of harvesting easier—at least easier than separating the barleycorns from dirt. Archaeologists have found domesticated barley near Jericho that dates back to about 9000 BC.

Why ferment? Plain water wasn't necessarily good for you—open sewers and all. Besides, beer, wine, mead, and cider taste better. Then there's the alcohol. Not just for the buzz, alcohol also means calories—something you need if you scratch furrows in the dirt for a living.

A stone tablet unearthed in 1981 describes fermentation in Sumeria (now Iraq) around 6000 BC. There is a recipe for beer from that area written about 4000 BC. It shows barley and pictographs of bread being baked and crumbled into water. The result is translated as "exhilarated, wonderful, blissful." Written on small clay tablets, these are now at the Louvre in Paris.

By 2000 BC the people of Babylonia (yep, another name for Iraq) had at least twenty styles of beer and exported it as far away as Egypt. A tablet in New York's Metropolitan Museum lists Babylonian beers translated as dark beer, pale beer, red beer, threefold beer, beer with a head, beer without a head, and others. They drank it through a straw (probably to roughly filter out the chunks).

When Khufu's men built the Great Pyramid at Giza, he had barley fields planted to provide them with beer. Beer was buried with the pharaohs. Ramses II had strict laws about how beer was to be brewed. It's thought he offered up thousands of gallons each year to appease the gods.

Hammurabi put down the first written laws (again in Babylon) around 1700 BC, and they

5

included a guaranteed daily ration of beer for all citizens. Workers got about two liters, civil servants three liters, priests five liters. These laws also set down rules for pricing of grain and beer and acceptable contents of wort for different styles of beer. Stone tablets of Hammurabi's code were found in 1902 and are now at the Louvre.

The Romans picked up brewing from the Egyptians through the Greeks, but replaced it with wine making once they got the idea of fermentation. Actually, beer was rarely brewed in Rome, and it was considered gauche. But the Romans did take the art of brewing north of the Alps to areas where barley was easier to grow.

Around AD 100, the Roman historian Tacitus wrote about the Germanic tribes, "To drink, the Teutons have a horrible brew fermented from barley or wheat, a brew which has only a very far removed similarity to wine."

Who was doing this "brewing"? It was the same people who were doing the rest of the cooking and cavehold chores—the women of the family. Tribes would keep some grain back for brewing in the winter when the climate was cooler and more suitable to fermentation—another reason to move from a hunter-gatherer existence to an agrarian society.

BEER COMES TO EUROPE: FAMILIES, ABBEYS, AND COURTS

Once Rome fell, the Middle Ages took over in Europe, and monks were "guardians of literature and science." Heck, they were the only literate people around. Kings and court hangers-on couldn't read. They couldn't write down a recipe. Only in the monasteries were people smart enough to brew beer. They used this near-monopoly in Germany, Belgium, and other Northern European areas to raise money.

Most abbeys had gardens and made beer to meet St. Benedict's decree that each abbey needed to be economically viable. Beer was sold in the nearby towns, and strong beers, like doppelbocks, were brewed by brothers mainly as a Lenten food.

The next step in the evolution was also invented by monks—the public bar. Monasteries had long been the hotel chains of Europe where travelers, mainly pilgrims, could get lodgings, food, and drink. If you could speak Latin or had a suit of armor, these early B&Bs sure beat a night under a tree listening to wolves howl. Kloisterschenken were formed at many monasteries where they could sell beer to passers-by and even to local citizens

Weihenstephaner has been in the German town of Freising since 1040. "Alteste Brauerei der Welt." Yep, the oldest brewery in the world. They are already making plans to celebrate its one-thousandth birthday. Hope to be around for the party. Monks were brewing beer on this site while England was still run by the Saxons. In North America, people were building mounds, making arrowheads, and trading mica. Natives may have been fermenting grain, but they didn't pass down the tradition to following brewers like they did in Freising. Sure, there have been changes. They didn't use hops in 1040. They didn't know what yeast was. All the buildings have been completely rebuilt. It's now owned by the Bavarian government rather than the Catholic Church. But that, in microcosm, is how the art of brewing evolved.

BREWING AS A BUSINESS

By the 1200s, brewing was not done only by the Church. Respectable professionals were brew-

ing in many cities in Germany. These were going to have a drastic effect on the monasteries, since the lay-brewers paid taxes on their beer. Kaiser Sigismund in the 1410s was the first to stop the public accessibility to cloister breweries—simply because they refused to be taxed and every drop they sold meant a drop of taxed beer wouldn't be sold.

In Bohemia, now the Czech Republic, some families discovered the advantages of larger production runs by building communal breweries that produced wort (the sugary liquid that is fermented into beer) that would be taken home by members for finishing. This is a practice still followed in eastern Germany.

In the 1600s and 1700s, royal courts took over much of the wealth of the monasteries, including their business interests such as brewing and baking. Courts bought existing breweries or started their own.

By 1800 only a few monasteries were left in Church hands. Today there are only seven that brew beer.

Wilhelm V took the opportunity of a fire in his castle in 1589 to build a new brewery in downtown Munich. Sometimes he would stop in with some friends, and quickly the brewer set up a drinking room for the boss. It was 1610 before the public was allowed to drink the royal beer, when the brewery was expanded and a real brauhaus was added. Today

The Background

that is the most famous pub in the world, the Hofbrauhaus.

The Confederation of Belgian Brewers in Brussels has had a guild house on the Grand Place since 1695. The Maison des Brasseurs is located in truly a premier spot, directly next to city hall on the most elegant square in northern Europe.

THE BRITISH ISLES

Across the channel, wheat was being used in the British Isles before the Romans brought barley with them. The patron saint of Glasgow, St. Mungo, was known to be a brewer in the sixth century AD. There is evidence of crude brewing in Scotland with grains, honey, and herbs as early as 4000 BC.

During the Middle Ages, monasteries weren't quite so powerful or commercial in England. Most brewing was done by individuals and coaching inns or on estates. It was fashionable to have a house brewery to impress visitors, but most of the beer was consumed by the staff and field hands as part of their pay.

Aberdeen records show 152 professional brewers in 1509—all women. Edinburgh had more than 300. London had about 290 breweries—110 run by men, 180 by women. Almost all of these were one-person enterprises. If the brewery was at a private home, an "ale wand" was hung outside the house when beer was available for sale—the origins of the British pub.

NORTH AMERICA

Columbus, on his last voyage, recorded native Indians making beer from corn and tree sap (thought to be the black birch). He compared it to English beer, but he was Italian, so what did he know? Both Sir Walter Raleigh's colony in Virginia (1587) and the Jamestown settlement (1607) had breweries. In the early 1600s, a commercial brewery was opened in New Amsterdam (New York City to us) after a brewer came over from London in response to an ad in the newspaper.

Stories that the Pilgrims cut short their trip in 1620 and landed on Plymouth Rock because they were running out of beer should probably be discounted, since there are many myths about the Pilgrims that just don't hold up. But we can reasonably believe they did set up a brewery in Massachusetts shortly after they landed.

By 1674 Harvard College had its own brewery, and by 1680 William Penn owned a commercial brewery.

George Washington had a brewery at Mount Vernon, but it was only for the family's consumption. He has passed down a recipe for small beer. Thomas Jefferson had a private brewery at Monticello. By the way, Samuel Adams's reputation as a brewer is mostly exaggerated. He did inherit a commercial brewery in Boston, but there are no records of him ever lifting a mash paddle.

If you are interested, here's George Washington's recipe:

TO MAKE SMALL BEER

Take a large Siffer [Sifter] full of Bran Hops to your Taste.—Boil these 3 hours then strain out 30 Gall[ons] into a cooler put in 3 Gall[ons] Molasses while the Beer is Scalding hot or rather draw the Molasses into the cooler & St[r]ain the Beer on it while boiling Hot. let this stand till it is little more than Blood warm then put in a quart of Yea[s]t if the Weather is very Cold cover it over with a Blank[et] & let it Work in the Cooler 24 hours then put it into the Cask—leave the bung open till it is almost don[e] Working—Bottle it that day Week it was Brewed.

As Europeans moved west across America, they took brewing with them. A small frontier town that could offer beer could be as proud as a modern city is of their NFL team. This was even more prestigious than having a distillery, since freshness is needed for beer whereas whiskey travels well.

> The first brewery in Richmond was commenced by Ezra Boswell about the time the town was incorporated *(in 1818)*. Of the quality of the beer we have now no opportunity of forming a judgment, but it is said that some of the Councilmen of that day—who, of course, served their fellow-citizens gratuitously—one day sent to Ezra for some of his brewing, and we presume, they quaffed it until they were satisfied, but, like all men in place, they, by this simple act, subjected themselves to the tongue of slander. By the citizens, who took it upon themselves to watch over the pecuniary interests of the place, a rumor was set afloat that the Councilmen were drinking beer at the expense of the corporation.
>
> The price of beer, sold at taverns, was in that day fixed by the court at 12½ cents a quart, while the same authority rated whiskey, per half-pint, at 12½ cents, the same quantity of common brandy, at 18¾ cents, and cognac, rum, and wine were to be sold at 37½ cents by the half pint. The care of the Court in this particular is further evinced by their allowing George Hunt, clerk, a certain sum for the purchase of whisky, during the sale of lots in Salisbury.
>
> (John Plummer, *Reminiscences of the History of Richmond*, 1857. It is thought that a tavern had been opened in Richmond in 1816 by Philip Harter in a log building.)

Other early Indiana breweries sprang up along the lines of civilization's advance—eastern and southern Indiana first and then moving north. Much of the detail of these early breweries has been lost, but we know of dozens that made an impact on their towns.

1820—Cambridge City—Owned by Henry Ingermann, an immigrant from Germany.

1820s—New Harmony—The Rappite colony had a brewery and two distilleries. After all, it was to be a utopian society.

1823—Madison—The Jacob Salmon Brewery became the Madison Brewing Company, which distributed Madison XXX beer as far away as New Orleans. It closed at the onset of Prohibition in 1919.

1830s—New Alsace (near Batesville)—Owned by Charles Zix, an immigrant from Baden-Baden, Germany.

1831—LaPorte—A brewery existed north of the courthouse in an area called "Ten Mile Strip." LaPorte's streets weren't laid out until 1833.

1833—Dover (near Batesville)—Owned by Balthasar Hammerle. "His occupation was tailoring, but this proved to be unprofitable, so he built a brewery—the first in Indiana [*sic*]. He managed this business until 1856, when he turned over the business to his son."—J. Wilbur Jacoby, *History of Marion County, Ohio, and Representative Citizens*, 1907

1834—Indianapolis—William Werweg, a contractor for the National Road, and John L. Young established the first brewery in Indianapolis. It closed about 1842.

1837—Terre Haute—Chauncey Warren and Demas Deming started the Terre Haute Brewing Company, which became the seventh largest brewery in the United States. It has been through six hands and two downsizings, and some parts are still brewing beer today, although the Champagne Velvet name is no longer used.

1840—Lawrenceburg—Owned by John Garnier, an immigrant from France. Enlarged in 1866, but closed at the onset of Prohibition. It was sending beer as far away as Fort Wayne.

1840—New Albany—Hew Ainsle left the New Harmony community to open breweries in Cincinnati, Louisville, and then New Albany. That one was destroyed by fire in 1841.

1840s—Michigan City—Owned by Christian Kimball and operated by his sons.

1842—Tell City—Wendel Hofmann moved from Darmstadt, Germany, to open a brewery that lasted until 1868.

1843—Goshen—Cephas Hawks operated a sawmill, woolen mill, store, tannery, ashery, and a brewery in Waterford, a small community south of Goshen.

1843—Aurora—Thomas and James Gaff opened a distillery in 1843 and complemented that with the Great Crescent Brewery in 1873. They went on to become the leading citizens (and employers) of the town. The brewery was big enough to export beer to Germany and send it to the silver mines in Nevada in the late 1800s. An explosion in the brewery killed two people, and it was sold to an English syndicate in 1899.

1845—Newtown (near Batesville, but no longer existing)—Owned by John Beckenholdt. He died in 1860, and the brewery and town seem to have gone with him.

1848—Lafayette—Wagner & Herbert Co.—It closed during Prohibition, but reopened as the Lafayette Brewery, Inc. Owner John Wagner, an immigrant from Weimar, Germany, changed partners from Dietrich Herbert to Frederick Thieme in 1862 and went on to become one of the most prosperous citizens of Lafayette with interest in several banks. It was reorganized through a subsidiary, the Lafayette Ice and Coal Co., after Prohibition, but closed in 1952.

1850—Indianapolis—Indianapolis Brewing Company—The IBC was formed by merging three breweries in 1887, the oldest being the C. F. Schmidt Brewing Company, which started in 1850. They closed the doors of this institution in 1948 when a federal judge ordered the company seized to pay tax debts.

The Saint Meinrad Archabbey in southern Indiana started a brewery in 1860, but the beer was so bad that the brewery was closed in 1861.

TIME MARCHES ON

At about this same time, other German immigrants started Anheuser-Busch, Miller, Coors, Stroh, Schlitz, and Pabst. The late 1800s saw refrigeration, automatic bottling, pasteurization, and distribution by double-walled, ice-cooled railroad boxcars. In the 1870s, this allowed Adolphus Busch to make Budweiser a national brand.

The most far-reaching factor affecting beer in the United States was the Eighteenth Amendment enacting Prohibition on October 3, 1919. By that time, twenty-six of the forty-eight states already were "dry" by local laws. Heck, three had already gone dry by 1905. Oklahoma and Kansas didn't go back to "wet" status until 1948 and Mississippi not until 1966. Today you still see dry counties in many states in the South.

Before Prohibition, breweries were consolidating, but when the Twenty-first Amendment ended Prohibition on December 4, 1935, only half of the breweries reopened. St. Louis, for instance had twenty-two before Prohibition, but only nine reopened afterward.

1880—2,300 breweries in the United States
1914—1,400
1935—160

WWII shortly followed, and this sent many more breweries out of business. In the 1950s and 1960s, another spate of local breweries bought by national giants such as Falstaff and Heilman left the United States with less than a dozen brewing companies by 1968.

In Indiana the Terre Haute Brewing Co., Indianapolis Brewing Co., Lafayette Brewing Co., Drewrys in South Bend, Kamm's in Mishawaka, Falstaff and Hoff-Brau in Fort Wayne, and F. W. Cook and Sterling breweries in Evansville were around in the 1950s. The last of the old-line brewing plants in Indiana, Sterling, closed its doors in 1997. By that time fifteen microbreweries and brewpubs had opened, starting the modern era of microbrewing.

www.indianabeer.com
www.BrewersofIndianaGuild.com

Brew Heads: Local Brewers Gather for First-Ever Roundtable

On March 15, 2008, the first NUVO-sponsored Indiana Craft Beer Roundtable was convened at the Indiana State Fairgrounds. Microbrewers, homebrewers, and beer aficionados were in attendance. This is a transcript of their lively conversation.

ANITA JOHNSON, OWNER OF GREAT FERMENTATIONS, SERVING AS MODERATOR: The reason for this first annual Indiana Craft Beer Roundtable is that eighteen years ago, *NUVO Newsweekly* and Broad Ripple Brewpub [BRBP] started quietly, without much fanfare, and both have had an impact on the community. NUVO has influenced arts and culture and what's going on in the community, and BRBP has influenced a lot of people who had their first taste of good beer at the brewpub. Now we have brewpubs all across the state. But it all goes back to BRBP.

Over the past eighteen years, both NUVO and the craft beer industry have engaged us with their philanthropy and civic responsibility and the love of craft.

We'll talk today about the love of craft.

Let's start by introducing the panel of brewers:

Eileen Martin, Upland Brewing Company, Bloomington

Jon Myers, Power House Brewing Company, Columbus

Ted Miller, Brugge Brasserie, Broad Ripple & Production Facility, Terre Haute

Greg Emig, Lafayette Brewing Company

Kevin Matalucci, Broad Ripple Brewpub

Paul Edwards, homebrewer, member of Foam Blowers of Indiana and Central Indiana Alliance of Beer Judges

Clay Robinson, Ram Restaurant & Brewery [as of 2009 co-owner of Sun King Brewery]

Omar Castrellon, Alcatraz Brewing Company

Jim Matt, homebrewer, member of MECA

JOHNSON Let's go back to the beginning. John Hill started this with the BRBP. We have three brewers from BRBP: two former brewers and one current. Talk about the beginning of the brewpub.

EMIG I went down and met John Hill. I'd heard rumors of him starting a brewpub in Indianapolis. I got onboard as fast as I could. I was a homebrewer. I wanted to be part of the first brewpub in Indiana. Unfortunately, John had hired a brewer the day before I met him. So I went ahead and worked with John as a laborer doing construction at the brewpub and then worked as a manager and bartender when

BRBP first opened up. After a while I started up my own brewpub project.

Then John called me back. The brewer he'd hired took a job in Germany, so I quit my job the next day and started working with John. It was great being at the first place in Indiana where people could come in and order a pint of beer and sit across the bar from you, and you could see them enjoying a craft beer, and being able to educate the public about the different styles and how good fresh beer can be. John had an innate taste for what he liked to drink and had enough basic brewing knowledge, so between us, we could put together a top-quality product.

MILLER My personal story of this is I lived and grew up about five blocks away from Broad Ripple Brewpub. I was at school at IUPUI. I drove by the building one day and saw there was a brewery open, so I drove home as fast as I could and said to my mom, "There's a brewery

five blocks away. I'm going to work there." I had one problem. I was 20. I went over there day after day. Finally, one day John [Hill] said to me, "If you don't come back until October, you'll have a job."

I was fascinated by this whole idea of a tiny brewery in my neighborhood. Greg [Emig] started me into the craft. Then Paul Edwards got me into the scientific aspects and into the idea of a career. I think BRBP changed a lot of people's lives.

MATALUCCI It was a love of craft. I started working there as a server, and after four or five months I was tending bar, and once Ted had left, John hired me as a brewer, and I've been there ever since.

EDWARDS I remember when it [BRBP] was Broad Ripple Auto Parts. It's a mile from my house. And now I have two brewpubs. The other one is Brugge. It's three-quarters of a mile from my house. Now I can walk up the street and have the good fortune to drink with these two guys [indicating Kevin and Ted]. Let me tell you, it's a lot of work. I would not want to be a pub owner because I don't have the back for it. It's a lot of work and a lot of dedication year-round. I'd been hoping for it for a long time. And now it's like I could quit homebrewing.

[Laughter]

JOHNSON There's a lot of status for being a brewer. People come into my store and say, "Well, Ted said dot, dot, dot." There's a lot of technology, and it takes being able to fix things. You can't make many mistakes in brewing beer and make it profitable. You might want to talk about that.

MATALUCCI Besides what else you've got going on any brew day, you have to be an electrician and a plumber, so you definitely have to be hands-on.

EMIG You know John didn't have someone come in and install the brewery. It was very much John hands-on. It was hodge-podge equipment, putting things together and making it flow. Engineering. Get into a rhythm. Not spend a lot of time. I learned a lot from John. When I started my own business, I didn't have to spend a lot of capital. I didn't have assets to order brewery equipment so I could put things together. You have to be able to fix things.

MILLER I've known a lot of brewers starting like that, and I've seen a lot of brewers using other people's money for a really fancy brewery. I was in China. You get that fancy equipment. They don't know how to fix it.

JOHNSON Jon, talk about being a homebrewer to being one of Indiana's smaller brewpubs.

MYERS I want to add to what Kevin was talking about being a jack-of-all-trades. The equipment we put together we've had to figure out how to use it over the past nine months. On top of that I'm tending bar, brewing, mopping floors.

[Laughter]

ROBINSON Part of what's true about all brewers that I know is that it's the whole workload —everyone working together. When people ask, "What do you do all day?" Sure, it's a craft, and you make things, but that's only part of it.

MATALUCCI The best brewers that I've met have enthusiasm for what they do. One of the things John offered me—he was so enthusiastic about the whole craft beer industry— call it microbrewery or craft brewery. We'd drive out to the Great American Beer Festival. It was twenty hours to Denver, but he'd talk to other brewers about equipment, what works, what doesn't, interact with a lot of people. John loved to travel. He went to Denver; he went to Boston, Madison, Wisconsin. We had a great time traveling around the country, being able to interact with all the small brewers, exploring the system, going to other places.

JOHNSON One of the things that impresses me about the industry is you are all kind of competitors, you are what you are, yet you share information between each other and support each other. You might want to talk about that, how you all share.

MILLER Here's a great story. Not everyone knows about the hops shortage right now. Two weeks ago, Samuel Adams, the biggest craft brewer, sent an email: "We have some extra hops. You guys tell us what you want. If there's too many who want to buy, we'll have a lottery."

EMIG They've had requests for over 100,000 pounds, and they're still coming in. The story is generosity to help competitors at cost.

MATALUCCI At $20 per pound, that's a pretty good sport.

[Laughter]

MARTIN Considering supply and demand, they could ask for a lot more. To offer that up at cost, that's generosity.

MATALUCCI For us here, it's interacting with one another. Talking, sharing recipes and ideas.

ROBINSON Downtown we've got Alcatraz, Rock Bottom down the street. People come over to the Ram, you start talking to them about beer. They ask about pale ale, and if I don't have any, I can say, "Look, you need to go over to Alcatraz or Rock Bottom." We send people to other places. Hey, it's collaboration. Say you come in and start brewing, and you think you've got 150 pounds of malt and find you don't, so you can call down the street and get what you need. It's a pretty small club. When you talk about brewers, you see what kind of camaraderie you have to have. We're not competitors. We have to help each other. It's a relationship.

JOHNSON That brings up a great point. That is, when you find you have several brewpubs in one area, you draw tourism to that area.

ROBINSON In each area—downtown, Broad Ripple—there's so much variety of beers, Belgian-style brewpub, American-style brewpub, English-style brewpub. People travel for that type of thing. Downtown we have different styles of pubs along Massachusetts Avenue and Fountain Square where you have unique places like Rathskeller. You get a synergy.

AUDIENCE Is there a profile of a craft beer consumer?

EMIG We looked at our customer base. We're talking about people who are university-related; we're talking about students, faculty, staff; we're talking about downtown businesspeople, local Lafayette workers and construction guys. We're talking about job diversity, age diversity. It's still a niche thing, but I don't think it has any real definable parameters.

MILLER It's a wide demographic.

ROBINSON I didn't think of craft beer as being important to people who are traveling, but travelers who come here like to taste different craft beer. It's important to them that we have this diversity here.

EDWARDS One thing I realized: when you stick to the same pub, when you've got a neighborhood pub, you see the same people. When the BRBP was brand-new, people were unsure about the beer they were drinking. When you see the same people over a time, they would start talking about the beer, and they would say, "Oh, I think this week the beer is . . ." They could detect differences that a year ago they couldn't even think about. They've become much more educated beer consumers. They were first attracted because it was a new idea, but then they became regulars.

I think the beer consumers now are a lot smarter than they were twenty years ago. They can now go to a pub and know the difference between a Belgian ale and an English ale. They know that when you get a factory beer, everything is measured out exactly the same way every time. But when you go to a brewpub, there are variations. For instance, I can go to Brugge and notice a difference from time to time. The tripel is a little different today from last time. It's still a great beer.

[Laughter]

MARTIN That's the difference between macrobreweries and brewpubs—you don't expect the same.

MILLER Macrobreweries are expected to be the same, but because of the economic environment of brewpubs, from the time you first brew to the next time, there are differences. It definitely changes.

AUDIENCE What is the percentage of beer to food?

MILLER It's close to 50-50 for me, food to beer. It's different for everybody.

ROBINSON I'm interested in the camaraderie that's part of food and beer. I like sitting down with somebody at a brewpub. I go to Brugge and notice what they're serving. You put those things together. You like good beer, good food. You like to link those up.

We use a lot of our beer in our food. You mix together onions and tomatoes with an IPA; you use beer to tenderize meat. You try to pair things for good beer and good food.

EMIG One time you could have one or the other, but you can't get away with that anymore. Now you better have both sides, good food and good beer.

ROBINSON For profitability you need the balance.

MATT For me it's great that with Terre Haute Brewing, Brugge now can have four or five beers on tap all the time.

[Laughter]

JOHNSON Let's talk about beer and food in restaurants. I've been to restaurants where, if they don't have good beer and good food, I won't go.

[Laughter]

MARTIN That makes for a lot of us.

MILLER I'm going for a tie-in. I talked with a distributor who said high-end restaurants don't have good beer. It's like molecular disarmament to ask high-end restaurants to offer craft beer. I'm going to get together with a distributor and do one and prove that people who go to high-end restaurants will drink craft beer.

EMIG We have the palate for beer. It's working with your chef to put a menu together. You get a better combination, a better presence, better pairing working together than just one person saying you need craft beer in high-end restaurants.

MATT The thing that is misunderstood about beer is its complexity. With wine you just have grapes. With beer you have the water, malt, yeast, hops. It's phenomenal what you can do with it. People pair wine and food, but when you look at the number of beers, there's a lot more you can do to pair food with beer.

AUDIENCE Can you talk about the water?

MATT From a homebrewer's point of view, it's a lot more economical for me to start with the water we have.

ROBINSON At the Ram, Dave [Colt] and I, we look at the water—we live in a world where the water is really hard. There's styles you can make with what you have. Others you have to make adjustments, treat it per style of beer.

MATT You take out, add in, according to the style.

EMIG Bottom line, with modern chemistry you add to your water what you want it to be. What's different here is we try to brew beer styles from all around the world. We learned how to make them, adapt them. I think that's why we're making some of the best beers in the world right now. We make American-style ale, American-style lager. Most places had their styles of beer before the craft-brewing boom.

AUDIENCE Are we getting gimmicky with water?

CASTRELLON I took a water sample to a lab, but that water changes every day. Levels will be different wherever you go. You manage the best way you can.

MYERS You work with what you have. We do not alter our water at Power House Brewing.

ROBINSON When I started brewing at Rock Bottom, I had a hands-on education. Over four to five years I didn't treat water. People come in with beer they're brewing, and you taste mineral deposits, and you say, "This is really bad beer." They're using well water for Kölsch, pilsners, and the light beers. You notice less with dark beers. At the Ram we send to corporate to test at least once a year. One thing we find, because of our water, our porter and our amber are recognized at the Great American Beer Festival.

AUDIENCE Do you break down to a base line and then build up?

EDWARDS I live in Broad Ripple. I know the water is good for darker beers. I run my tap water through a charcoal filter to remove chlorine. For lighter colored beers, I'll mix it with reverse osmosis water. I had to learn that I can build it up. It's different for homebrewers brewing five gallons; for a brewpub's multibarrel system, it's a whole different scenario.

ROBINSON We boil our water beforehand.

EDWARDS Without a chemistry background you can be overwhelmed by water pretty quick. There are water profiles out, but water profiles need to be taken with a grain of salt.

AUDIENCE What's the profile of a brewer?

ROBINSON It takes a lot of different people to brew. Some, like MECA members, are scientists and engineers. Some are pushing it for bigger beers. Some brew classic styles. Some hands-on guys who like to fix cars get into the mechanics of brewing.

JOHNSON Let's talk about the percentage of craft beer consumption in Indiana.

MILLER Jim Schembre can answer that.

JIM SCHEMBRE [an audience member, who is head of World Class Beverages] Indiana is the third worst state in the nation for craft beer sales.

COMMENT FROM AUDIENCE Is it because we have all those races? I learned the largest Budweiser account was the Speedway account in May.

SCHEMBRE We've not done a good job with the education process for craft beer. You travel, and other places provide tons of information about craft beer styles. We have to do a better job.

MILLER The point is we have an opportunity. Meeting at the Brewers Guild recently, we said, "We're all brewers. What's the most important thing collectively as a guild?" The answer: "We're neglecting the consumer collectively." We have a new initiative to get out there and reach consumers. Get away from brewpub. Get out and reach thousands of people at a time.

JOHNSON [sharing a flyer] Here is a new education program for consumers: Master of Beer Appreciation. Log on to www.BeerMBA .com.

EMIG To educate consumers about different products, aside from big beer festivals there are opportunities for people to educate themselves about craft beer. There are a lot of small festivals going on. I do a class every year at Purdue. We started with 20 students, and now there are 114.

ROBINSON Omar is teaching a class at IUPUI.

CASTRELLON I'm teaching 10–12 students. It's a very small moment for the craft industry. I don't teach it per se; I manage it. I'm not a great speaker, so I get others to teach. Every year I get more people involved. Sensory evaluation taught by Bob Ostrander. I pass on the Beginning Brewing section to Dave [Colt] and Clay—they do a great job—refrigeration, laws pertaining to brewpubs, etc. Students get an overview of several things. Of course, we taste and evaluate plenty of beers. The students receive extensive information on the brewing process. They learn how style guidelines work. They do a final project on a brewpub concept, complete with beer styles, a menu, a location, and most of the suppliers they need for the business.

Most students who take the course are simply interested in beer. A few need it for a certificate program the school provides. Most students honestly expect a rather easy go, but it is a 300 level class, so the work is a bit overwhelming. They are surprised at the amount of information, but once they realize the work involved and that a grade is at stake, they usually do pretty well. Their eyes are certainly opened to a new industry.

I enjoy managing the class because they get to learn from different people who are experts in their fields. That is, refrigeration technicians, water specialists, and people who have studied certain aspects of the industry in more detail. Also we get to share many styles of beers. One message that emerges by itself is

that drinking fresh local beer, if made responsibly, is almost always the way to go.

ROBINSON There's education from different sources people don't know about. World Class Beverages teaches classes. There's the Purdue class. My own staff at the Ram will ask me where I'm going, and I'll say, "I'm going to teach at Omar's beer class at IUPUI," and they'll say, "There's a beer class at IUPUI?"

[Laughter]

ROBINSON Everyone who hears about it wants to take it.

AUDIENCE Is it a regular class?

CASTRELLON It's an elective class offered in the spring and fall semesters, 6–8:40 PM on Thursdays.

MILLER Brewers Guild authorized a scholarship.

SCHEMBRE How do we get that message on a consistent basis to consumers?

ROBINSON Indianabeer.com. I like to do tappings to introduce people to new experiences. A lot of people out there don't like beer because they think all there is is yellow and fizzy. You get these people in and they say, "I like vodka and pineapple." I say, "Why don't you try a hefeweizen." They taste the cloves and they say, "This is terrific." I'll ask, "Do you like chocolate? Try porter or stout." They were people who didn't like beer and now they say, "I had no idea." It's like their minds are suddenly opened. Most people drink the same beer. They don't go out and seek. We have to train our staff to talk with them: "Try this. What tastes do you like?" Blow minds open.

The Background

MARTIN Since we have seven different beers on tap at Upland, there should be something. It does take an open mind for a customer to be willing to try something. Samplers are great to be able to try different styles. We'll give them a sample of something compatible with what they normally drink.

EMIG One of the most successful events was a wine tasting at the Lafayette Museum of Art. I invited myself into it. We took a Scottish ale. We were completely snubbed for the first hour and a half. We finally got a couple of people to try it. We said, "This might be a little different from beer you've usually had." By the end of the evening we had a line. It had a big impact on people. They came to the realization that there's more to beer than yellow and fizzy.

AUDIENCE Do you use ingredients grown in Indiana? Is anyone growing hops?

MARTIN Upland grows hops on the front of the building. In the spring we put the trellis up for them. We harvest them in August. We used them last year in our Lambic.

ROBINSON In Indianapolis it's a climate and space issue. We won't have the varieties. But mainly it takes dedication. It takes a lot of hops to pulverize down into the packages we use. You need this huge amount to crush down into an eleven-pound bundle. Hops have a short shelf life. A couple of guys will come in with fresh hops they've grown, and we'll use them, but it's not consistent. Ethanol is playing a part in Indiana agriculture. Farmers are plowing under hops fields to plant corn. Ethanol is playing havoc with our hops crops commercially worldwide.

EDWARDS There are still wild hops growing along the Monon.

EMIG Hops were undervalued. Fifty percent of worldwide hop acreage is gone. It was a perfect storm. All things came to a head this year. Hop weather conditions in Europe made a poor harvest—they lost 60 percent of the harvest. There was a fire out west. On top of that, hop usage is up.

EMIG Prices are up. If you can't get hops, you make adjustments. There's a pinch on barley as well. It takes capital investment to keep costs down. Six-pack cost has gone up slightly.

JOHNSON Let's talk about the philanthropic impact of the craft beer industry.

MILLER We have given $350,000 for philanthropy [annual Brewfest sponsored by the Brewers of Indiana Guild].

[Applause]

EMIG We have an annual Winter Festival. In 2007 we had 250 people. We've raised over $30,000 in scholarship money for Purdue. We participate in a lot of community events. If someone wants to do a fund-raiser, we'll have a community night in our place, and we'll give a percentage of our gross sales that day. We've got to be involved in the community. It's giving back to the community, to the people who support us every day.

ROBINSON Brewpubs have solidified community. They've become synergy for community. Since Rock Bottom came to downtown Indianapolis, we've done a lot of corporate sponsorships, like annually with the Fire Chiefs.

JOHNSON Let's talk about the effects of brewpubs and homebrewers.

EDWARDS Well, brewpubs have taken brewing to a different level. We're all at different levels. There were a lot of styles dying out. They were European styles; beers in England like a porter. You couldn't get a good porter in the USA; these styles were being neglected by the larger commercial breweries. They were going out for that yellow fizzy stuff. Homebrewers twenty-five years ago were brewing stuff you couldn't buy anywhere. Now you can. A lot of small breweries saw the value. They took homebrew recipes and scaled them up and started brewing them commercially. Now you can find a porter at a lot of places. [Speaking to Kevin] You guys have a really great porter. We do a lot of whacky things that would never be commercially viable, like Pumpkin-Coriander-Raspberry Dunkelweizenbock.

[Laughter]

MILLER I think the best thing about homebrewers is that they are immensely proud people. They bring their brews over. They are so proud of their products. They are ambassadors of quality. We have a lot of homebrewers talking it, teaching it, going for quality.

SCHEMBRE Homebrewers initiate the other consumers.

EDWARDS When I traveled for work, I liked to go to towns I knew had good brewpubs. The owner is there. The brewer is there. I give away a lot of my homebrew. We're not allowed to sell our homebrews, but I'll have a party and invite people, and they'll have a chance to taste different brews, and we'll talk about them, and they'll say, "Oh, we didn't know beer could taste like this." Then they'll go try a commercial craft beer.

EMIG I got into homebrewing the opposite way. I was a bartender at a beer bar with people coming in bringing their beer, and they inspired me to go to the Great American Beer Festival. They were passing on the passion of what they were brewing.

EDWARDS It used to be that homebrewers in Indiana couldn't take homebrews off their property. It was an old Indiana Prohibition law that didn't get changed. I could make it at home. I could drink it at home. But with a strong lobbying effort by our club [Foam Blowers of Indiana] at the State House, we finally got the law changed so we could have things like beer competitions for commercial and homebrewing. We got judges in here. We got people interested in craft beers. I was off in the woods by myself twenty years ago. Now how many brew clubs do we have?

JOHNSON Let's talk about professional and amateur brewers brewing together as catalysts.

MATT The 2006 Pro-Am competition solidified relationships between homebrewers and professional brewers. There was always a good relationship, but this gave them a chance to brew together. It's a great experience for homebrewers.

ROBINSON I didn't start out as a homebrewer. I started out as a professional brewer, but I have a fascination for creating things. MECA [homebrew] club members come in a lot, and they bring their brews. It's nice to come up with different things. About ten years ago I tasted rye beer and wasn't interested in it, but now I like to come up with something new. I'll ask, "What can I use this for? Can I use a different hop?" With the hops shortage, breweries with good beer will start to create. Even with the hops shortage, we will have to stay consistent, so we'll use rye to accentuate hoppiness. We'll put different things together. Stylistically, Omar is an awesome brewer.

JOHNSON Omar, how do you address that situation where not everyone looks for big craft brews?

CASTRELLON I have been at Alcatraz since 2002. Most of the beer made at that time was on the light side. Not many of our customers were drinking true craft beer, I believe. So I had to proceed slowly. At Alcatraz we are sort of stuck in time. Not many craft beer drinkers even now. But I manage to make some bigger beers that do sell well. Then Ted started making Belgians, and I got interested.

[Laughter]

CASTRELLON I make a Belgian here and there, and they do move. But our top sellers are still the light and the wheat. The pale is up there, since that is the style that is growing fastest in the craft industry. I heard this from Jim [Schembre] from World Class. I continue to make mostly light beers because we have to make money, serve the clientele we have. It would be suicidal to do otherwise. We tried a gastro pub menu and almost went out of business. It just does not work at that location.

JOHNSON Let's talk about brewing Indiana beer to increase taste awareness of categories.

SCHEMBRE Indiana is so behind. Indiana does not produce enough beer. We have to grow categories for our consumers to drink a variety that includes domestic and import styles. It's a struggle to get Indiana brewers to produce enough beer to grow consumers. If the category grows, everyone grows.

ROBINSON Belgian is impacting our business. People are starting to pay attention.

SCHEMBRE How do you get from Miller Lite to an IPA?

JOHNSON Macro drinkers drink only one beer. Craft beer drinkers don't drink the same beer all of the time.

ROBINSON The beer I remember from my parents' refrigerator was Schlitz, Pabst. I started as a server at an English pub and could drink a variety. I started with brown ale and moved to beer with hops.

AUDIENCE What about gateway beers?

MARTIN They're great to get people interested in trying micro brews. The wheat is our crossover beer. It's about getting people into quality drinking as opposed to quantity drinking.

ROBINSON Gateway beers are super important. "No Budweiser here? What is the lightest that you've got?" They try it and say, "That's good. I like it."

MILLER When we opened Brugge, we opened with dubbel, tripel, and a pilsner. My gateway beer is pilsner. Still, why are you drinking pilsner when you can have a tripel?

SCHEMBRE It's important to have a local brew with a local personality. You have to put your story on the bottle. You have to put a face on the name of the beer and clearly define your difference. Indiana can get a bigger share of the market.

Beer Judging
Paul Edwards

Paul Edwards, veteran beer judge and "Indianapolis's grandfather of homebrewing," is at his favorite Brugge Brasserie perch just outside the brewing room. Paul is a founding member of Foam Blowers of Indiana (FBI). Paul talks about the dichotomy between judging and selling alcoholic beverages at the Indiana State Fair. He is a founding member of the FBI Indiana Homebrew Club.

The FBI is, I think, the largest HB club in Indiana. But the FBI is far from the oldest club. Both Tippecanoe Homebrewers Circle in Lafayette and the St. Gambrinus Benevolence Society in Bloomington are older.

Beer gets awards but isn't allowed at the Indiana State Fair. This is the story behind Indiana State Fair Brewers' Cup competition and why the competition is held prior to the State Fair itself.

In 1996 Indy Parks asked me to teach a class in homebrewing. At that time, I'd been homebrewing for about ten years. I said I wanted to bring my homebrewed beer as samples for students to taste and learn from. The city attorney said, "You can't do that. It's against the law to take homebrews off your property."

Title 7.1 is the alcoholic beverage law that the Indiana Alcoholic Beverage Commission upholds. Well, the Indiana State Fair had been breaking that law because they already had a wine competition under way in July, prior to the State Fair itself. They were very interested in changing the law.

In 1997 and 1998 Brian Hasler, then state representative from southern Indiana and a lover of craft beer, introduced bills to change the law to allow homebrews and homemade wine to be taken off one's premises. The bills got nowhere during the first two sessions. By 1999 we had a better understanding of the Indiana legislative process, and I had collected other state laws on homebrews. After one of the hearings I was approached by a lobbyist who represented Miller Brewing Company. He wanted to know just one thing: "Do you want to sell your homebrew?" When I told him no, his objections disappeared. The bill passed out of committee, was passed by both houses of the legislature, and was signed by Governor Frank O'Bannon.

In 1979 Congress fixed the law for homebrewing, so the standards are set. Everybody brews differently. But that was only at the fed-

eral level. Each state has its own rules regarding homebrewing.

Anita Johnson and I wrote the bill that became law on July 1, 1999. Wine makers and homebrewers living in Indiana are now allowed to take wine and beer off their property, not to sell but for personal use, educational purposes, competitions, and into licensed premises (of course, we need permission from the management of the licensed premises). Many of the places where homebrew competitions are held are licensed premises, so we made sure we could still do that when we wrote the language of the law. Selling homebrew is still strictly forbidden.

We immediately set up the Indiana State Fair Brewers' Cup, which has brought positive attention to an Indiana industry. We were just doing what makes sense. Since it didn't cost anything except for the minimal amount for the State Fair to run the competition, we got the votes. It's a state event like all other competitions at the State Fair, except that since you can't sell or have alcohol on the fairgrounds during the State Fair, the judging has to take place on Fair Grounds on a date separate from the State Fair itself. The second Saturday in July was set as the date for the Indiana State Fair Brewers' Cup judging. The State Fair is in August.

I made wine in college, working for a winery in Cincinnati. After graduating from the University of Cincinnati and taking a job in engineering in Indianapolis, I tried making wine, but it wasn't very good. In 1987 my wife gave me a book on homebrewing. I finally read it and started brewing. In 1989, I attended an American Homebrewers Association conference in Oldenburg, Kentucky. Among the 500 present were people from Indiana. We formed a loose-knit group to meet at each other's homes to compare processes and generally help each other.

In a short time, we organized as the Foam Blowers of Indiana. Ron Smith created the logo. The slogan, "We Tap Kegs, Not Phones," was coined by another of our founding members, Chuck Durant. Even though it wasn't strictly legal, the FBI started meeting in 1990.

In 1992 I decided to study on my own to get certified as a judge. There were very few Beer Judge Certification Program (BJCP) judges in the state at that time. Anita Johnson, who has been coordinating judging for the Indiana State Fair, has had to recruit qualified judges from Illinois, Ohio, and Michigan. So I felt we needed to start getting certified in Indiana. I also felt judging would help me become a better brewer. I achieved "national" status with the BJCP in 2006. Judging is a way of learning what other people are capable of doing at home and in microbreweries. I've learned how society has developed in different parts of the world in relation to beer.

Basically what's involved in certification is a lot of drinking of different styles and knowing what the standards are for each based on the Beer Judge Certification Program (www .BJCP.org). We take a three-hour comprehensive test that is graded by three qualified judges. These rankings are reviewed by a fourth judge, who gives the final grade. We are rated on our depth of knowledge, including stylistic accuracy, technical merit, and intangibles like writing a report that helps the

brewer make a better beer. We're not allowed to write, "This beer stinks." We don't get the recipe, just the beer. So by tasting we have to know what the ingredients for that particular style should be and what we think is good or not so good. We get into the complexity of a recipe. Hops is what makes beer, and their use makes a brew distinctive. Different hops are used for ales versus the hops used for lagers, but these are just generalizations.

A study group of about a dozen of us met for several months to prepare us for the test we took in March 2006. It was September before we had results. We always help each other. We're people with a passion for brewing and judging. We formed ourselves into the Central Indiana Alliance of Beer Judges [CIA].

With beer, most people think in twos— pale or dark. People think dark means strong and pale means weak. Wrong. Guinness, probably the best-known stout, is about 3 percent alcohol. Some pale ales are 8 percent. Knowing the profile of a beer makes drinking it more pleasurable. For instance, while stouts share some ingredients in common, a range of differences make each distinctive. Knowing what judges look for in taste, aroma, and visual qualities to earn a medal helps a craft beer drinker make good personal choices as well.

Craft beer drinkers tend to be people who like to be informed. Professional brewers brew what will sell, and they like to get feedback from knowledgeable patrons who have a "discerning palate." Regulars are a brewpub's best friends. We tend to follow our nose when we travel and find the brewpub with the best food and beer. We make a lot of friends.

Beyond that, we have to know what the color of the bottle does to the beer that we're buying off the shelf. Shelf life is about three weeks to a couple of months for best quality for most styles of beers. (Some styles of beer, however, can be "cellared" like wines for many years.) Check the code for freshness. Heat and light are enemies of finished beer. Brown bottles keep out ultraviolet light. Green lets ultraviolet light (UV) through. Beer is harmed quickly in green bottles. UV light creates a skunky aroma. Is the store you're buying from turning over quickly enough?

Is there more diversity in beer than in wine? Some experts say yes. And that's where the competitions play a part. There are seventy-four, and still counting, styles of beer. It's most often the competition beers that introduce innovations, and most of the experimentation is by homebrewers who can more easily try a lot of different combinations of the basic ingredients in five- to ten-gallon quantities. It's harder to experiment when you're microbrewing in 1,000 gallons, which is why even professional brewers may test their ideas in smaller batches.

Discerning beer drinkers follow the competitions to learn what's next in the constantly evolving craft beer industry. The public in general can learn a lot by following the awards, festivals, local tastings, and the opinions of judges.

Interview August 8, 2008, at the Brugge Brasserie, Indianapolis

Homebrew Supply
Joan Easley

Easley Winery

205 North College Avenue
Indianapolis, IN 46202
317-636-4516
www.easleywine.com

JOAN EASLEY, FOUNDING OWNER,
WINEMAKER/HOMEBREWER

I think there is a resurgence of homebrewing. They are young fellows who like the real good beers and the brewpubs, but we're into hard times, and they now prefer to commit themselves to making beer as good as that. Now then, if they come in and tell me they drink Miller Lite or something like that, I tell them they're wasting their time homebrewing and to just go buy a six-pack because they're not saving money homebrewing. But if they are into the Guinnesses or good ales, then they should start brewing because they will save a lot of money.

It just seems like a whole new generation is coming along. We are still carrying kits, only now they are professionally made kits. Back when I started in 1974, they were not. We would just get a good recipe and put a kit together. What started me on all this is that I went to a meeting, I believe, in Akron, Ohio, and Char-

lie Papazian sat next to me at this conference for people who sold beer and wine. I got all excited by meeting him and reading his book, *The Complete Joy of Home Brewing,* and seeing how he got going at it, and I started making beer myself. What's so funny is at that time there were these little tiny bottles that Miller's had put out, and I started making homebrew and bottling some of those. When people would come in, I'd say, "Here's the recipe, and this is what it tastes like." And I'd make up a kit, and they'd go home with it. But now the kits are fabulous. They don't go as far as whole grain; they are concentrate [malt extracts]. A lot of people don't want to go to all-grain, and I had to get out of the all-grain business because it attracts too many little critters. But I have all the other grains that are flavor grains. The brewers who are into whole grain are getting their big sacks and other things at Great Fermentations. Anita Johnson is wonderful. She takes care of those guys. When I get whole grain people, I send them to her. We're very, very happy competitors.

In the early days I'd brew a batch almost every week from some recipe Charlie had in his book so I could get people to try them and buy the kits I put together and homebrew.

Back then there weren't many homebrewers. John Hill was one of the first ones, and Paul Edwards, who was president of Foam Blowers for many years. And I remember Greg Christmas. They encouraged me to start carrying a lot of hops, so I planted hops. In the fall when the hops were ready, I'd give them a bag and say, "Go over there right in front of our garage building on the next street and pick your hops." So they had fresh hops to throw in, and they were just so excited. When I planted those hops, I bought three different kinds, but what happened was I had a little boy help me plant that day, and he mixed them all up, so I never really knew which were the Hallertauer [German "Noble"] and which were the others. We just knew they were good hops in mixture. Mystery hops started growing up around the telephone pole, and the telephone people don't like that, so they would send someone out to cut them down. Of course, cutting them down didn't do the job. They're still growing. They come up no matter what. That's neat. A lot of the guys are growing their own hops now. I used to sell hop plants, but I don't now.

From the beginning I thought there had to be a club because they needed to get in contact with one another. In the very beginning it was just individuals. It was Paul Edwards, I believe, who called a meeting. Paul was the big guru then. [Laughter] I don't think I formally joined the Foam Blowers. They had meetings here in the early days. We learned so much from each other. Charlie Papazian came to town, and we learned you had to keep your hops refrigerated. I didn't at first, and I noticed they were changing colors. You had to figure it out for yourself. Some of the guys were always talking about going to Seibel in Chicago, so I'm glad to know some did go.

My husband and I were home winemakers. He was a lawyer, but he always wanted to go into some business. He came home one day and said, "What do you think if we started a vineyard? Some land is available in southern Indiana." So we went down there, and we started planting in Crawford County. It all started because some newspaper editor from the East brought some hybrid grapes over from France and found out that they did really well in the Midwest. Until then, the only grapes around here were Concord, Delaware, Catawba, the sweet grapes. His article in a wine publication got my husband really interested. So after that it was back and forth, back and forth every weekend when the kids were little, taking care of these grapes. And then after about four years we had grapes, so what were we going to do with them? He knew we were going to start a winery; he just didn't warn me about it. [Laughter] We could have gone down there and done a farm type thing, but his law practice was here and the children were in school, so we looked at three places in Indianapolis. This place was for sale, there was a house out on 16th Street with land to plant grapes around it, and the Water Company pumping station that's now in White River State Park. It's a little building that would never have been right for us. We bought this building and put his law office over here in the front of the building and made wine back here, with a little tiny tasting room. He died in 1997, and Mark, my son, took over. Jack wouldn't have been happy about that, because he felt there was no money in the wine business. He had talked with people in California who said it took them three generations before they made any money because you keep putting back into it and back into it. Mark married Meredith, and she's the best thing that ever happened. She just loves this place, loves putting on the parties, loves buying for the gift shop. I feel so good about handing the whole thing over to them because they have connected tremendously with the community.

We were selling the winemaking things, so I said, "Let's sell beer making things, too. I'll learn how to make beer." I started reading the books. At the very first wine competition at the Indiana State Fair, I got a medal for my Concord wine. We were home winemakers then. I look back and think, if only I had known where it was going to reach. Concord was what we were growing then, so it was from our own grapes. We didn't yet have our good hybrid grapes. But now we get grapes from everywhere. We don't grow all of our grapes anymore. We buy from farmers in the business, so we have Indiana hybrid grapes, and we bring in some from California and some from Michigan. We got a gold medal last week at the competition in Story, Indiana, for our Cayuga White. I just love this kind of work, whether it's wine or beer.

It's so much fun to read Charlie's book. He's a fun person and so well recognized in Colorado. He was the guru. There's no doubt about it, and that book of his made more brewers than anything or anyone else. I say to people who come in and want to make beer or are thinking of making beer, "Don't buy the kit now. Just buy this book, and if you decide you want to make beer after you read this book, come back and I'll give you the money back when you buy the kit because there is a book as part of the kit." Once they read Charlie's book, if they are at all interested, they become sold

100 percent. Charlie is the funniest, happiest brewer I ever knew in my life. All of these early guys were all of his fans.

We had our picture taken together when Charlie came to the Ram for a new edition of his book several years ago. He went around to the brewpubs across the country. The one we sell now is an even newer edition.

Most of the new homebrewers who come in here start out independent. If they get really interested and go to all-grain, I ship them to Great Fermentations, and then I think many join a club. But I've got customers who have been homebrewing for years and years, and they are still using kits. They don't want to be bothered with all that other stuff. But some of those fellows actually have little breweries at their home. I have found they are usually in the technical type professions, and through the years I've noticed a lot of them have facial hair. They are computer people and engineers. I don't think I've ever sold a beer kit to a salesman! I always ask them what they do, so that's just a personal observation.

Right now we're going back to homebrewing. I'm selling lots of kits to first-time brewers. They don't know a thing about it, but they've heard you can make it much cheaper than you can buy it. The complete kits are just fabulous—for example, this kit for Bold Russian Imperial Stout. These kits are what gets them going. In the early days, everything was just basic. Now there are so many options for homebrewing. We're expanding our storage space to accommodate it all.

Interview April 30, 2009, at Easley Winery

Homebrew Supply
Anita Johnson

Great Fermentations

5127 East 65th Street
Indianapolis, IN 46220
317-257-9463
anita@greatfermentations.com
www.greatfermentations.com

ANITA JOHNSON, OWNER

I have loved beer most of my adult life. When I worked in Chicago during the summers—I worked for my brother and we worked all of the time—one of our favorite things when we came home at night was to have Augsburger Dark, which was my favorite, with a salad, go to bed, get up, and do it the next day. So in 1980–81 I was drinking Augsburger Dark, and I loved it, and then we always tried to drink different beers when we traveled, and we enjoyed that. I can remember hosting a huge Brazilian Carnivale here in Indianapolis, as part of Partners in the Americas, which partners Indiana with Rio Grande de Sud. We imported beer from Brazil. There was a lot left over, so we went through that, and it started us on a craft beer journey. I remember being in Washington, D.C., and going to a pub and saying, "Are there any local beers?" We got Sam Adams, and we loved it. Just taken by it. We came

back here and couldn't find it for a couple of years. We'd ask for Sam, Sam something. And they'd offer us Sam Smith, and it was always a disappointment.

I love food; I love beer pairing; I love to cook. Then a friend said, "I make beer; I make beer; I make beer." I kept trying to get my husband to make beer, and he would never take the bait. So my friend invited us over to his house to try his homebrew, and I remember going down to his basement to pour a pint from his Keg-o-liter, and my eyes opened as I tried it. It was the best beer I'd ever had in my life. I asked him to come over and teach us how to do it. He said, "Sure, as long as you make me dinner." I asked, "What do you want?" He said, "Fish sticks and macaroni and cheese from a box." He took me to another homebrew shop here in town. We looked at equipment, then came to Great Fermentations and bought our equipment and started on this journey. Then the store was going out of business, and my husband said, "How would you like to own your own homebrew shop?" The roles were reversed. I was badgering him to start brewing. Now he was badgering me to quit my job and open a homebrew shop. With very little forethought and business plan, we did it, and I'm

glad we did it. That was in 1985, at 86th Street across from North Central High School, then Broad Ripple, and now here. We've gone from 1,000 square feet to 4,000 square feet, and we're starting to burst at the seams.

It's exciting. There are a lot of changes. It's growing, and it's growing a lot. I see that people are more interested in the food and beverages that they consume; a "buy local" kind of movement, slow-food and the craft beer side of things talking about beer/food pairings, not just consumption. I see interest in the quality of food and beverage. The quality of the collective brewing and beer knowledge is so much better than even thirteen years ago when I started. You have the internet. You have the people who come in who have watched videos of brewing on YouTube, which is for learning as well. You have podcasts that talk about very technical, geeky parts of brewing which are available to anybody at no cost. You have shows that are brewing to style. You have the brewing network, which talks about technical brewing subjects weekly. The collective brewing knowledge is so much greater. On a local level you have a couple of homebrew clubs that have inner competitions. There's so much more knowledge; it can be knowledge of technical or scientific parts, or it can be creative. We've seen an interest in wood-aged beers, and that came from the craft industry. We've seen a greater interest in Belgian beers, which Brugge in Broad Ripple started. It goes both ways because homebrewers influence commercial and craft beer brewers. We have the Pro-Am Competition at the Great American Beer Festival, where a homebrew recipe that has won an award is brewed by a home and professional brewer in a brewery and submitted for competition. You have styles like classic American pilsner that were reintroduced

by homebrewers. There is a nice transfer of knowledge.

There is a rhythm to life. In your late 20s you still don't have a lot of disposable income. When you are closer to 30, you have a little bit more income, you have a little bit more time; then you get a girlfriend, so you brew a little bit less—or a little bit more. And then when children come, it trails off quite a bit, and then when the children are a little bit older, you pick it back up. Probably 35–55 is where we see most of our brewers, and most of them are men; very few women. There is a study going on in Colorado to find out why there aren't more women brewers. I don't know why that is, since I'm active in the community, yet we just don't see a lot of women brewing. Professionally in Indiana we have two female head brewers and one assistant.

Our store is a lot more technical than most stores. We probably have a larger percentage of all-grain brewers than most, but the vast majority are still in extract and green brewers. I think the reason is we are all so pressed for time that you can't always dedicate six or eight hours to a batch of beer on a Saturday. There is too much negotiating with your spouse. You've got to negotiate with your job to find that block of time.

We still get the occasional customer who hasn't heard there's a hops shortage, but as soon as they see the price of hops, it is driven home that there is a hops shortage. I think it's going to make us better brewers. There is going to be something good to come out of this. I think we wasted a whole lot of hops for the wrong reasons. I think we can't hide behind hops; we can't hide behind malt anymore. We're going to be making more delicate beers that are harder to make. It's going to make us better brewers. We all go through a time when we want to make higher alcohol beers, more hoppy beers, and then we try to go back and figure out, "Hey, am I really a good brewer? Can I make a light beer that's good?" So I think we'll come out of this.

A lot of brewing to style has to do with having a very good competition here in Indiana where you have to brew to style to get a medal. With the local judge class where more of us are aware of it, there is more talk about brewing to style, but I also want to caution people to step back a little and enjoy it for the taste and not just that it matches a style. There's good beer that doesn't fit in a style. I would caution that it can't be so rigid.

I hope there will be a growth in small competitions statewide. There is a porter competition in New Albany. There is the Upland competition in Bloomington. It's more of an informal competition; you get feedback on your brews. It creates a sense of community and increases your knowledge.

By state law you can't serve beer at the Indiana State Fairgrounds during the Fair. You can serve beer during the rest of the year, but you can't during the Fair. It really has to do with the state of religion and how people perceive beer. I think it's possible now because we are looking at beer more as flavor than as alcohol, as enjoyment and savoring rather than just consuming. The way we look at beer as a complement to food or as something to savor rather than just to get the effect of the alcohol has something to do with that. But I also think because we have so many brewers in Indiana and they are becoming more organized at promoting their product—they are more passionate about promoting their product—we have the ability to change the state law and make local beer available at the State Fair. I'm excited about that openness because so many

venues are purchased by a major brewery. They have the marketing budget to buy the exclusive right, but they can't do that at the State Fair because it promotes local agricultural products, and so I'm excited about that for small brewers' sake because small businesses don't have a lot of money. They have to band together to get it done. There are a lot of people who have no idea there is a new brewery in Crown Point, that Mishawaka Brewing even exists, that Mad Anthony in Fort Wayne exists. And if you ask, "How many breweries are there in Indianapolis?" they don't know. It's an opportunity for Indiana breweries to get their name out. I know that changing this law is going to be hard. When they tried to change for Sunday sales of growlers, one of the quotes was, "We are going to keep the Lord's Day" [an inequity with wine sales].

I think it's important to get people to look at beer as a savory thing, to appreciate the nuances of flavor, the explosions of flavor, because if you don't, it is just a beverage. The many layers of a barley wine—when you can lead a group through a tasting and say, "I'm serving this barley wine at a warmer temperature so that you can taste all the flavors." And then I teach by analogy, talking about vanilla ice cream with the vanilla beans. It doesn't taste as vanilla-y when it is really frozen. So I have them take a taste of the barley wine. "Do you taste that caramel in there? Do you taste the chocolate and the coffee?" And then we go through the layers of everything. I'm always willing to lead people through a discussion. When people tell me, "I don't like beer," I tell them, "I am going to look at that as a challenge. I bet I can find a beer that you love." And a lot of times I do. That is gratifying to me. So I make beer and serve it at beer festivals. I talk to groups whenever they want me. I hope people here see the possibilities. I don't do as much outside work as I used to, but ask me and I'll do it.

The best way to describe Bill Friday is like a humming bird. He was nowhere, and he was everywhere. He would show up. He would be a fixture at Chalkies, a Greek beer bar on the Northside; he would be at homebrew club meetings all over the state. He would show up at beer tastings; he would show up at your house. He was like a humming bird in that he would pollinate and carry things all over and spread it all around. One Christmas he showed up at my house with a gift for my husband. We didn't have a gift-giving relationship. Bill had seen or he had heard; he gathered information that my husband needed some way to hold a tube. Bill had been at Purdue one day, and he found a lab stand and snagged it out of the trash and brought it over one Christmas morning. Jim didn't ask for it. It was just in passing that Bill found out about it and thought of my husband and brought it over. Everywhere he went, he promoted good beer and good beer with food. He loved to start with Bet Noir, a chocolate flourless cake. His card read: "Will talk beer, baseball, music—and something else." I said,

"I'm looking for a book about Indiana historic breweries," and he went to great lengths to find that out on the internet. He went far and away, above and beyond, to promote good beer. He really loved it.

At the National Homebrewers convention in Cincinnati, I happened to see one of his best friends, Ed Bronson, who helped found Tippecanoe Homebrewers Circle. I said, "Ed, it's Anita Johnson." And he recognized me. And I said, "I have a button on for Bill. Bill is here." And he kind of cheered up.

Before Bill died, I had never seen a funeral where they had a toast. But they brought a homebrew in, and they had a toast for everyone around to join in—the essence of Bill Friday. He didn't have a lot of family. His beer went to a lot of people in the homebrew community. Occasionally someone shows up with a Bill Friday beer. One of them had sludge about two inches thick from the chocolate he had in it. He loved chocolate.

He was a librarian at the public library in West Lafayette.

Interview August 5, 2008, at
Great Fermentations

Notes

2

The Brewers

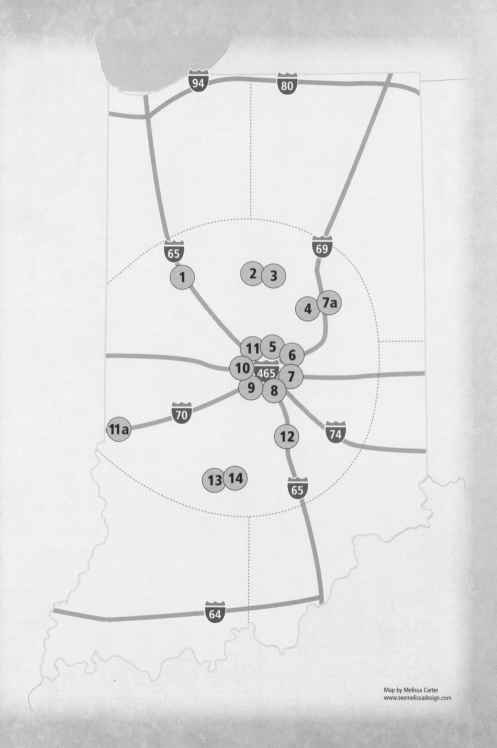

Map by Melissa Carter
www.seemelissadesign.com

Central Indiana

Central Indiana Brewpubs & Breweries

1   LAFAYETTE BREWING COMPANY

2   HALF MOON RESTAURANT & BREWERY

3   BRASS MONKEY BREWING COMPANY

4   BARLEY ISLAND BREWING COMPANY

5   ROCK BOTTOM RESTAURANT & BREWERY DOWNTOWN

6   ROCK BOTTOM RESTAURANT & BREWERY COLLEGE PARK

7   RAM RESTAURANT & BREWERY

8   SUN KING BREWERY

9   ALCATRAZ BREWING COMPANY

10 BROAD RIPPLE BREWPUB

11 BRUGGE BRASSERIE

12 OAKEN BARREL BREWING COMPANY

13 UPLAND BREWING COMPANY

14 BLOOMINGTON BREWING COMPANY

Lafayette Brewing Company

622 Main Street
Lafayette, IN 47901
765-742-2591
www.lafayettebrewingco.com

GREG EMIG, BREWMASTER/PRESIDENT

I was raised in northern Indiana, in Valparaiso. My parents lived there until 2004, having lived there for almost forty years. When I came to school, I came down to Purdue, so my brewing started here in Lafayette, learning homebrewing from Bill Friday, Steve Robertson, and Ed Bronson, who now lives in Chicago. Those guys were all big into the homebrewing scene at the time. Bill was the one who brought the supplies for the local homebrew club. When I was working at the Knickerbocker, these guys were sitting at the bar telling stories about going to the Great American Beer Festival and doing all this beer-related travel, and I thought, "Man, what a great concept that you can make a living doing this." I'd ask, "Oh, hey, what do you do with this? What's the best way to go about this? What yeast do you use? What do you do?" These guys had ready information for me and were able to point me in good directions. They brought in homebrews for me to try. I was like, "This is beer? You're kidding me." I was a guy making beer in my kitchen, sticking it down in the crawl space to condition if I needed it to. Even though it was my hobby, I knew I wanted to make beer, make it a job. I was getting into it, and right away I thought, "Hey, this is something I'd like to get involved in."

I moved out to Kansas for a short time. My wife and I lived out there for about a year and a half. The same time we moved out there, the Free State Brewing Company, the first brewpub built in the state of Kansas, opened up.

Unfortunately, I didn't get employed down there, but I did spend a lot of time down there drinking their beers, and that was actually the first brewpub that I had ever experienced, so I was knocked off my bar stool by what a nice fresh beer can taste like. It was an experience I will not forget.

We moved back to Indiana and were living in New Castle, but I kept in contact with Bill, and he told me there was someone in Indiana who was going to open up a brewpub. That turned out to be John Hill, so the very next day I drove down, and I found John working away at the Broad Ripple Brewpub. I approached him about possibly being a brewer for the company. Unfortunately for me, he had hired a brewer the day before. Gil Alberding was the initial brewer. I went ahead and took a job with John, and I helped him while he was under construction. I worked in the restaurant as a bartender and a shift manager, running the service end of things, and stayed there for a while, then eventually moved on and did some other things.

During that time my wife and I said, "This is something we'd like to pursue—open up a brewpub." So we started looking round everywhere from Cincinnati, Ohio, out to Kansas City and points in between. We had a couple of tenants; we owned some property, which was one of our goals in opening a brewpub, because if all else failed, we had something left. The economics of doing something in a bigger city like Cincinnati or Indianapolis or Kansas City wasn't really viable for us from a financial perspective, so we started looking at smaller communities—Oxford, Ohio, where Miami University is. We were focusing on university communities because we wanted a more open-mindedness in terms of beer from people who had traveled a little bit and had experienced

different styles of beer. And of course Lafayette kept coming back on the list. We had ties here, obviously, to the university community.

When we finally came and looked at downtown Lafayette, there were certainly opportunities from the perspective of "This is affordable for us. There are a lot of vacant buildings downtown that would work well for us." We had talked to people in other communities who wanted a big industrial brewery. They wanted nothing to do with our plans. That was just the reality of the situation. Here in Lafayette we had a few ears that were sympathetic with what we wanted to do and thought it was a good idea for downtown, and things fell into place. But it was nice just at that time for John Hill to call me and say, "I need a brewer." I said, "I'll be there tomorrow to brew, but I do want you to know that I'm going to open up a brewpub at some point."

I think John thought, "Yeah, maybe you will and maybe you won't, but come on down here and start working."

During this phase of finding a location, I had the opportunity to work in a brewery and get hands-on experience. For John, this is kind of a retirement thing. He wanted to have fun doing it, so it was a great opportunity for me because we would travel to beer festivals. We went as far east as Boston, as far west as Denver, and points in between. We would take the beer that we brewed going to festivals and would stop at every small brewery between point A to point B to talk to brewers, talk to owners about how things were going for them, what things worked for them, what styles of beer they were brewing. We'd taste their beers and ask them where they got their yeast, where they got their equipment. During that year and a half of working with John, we

visited between 120 and 130 breweries. Considering there were only about 200 in the whole country, we hit a lot of them.

At the end of 1992 in December, I stopped working at Broad Ripple. On January 2, we took possession of this building and started working. When I was leaving Broad Ripple, I trained Ted Miller, who now owns Brugge and Terre Haute Brewing Company. Ted had been working there in the front of the house as a server and a bartender, so he came over to the brewery side, and I trained Ted. At the time Russell Levitt, who used to work at Broad Ripple Brewing Company as a server, went down to help Jeff Mease start up the Bloomington Brewing Company. After Russ left Bloomington, Upland was his project, and that has come full circle with Doug Dayhoff at Upland now. So John spawned all these guys. In the meantime, Mad Anthony opened up. The guys in Mishawaka came down and talked to John about running a brewery and the legalities of it. That was something Jeff Mease got involved in, helping legislation getting written and passed so that brewpubs were actually legal in Indiana. That law was passed in 1993 when we were opening, so Lafayette Brewing Company was the first true brewpub to open up in Indiana under that brewers legislation.

When we came back to Lafayette to open the brewpub, Bill Friday was ecstatic. The guy he got into beer was coming back and opening up a brewery. He was just a fantastic supporter. He talked us up, and I honestly believe he enjoyed the product we were putting out. He had a lot of ties in the homebrewing community, not only here but nationally. He was a pretty complex character. I knew him as a homebrewer, but he was a librarian and a collector of books and music. He had a solid beer knowledge, a good idea of what he was tasting, stylistically what made each different. Just to be able to talk with him added to my education, as did talking to other brewers and obviously having the hands-on experience to brew at Broad Ripple, at a commercial brewery. Those were all the basics before I had the opportunity to go up to school and take classes.

I'm still connected with the homebrewers. We hold the Tippecanoe Homebrew Club's annual holiday meeting here every December, and they are in the Mug Club. It is good to have them as part of Winter Warmer for people who want to talk about brewing. It allows for a more hands-on educational experience. A lot of times we professional brewers can spout off about our beers, but when you can talk to someone about what they are doing in their kitchen, it's easier for people who attend Winter Warmer to get a feel for some of the things homebrewers are passionate about. For some of us, it's been fifteen, twenty years since we started as homebrewers. But that's where our passion came from.

In 1999 or 2000, for whatever insane reason, my father and my sister decided to open a brewpub in Aberdeen. I tried to talk them out of it. You have to make a life choice when you run a restaurant, and it's not for everybody. For my wife and me, it's a lifestyle choice. We're not going to get rich, but we enjoy what we're doing. I wouldn't do anything else. Anyway, they got that place open, and I traveled up there for the first year to do the brewing, going back and forth. And then they had different people do the brewing. Sam Strupeck from Shoreline was one of those guys. Also Ryan Neff, who had worked a little with Three Floyds as a volunteer. I trained Ryan. Aberdeen was sold to Skip Bozak. Skip went in with the intention of a career for himself and for his son, but they ended up selling off the brewing equipment and leasing the restaurant space out. Aberdeen Brewing Company was somewhat short-lived. The building was built from scratch. My brother was the general contractor; he worked for my dad. They had the restaurant and a couple of retail spaces in the same building. It was a great setup for a brewery because it had solid foundation floors with drains to the basement and stuff you did not have to retrofit into a building. It's a whole lot nicer to start out from scratch and know what you need than to retrofit.

At the time we moved here, downtown Lafayette was pretty rough. We recently looked at pictures of Main Street when we opened in 1993 and we said, "Wow, we did what?" But it's come miles since then. The railroad relocation project was a huge 20- to 30-year project, obviously multimillions of dollars, but it was going on for so long when we came to town that people said, "Yeah, this is not really going to happen." Well, it was done two years after we moved in. That's when the tracks started coming up and they moved the depot. It was the first time you could see anything tangible with the whole project, but it had a huge impact. There used to be traffic backed up to the top of the hill. People couldn't move because of the gridlock of a train coming through town in the middle of the afternoon. Tearing up the tracks and rerouting the trains happened relatively quickly after twenty-three years prior to that for laying all the foundation for the infrastructure.

Part of what we do is get involved with the community. An example is Friends of Bob, a quintessential grassroots organization that motivated people to put a lot of time and effort into bringing world class musicians to play here in an affordable way. What they've done for the music scene in Lafayette is outstanding. We refurbished the upstairs and made it available for special events, but Friends of Bob was the main reason we did it.

This building for much of its lifespan, as far as we can tell, was either a furniture factory or a furniture store. In the 1940s or 1950s, it was Wagner Dry Goods. Wagner ironically was a local brewer. It was Kaplan's Furniture when we bought the building. Prior to that, it was a Kittle's franchise, but the Kaplans owned the building. When they moved out, it became Michael's, their son's. When we bought the building, it had been up for sale for a year, and they were in the process of moving to the new location, so it was literally on its last days when we came in here and started looking at it.

We had to redo everything, which made for a rough existence. There was only one small bathroom in a corner on the second floor. My wife and I slept on a mattress; we lived on the second floor from January 1993 until July 1995 with three dogs. We'd take them out for a walk every day, and we had a coldwater shower that we rigged up on the second floor in the bathroom with a broken window, so in the winter we'd take a one-minute shower. [Laughter] We were so excited when we opened because we had hot water down here. We went out and bought a camp shower, and we'd come down here and fill it up with hot water and take it up to the second floor so we could take a hot shower. [Laughter] At the time that's what we had to do.

We worked hard, but part of it was the luck of timing and the simple naiveté of it all. We had a great idea; we thought it was going to work. When I look back, there were so many things we could have done differently and a lot better, but the reality is it all did work out. Having worked in Broad Ripple Brewpub, we tried to bring the same attitude that was going on in Broad Ripple, which is a very busy area where there were plenty more out the door. Well, there weren't plenty more out the door in Lafayette. We had to adjust that to bring in more traffic. We had to adjust ourselves to the way we had to do business from the way we thought we would do business initially. The building was five times the size we ever anticipated, but when we were looking at properties, this was just the best value at the time. You just had to be willing to take a chance. We didn't even have a concept to fill the whole building. One floor was all we had an idea for, and I thought, "Let's see what it brings."

The second floor is now the community room, but the third floor is just like it was when we took over the building in 1993. It's laid out as a furniture display area. We have some storage up there, and I have a small office. It has had its share of water damage coming through the roof until I had it fixed up. That's the thing with old buildings. You never know what you are going to get into. The simplest repair all of a sudden turns into a catastrophic series of events. But we wanted an older building, wanted to be a part of historic perspective. We wanted to be downtown.

We grew into the Winter Warmer. It started out as a series of beer tastings that we did for our local mug club. Some of them were popular, and some weren't. When we did the barley wine, it was the most popular. But still, until we built the upstairs, tastings never attracted more than fifty people. It was always exclusively for members who came in to sample beers. At the time I would bring in other beer, not exclusively from Indiana because there weren't too many of them, but from craft brewers around the country.

In 2001 we were getting ready to open the second floor. My wife's sister had passed away the previous year, and we decided to try to do something with Purdue to set up some sort of scholarship. In order to raise money for that, we decided to open the winter beer tasting—Winter Warmer—to the general public and invite other brewers from around Indiana and try to get them involved in having a small beer festival. We got a dozen other brewers to bring beer, and tickets were on sale for about nine weeks, and the day before the event we ended up selling out. We raised enough money to set up the scholarship in the School of Consumer and Family Sciences, where my wife's sister, Laura Williams, had worked. We also raised a little bit more money, so we opened a bank account and said, "Well, we'll do this every year to raise enough money to fund a scholarship for that year and eventually endow the scholarship at Purdue," a $20,000 commitment. We were hoping to do that in ten to twelve years, but we ended up doing it in a little over seven. Since that scholarship has been endowed, we formed a new organization called Laura's Kids, obviously in her memory, that makes money from our Winter Warmer. We do a golf outing in the summer to put money into it, and a portion of the money from our in-house root beer sales goes into this fund. We just try to benefit children's organizations. We had a benefit for Big Brothers and Big Sisters on St. Patrick's Day 2009. In addition, we're going to donate money from Laura's Kids to Big Brothers and Big Sisters. We also donate money to one of the local Montessori schools for the kids to have cubbyholes to hang up their coats. We pick

organizations that are in need, not-for-profits, but even if it is a for-profit organization and we think it is doing good for the community, helping children with their needs, we try to help them out.

Tippecanoe Common Ale is one of our flagship beers. We didn't start producing it until 1998, but it was something that utilized the Amarillo hops that had not been commercially available until then. It's a relatively new strain of hops. We got hooked up with it through an event that the Real Ale Festival had. They had gotten hooked up with an Irish importer and had nine or eleven relatively new varieties, so they got individual breweries to brew a single varietal beer with these different hops. The hop we were assigned to brew with was a citrusy hop that we used to make a strong ale. But at that time I was exposed to this Amarillo hop, which I was taken with. It has a citrus orange flavor, and as I mulled it through my head, I put together an English common ale that I really had a taste for. Even before I brewed it, I knew how I wanted it to be. We brewed it, and it went over very well. The first year we brewed it as a specialty beer. We probably brewed it about a half dozen times, and people took to it so well, we brewed it more frequently, and then it just became a flagship beer. We added it to our regular lineup, and pretty soon it was outselling the best of the rest, two to one. It's a very popular beer with us. It was the first logical beer for us to put in a bottle.

Then looking at the next one to bottle, we said, "Our Black Angus Oatmeal Stout and our East Side Bitter sell very well, so either would be a good contrast with the Common Ale." The stout was one of our flagship beers we've been brewing since day one, so we said, "Let's go with the oatmeal stout." The reason we decided to get into the bottling was looking at a different revenue stream but also looking to get some more exposure. Even though we've been in downtown Lafayette for sixteen years, there are people here who have absolutely no idea who we are, so maybe just getting the bottles out with a six-pack carrier will generate a little more exposure for the restaurant itself and get folks to come down here.

Unfortunately, they are not returnable bottles. It is a whole other industry. For whatever reason, here in the United States, given all of our recycling and sustainability efforts, we have gotten away from returnable bottles. I think it's because of the economics. Returnable bottles are a lot heavier, so you are increasing the shipping cost and increasing fuel usage. On the other hand, why are we making all these new bottles? In Canada beer markets are driven by returnable bottles. Yes, washing bottles is a pain in the neck, but that has to be more efficient than manufacturing new bottles and throwing them away. Here returnable bottles are almost impossible to get. When we first thought of bottling, we explored different avenues for bottle suppliers. Initially we were looking for a unique shape. We found out that glass molds are limited in availability, and if you want a unique shape, you have to buy a mold, and that's a $100,000 investment, so unless you plan to produce 100,000 barrels a year, that $100,000 would not be very well spent. So we started looking at other sources in terms of returnable, refillable bottles, European-style liter bottles. But no one could guarantee a consistent supply of anything, so we ended up doing what everybody else is doing, unfortunately. To be honest, my first preference is a can. The canning equipment is accessible, the packaging is better than a bottle, it's environment-friendly, and it's cheaper. On every level, cans are better than bottles, even though there is a negative perception, which is unfounded completely, but it's out there. Our biggest problem is the egress of the building. I can't get a full pallet of cans in here. We'd have to start disassembling it; that's labor-intensive, and sanitation becomes suspect with unpacking and repacking. It just didn't work out in this facility. If we were ever to do a different production facility, I would buy a facility that could accommodate full pallets, and I would can.

Beverage Management is the class I work with at Purdue University. It is a required course for restaurant tourism students. When we started in 1994, the class had about 20 students. It has 65 this semester; it's been as high as 110. It's an evening class that meets every week. They do a different alcoholic beverage every week. When it's beer week, Bill [Dr. Bill Jaffe] brings the students down here. I basically go through a little bit about the small brewery industry and what we do; then we talk about the brewing process, how you make beer, what's involved. We take them through a sampling flight. Before we do the sampling flight, we talk about tasting beer and what kinds of things you are looking for in terms of flavors and body and aromas. We try to get the students to be aware of some of the things. Some are interested, some aren't. I'm thinking, this is the greatest course I could have had when I was going to college. We've done it thirty times since we opened; we've been doing it for fifteen years.

At LBC I think we make American ales best. When we first opened up, I didn't want to be too much like Broad Ripple. We needed to make our own niche, so we started out with just one yeast, an American-style ale yeast, and we brewed all of our beers pretty much based

Around 1978–79 the name Tippecanoe Home-brewers Circle (THC) just fell out of the sky. No formalities, no vision, no mission state-ment. Ed Bronson made a button that became the enduring logo for the group. The founding members included Bill Friday, Joe Rogers, Ed Bronson, and Richard Fudge. There was never much formal structure.

Homebrew clubs have a long tradition of silly names, starting with the Maltose Falcons (Woodland Hills, California) in 1974. In In-diana there are the FOSSILS (Fermenters of Special Southern Indiana Libations Society), IBADS (Indiana Brewing and Drinking Soci-ety), MASH (Mad Anthony's Serious Home-brewers), and of course the FBI in Indianapo-lis (Foam Blowers of Indiana). In Ohio there are SNOBS (Society of Northeastern Ohio Brewers), a Bloatarian Brewing League, and DRAFT (Dayton Regional Area Fermenta-tion Technologists). Not all clubs have silly names or acronyms, but the list does go on: Foam Rangers, OAFS, BUZZ, BURP, Mid-night Carboys.

In March 2002, Bill asked me if I'd take over scheduling the club meetings, something he had done single-handedly (with non-trivial griping and whining about it) for nearly twenty years. And then a couple of months later, the cat was out of the bag; he had cancer again. The same type of cancer that had taken one of his kidneys back around 1998 came back and took the rest of him in October 2002, a month after his fiftieth birthday. It was a pretty intense experience for the club. And it left the club "leadership" squarely where he had shifted it—in my hands. I've been trying to get out of the club leadership business since then, and it's a big catch-22. If I were a good leader, I'd be better able to effectively transfer the

leadership. So far we're making progress. I think. The problem with a college town homebrew club is turn over. We have a small level of formal struc-ture now, a board of directors, a membership fee ($10/year), a membership agreement, but prog-ress is slow and the membership is growing but very slowly. And all but a very small core of a dozen or so people is changing yearly.

Most of the members live within twenty miles of the city centers of Lafayette or West Lafayette. Some of us belong to, or receive list email from, other Indiana clubs (and Ohio clubs, too). We share announcements from club to club electronically. We have histori-cally had routine interaction with the clubs in Indy and Bloomington, although the dis-tances make it a less frequent phenomenon than would be nice. Ron Smith of the FBI has been a powerhouse of support for helping to get clubs networking a bit more, with the "Indiana Homebrew Club Day" event he has planned for the past two years and with his ef-forts in BJCP education.

I blinked (spent a few years helping my husband raise our kids, back-burnered the homebrew club meetings) and Greg Emig was a part of the THC while I wasn't paying attention. By the time my kids were teenagers and wishing I would leave them alone and I started hanging out with the club again, Greg had turned pro and opened LBC. From what I hear and see, he is an amazing and driven man who focused very well on learning to home-brew, working as a pro brewer or assistant, and moving right along to establish and own an incredibly popular brewpub in Lafayette. He has always been generous to and supportive of our club, and we are very fortunate to have the situation we do.

A friend brought me to homebrewing. In 1977, I moved to West Lafayette for grad school and fell in with a group of . . . librarians of all things. Well, not just librarians, quite a mixed group of twenty-somethings, but the mix included a couple of people who were studying library science or would go on to study it, and Bill Friday was the tall, prematurely balding, somewhat shy one. He was a year older than I, and he was excited, tickled pink, and passionate even, in his fairly quiet way, about the fact that by 1978 or 1979 it was now possible to obtain ingredients and instructions for making almost any beer style in the world. I knew very little about beer, but was somewhat acquainted with the pale, somewhat standardized American Lagers available to me: Olympia, Coors, Miller, Stroh's, Budweiser, Pabst, others. One of the local pubs here in Lafayette had Bass Ale on tap, and that was a bit different, but the homebrew that Bill made, and beers made by other local fellows, Richard Fudge, Ed Bronson, Joe Rogers, and others whose names I don't recall, those beers were usually much darker brown, and they tasted rich and a little sweet, like malt, and they had some bitterness and hops aroma and flavor. They were complex and mysterious and were not supposed to be served "ice cold." They were not highly carbonated, "reduced burp content." They were foodlike while not being heavy, and they were so tasty and enjoyable it amazed me. And homemade. I just loved the idea instantly and got started sometime around 1979 or 1980.

My specialty is probably teaching. Beer Ed. In truth it's a somewhat potent weapon in the fight against the kind of binge-drinking abuse that plagues the youth in much of our society. I disapprove of beer snobbery in general, but I will promote and accept it under certain conditions if it is likely to be responsible for helping even one young person start to understand that quality is more important than quantity.

And that beer is much more than simply an alcohol delivery system.

I don't have one specialty beer. For years I made porters, then it was stouts. When I got my first chest refrigerator I made Balkan Porter and Maibock over and over. The beer I've been making most often is American IPA. Been on a hops jag. Maybe my 54-year-old body craves the estrogenic qualities? When I stumbled across this info (about the pharmocognasy of Humulus lupulus including estrogenic activity), I wrote my husband an email with the link, and a subject header, "Maybe this is why I haven't grown a mustache yet." I think he wrote back and offered to pick up some Alpha King on the way home.

Brewing is a huge adventure in itself, and the club is another adventure. Studying for and taking the BJCP exam was a nerve-wracking adventure. (BJCP = Beer Judge Certification Program.) Teaching beer judge classes has been a strenuous and time-consuming adventure. The biggest adventure so far, and very recently, was helping organize a first-year competition with a friend who had no competition experience whatsoever, in a city over 300 miles from my home.

Misadventure? Burned the palm side of the three biggest fingers on my left hand very badly once, grabbed a very hot piece of kettle, which had recently been as hot as they get. Probably should have gone to the hospital. I instantly stuck my hand in the snow. (February. Snow on driveway. Most homebrewing is done outside with propane burners.) Keeping ice on the burns all day worked like a miracle. It is not medically recommended, but it sure worked.

Email interview following telephone
conversation July 2008

on that. But then as we got a little more comfortable with our niche, we started opening up more styles and doing not the exact same beers that John was brewing but the style of beers—the bitters, the dry stout, the St. Paddy's, the brown ale—and we started looking into doing the occasional lager. This past year for Christmas we did our first Belgian dubbel. Our bread and butter are the American ales, but over the last year or so, we have tried to stretch ourselves a little bit more, making more lagers, Belgian-style beer. Nevertheless, our Tippecanoe Common Ale is very much an American style, so is our Eighty-five; our Prophet's Rock Pale Ale is one of our introduction beers that's very much an American pale ale.

In 1996 I was fortunate enough to win the Siebel Institute alumni scholarship, which paid for tuition for their intensive course in brewing studies. At that time I didn't have an assistant brewer in here. But D. J. McCallister, who was attending Wabash College, came in here and said, "Hey, if you ever need a little help, I've worked down in Greenwood at Oaken Barrel Brewing Company with Doug Ellenberger."

Well, about two months later, I called him back and said, "Hey, why don't you stop in? I've got some things I want you to do." And then I got the scholarship offer and I was like, "OK, these two weeks in December, if I can get you to brew some of the beer during the course of the week, that would help me out so that on the weekend I can come home and brew and make sure we have plenty of beer." So it was able to work out. I had a little bit of coverage while I was gone. I could brew beer on Saturday and Sunday and zip up to Chicago to go to class. It was a great experience. I was really fortunate because I had applied to Siebel before I got the job at Broad Ripple, and things just didn't work out where I could go, and I was really glad that I had gotten to spend time not only working at Broad Ripple but setting up my own brewery and working in my own brewery and being able to go to classes after that because I would have been overwhelmed. I wouldn't have been able to get as much out of it as when I went. It was fortunate I didn't go the first time. I talked with other people in my class who were homebrewers jumping into it, and I know I got way more out of it than they did.

I always say the best breweries have the most passionate brewers. This holds true for any successful brewery whether it's here in Indiana or out in Oregon or whether it's on a big scale or a small scale. Those are the folks who have lasted over the years and have done well whether it be in Chico at Sierra Nevada, who started out small and now are producing 150,000–200,000 barrels a year, or a guy like John Hill, who is dedicated to Broad Ripple Brewpub and not being a distributor and not being anywhere but his little corner of the world and being passionate about the beer. Whatever facility you want to be, you really need that passion and the integrity to stick by your guns and say, "You know, we are going to produce good quality beer and serve it the right way."

Some of the people who got into the brewpub stuff particularly in the late 1990s were thinking, "Oh, this is up and coming, we're going to make this big dollar." They didn't know about beer; they didn't care about beer. They just thought they'd open up a brewery and ride the success. Those guys are all gone now. Unfortunately, some good breweries are gone, too. I know the guys at Circle V [1996–2001] struggled a long time, but that area at 82nd Street was such a nightmare for so long under construction. They were off the path. You can't plan for something like that.

What I think is a nice story for us centers around John Hill, but it even goes to a West Coast brewery, which is the White Salmon Brewing Company. It used to be the Hood River Brewing Company. One of the owners is Jaimie Emerson. Jaimie and John met while they were both attending Siebel. At the time Jaimie had accepted a job at the old Indianapolis Brewing Company, but Jaimie had also been offered a job at Hood River Brewing Company, so he went out there, and John came back to Indianapolis and started setting up Broad Ripple. Then John took a trip to Hood River to visit Jaimie to understand their facility and how it operated. Of course, Hood River was very small, a 15 bbl brewery.

So Jaimie and John, both from Indianapolis, hooked up originally in Chicago. John gave me the opportunity to learn in his commercial brewery. I taught Ted, who followed me. Now I've got a brewery, and Ted's got a brewery—Brugge in Broad Ripple and Terre Haute. Russ Levitt, who worked at Broad Ripple, helped set up Bloomington Brewing Company and Upland Brewing Company. Through my family opening Aberdeen and me brewing at Aberdeen and Sam Strupeck's relationship with Aberdeen, now Sam's opened up Shoreline Brewery. Jim (D. J.) McCallister, who helped us out here, is currently living in Chicago, and he is looking to open a brewpub in Dubuque, Iowa. The brewer after him was Doug Ellenberger. Doug brewed here for about two and a half years. He left here and ironically went to the Hood River Brewing Company out in Oregon, where Jaimie had gone. In September 2008, Doug opened Everybody's Brewing Company in White Salmon, Washington.

What's interesting to me is how John's influence has spider-webbed out, not to mention the consulting he has done with the guys at Mad Anthony, and I know he talked to the folks at Mishawaka before they opened their brewery and the folks at Oaken Barrel before they opened up. It's been nice to see how Indiana has grown and expanded upon itself by going back and back and back to the original guy who came and put in a brewpub.

It is such a unique thing about this industry; you wouldn't find restaurants cooperating like this. You couldn't find any other business where you can call up the owner and ask, "Where do you guys get your bottles?"

When my wife, Nancy, and I were going to do this, John and his wife said, "Anything you need from us, business plan information, sales plan information, you'll get it." He also said, "Do you know what you are getting into? Let us tell you a little about that."

Of course, you can listen to them, but at the time we were naïve, and now we know what it all meant. But it was really good to have them mentor us and give us the inside information. It's not all fun and games. It's a lifestyle choice you are making, and now I've given that talk to other people. If you knew any better, you wouldn't do it.

We get excellent support from the Purdue community and excellent support from the downtown community. The Purdue community ironically is not students. It's faculty, staff, and graduate students. Obviously it's not the undergraduates—you've got to be 21 to drink, so that eliminates 75 percent of the student population. But on top of that, those kids are looking for something different than we're offering. There's a small niche that will come over here, but the vast majority will get beer over on campus and drink themselves into a stupor. That's not what we're into.

When I was in school, the Knickerbocker had lots of imports and the occasional craft beer, but it was a very small niche of the Purdue students. For the most part, we do our business with the faculty, staff, graduate students, and people who are coming to town for football games, basketball games, or other sporting events. When we first opened up, there were virtually no downtown residents. Now it has considerably opened up. The city is making a concerted effort to make the downtown better. When we first opened up, people would come down to the Lafayette Brewing Company to have dinner, and then they would go home. Now people come downtown. They'll come here for dinner and go next door for a show or they'll go bar hop from place to place until the wee hours of the morning, and that stuff is great because it never happened before. Every time you get a new business opening up, it contributes to the whole. If you've got foot traffic coming by here continuously, you are going to have more people coming in. A few individuals in the last four or five years have done a lot for downtown Lafayette. These are people who have a stake downtown, who have come in and said, "Hey, let's try to do things downtown that makes it more attractive, that gets people down here."

We've been doing this thing called "Mosey Down Main Street" that we started in 2008. We did four of them. Basically, the city closes off Main Street to vehicular traffic from 6:00 PM until midnight on a Saturday night. We set up vendor booths and a stage up at Sixth and Main and at Eleventh and Main for musicians who want to play. It's a street festival. We sell bratwurst out front. There are people selling crafts; people from the farmers' markets come. People who came downtown four times last summer, I'll bet, haven't been downtown ever, but they came and started coming back to visit some of the shops. It's just huge for us because the summer has been so dismal at night. It has a little to do with the campus and with the time change because it stays so light so late. We really noticed a drop-off in our business in the summer because of the time change [to Eastern from Central].

Interview March 19, 2009, at Lafayette Brewing Company

Half Moon Restaurant & Brewery

4051 South Lafountain
Kokomo, IN 46902
765-455-2739
www.halfmoonbrewery.com

JOHN TEMPLET, HEAD BREWER

A lot of people ask what brought me to brewing—especially homebrewers because this is what they would love to do. I just kind of stumbled into it. I was looking for a job as a bartender or a waiter after I finished college at Louisiana State University. I was in northern California, where I had grown up, and I needed a job. I got hired as a cook at the Mendocino Brewing Company. I had never done that before, other than that I grew up cooking at home with my mom and my grandmother. We raised all our own food from goats to chickens, acres of gardens, so I was very familiar with cooking and food. But I worked in restaurants through college and have a background in the sciences,

so I worked there for five months as a cook, and they got to know who I was. When one of their brewers quit, I just said, "How do you get a job like that?" I was just as intrigued as anybody else is out there today. It's work you don't hear about very often. It's interesting, and the beer is fantastic. It's something I had never been introduced to.

So I filled in an application, and they hired me as a brewer-in-training. I fell in love with it. That was in 1992. That's how I got into it. It was by accident, but it was something I really had an affinity for once I started learning how to do it through cooking.

I drank plenty of beer in college. I had an affinity for the natural flavors and ingredients that are used and how to blend all that together. A background in chemistry, microbiology, and physics helped me understand why I brew like I do. It was just a natural thing. I love it. It is something you do have to have a passion for. I tell this to people who ask how you get a job like this because the paychecks aren't quite as big as some other jobs that I've had,

The Brewers

but it's definitely the love of it that keeps you doing it.

Mendocino was actually the second brewpub in the United States since Prohibition. They passed a law in 1982 that you could brew beer and serve it on the premises. The first one was Grants Brewing Company in Grants, Washington. The Mendocino Brewing Company was the second, and that's where I learned. They've been around for a long time. They taught the traditional methods that still to this day is my philosophy behind beer—old world craft. It was pretty fascinating to learn from them, but after eight and a half years with Mendocino Brewing Company, they had gone through changes—many growing pains—we went from a small 20-barrel facility to a large 100-barrel facility, and fully automated. So there was a lot of learning and growing in there. There were also some organizational changes that took place, public sale offerings that didn't quite go as well as they wanted. In 1999, a group from India bought them out—a group from Bangalore, India—United Breweries Group. It happened the summer before I left.

Why Kokomo? I get that question a lot, too. I was in Little Rock, Arkansas, before I moved here. I really didn't have any ties to the Little Rock area other than work. I had met someone and had just gotten remarried, and she had a job offer in north Indianapolis, and we were looking for a place to move because we wanted to start raising a family. We were looking at Tampa, Florida, because that's where her family is and we would have some support, or northern California where some of my family is, or southern Louisiana where some more of my family is, or Indianapolis because we had both been here and liked the people. She had

the job at Beef & Boards as musical director there, and she really likes working with them. And then Half Moon popped up with an ad wanting a brewer. Funny thing is, my wife replied to the ad for me just to see what was going on. I got to talking with Chris Roegner, the owner. A month later, we were making plans to move to Kokomo. Everything was just falling into place for us. I like to bring beer culture to places that don't have it. I needed a challenge, a new start on life. There was nothing we were running away from. It's just moving forward. It's been good so far.

Half Moon is really the first brewery in Kokomo. We opened May 2, 2007.

It's the smallest system I've ever worked on. It's a three and a half barrel brew house. It's all electrified. I've always used gas or steam in the past. It's just like any kitchen; if you're a chef you can go into any kitchen and make your best dish and it ought to be good. This was the same here. It's a system where I've never worked, but it's all in top quality condition, and I've been able to make just as good beer as I've ever made, if not better. I learn something new all the time. We've added two fermenters since we opened. The demand for the beer grew rapidly. We did not expect to sell as much beer as we've been selling, so we've already added to the system that we bought originally. You can find quality used equipment out there. What's wonderful is Chris was able to buy the stuff, not having hired me yet. After he hired me, I was able to take it from the warehouse and install it and have it laid out the way I would like it. So it was great. It's a brewer's dream.

Within a year of Half Moon opening, Andrew Lewis opened the Brass Monkey in Sycamore Marketplace. By the end of 2008, Sycamore

Marketplace closed just after Andrew Lewis purchased new equipment. Half Moon immediately put Brass Monkey beer on tap. This is what John Templet said just after Brass Monkey opened at Sycamore Marketplace.

It will be interesting to see what happens with Brass Monkey because I've seen it in the past. It's Andrew's passion obviously. He's been a homebrewer, and he's turned it into a professional dream, and it will be interesting to see the next purchase that he makes. It will be much bigger than the ten gallons that he's working on now—much more state of the art, and that will be a defining moment to show that you can create a beer culture here, teach people about something they've never seen before, and it will take off.

Kokomo tends to be looked at as a blue-collar town, and it is. There are a lot of factories here, so I was not sure what was going to happen when I came. I knew I could make good beer, and I knew that I would be able to turn it on to some people. But I thought it was just going to be this blue-collar Budweiser, Coors, Miller Lite drinkers. However, from these factories you also get a lot of engineers from all over the country, all over the world. We get Germans, Japanese, all coming to these same factories, so it's an interesting cross-section. The reaction to craft beer here surprised me. It already had this taste, so introducing beer last year in Kokomo is way different than it is now. Last year I had six beers on tap that range from a pilsner—a very light American-style pre-Prohibition beer—to a porter. There's a wheat beer, so two very light American style beers, a red ale, a brown ale, an IPA, and a porter; very basic flavor range and concept for the design of the six beers to slowly introduce them from the lightest, which is the pilsner, which is what they are used to with Budweiser,

the Coors, the Millers. The wheat beer, which is also light in body and flavor, has a sweeter, earthy character than the pilsner, so it stands out. Then slowly graduating them to the red, which has a caramel flavor but not overly bitter, which I thought would scare people away; and then the brown and so on. My idea was they would go slowly from one and advance to the next and eventually they would get to the porter and not realize that a year ago they didn't like anything like that at all.

Well, we sell as much IPA as wheat beer. We don't sell much of the pilsner at all. The wheat beer takes care of the light to whet the appetite for pretty much everybody. And the IPA, which is at the opposite end of the spectrum from the lighter beers with the heavy hop flavor and bitterness in the content, is right behind the wheat, so these people were ready for beer. My job was a lot easier than I thought. I just have to brew them. Now a year later—actually halfway through the year—I added two more fermenters so I could start making seasonal beers. Those six were not broad enough in the flavor spectrum for the people of Kokomo, which I thought was more than enough when I first got here.

Half-Batch Honey Rye goes on tap tomorrow. It's one I've made three times. It's one of the town's favorites. It will be the tenth beer on tap. I haven't had that many beers on tap. We have nine on tap right now, and usually it's eight—two seasonals. As long as I have room, I'll keep them coming. I don't expect to have ten all the time. It will be mostly eight, but it's really exciting to see just over a year later I've almost doubled the amount of offerings I have on tap and the sales keep chugging along and going in the right direction. There's a story behind the name Half-Batch—it's just to remind me of the first time I brewed it.

Half Moon Hazelnut Brown is the name I have for the beer you are drinking. I'm very traditional about my beer philosophy, so flavorings are something I've not been big on, but I've been flavoring beer at the Half Moon. That's what they want. I have a brown on tap all the time. It's a basic English-style brown, maybe a cross between English and American-style with a balance with the hops. It's certainly not hoppy. But the Hazelnut Brown I made quite a bit differently, not just the hazelnut but the type of malt that I used has made a difference in the mouth feel. It turned out really well, but flavored beers is not something I usually make. I've made a blueberry wheat, a strawberry blonde, a hazelnut brown, and a chocolate stout, so I'm broadening my horizons. This is the fourth flavored beer that I have, and they're all different flavors. Everything acts differently. I'm getting to a balance between the customers' feedback and my personal philosophy of how the flavor should interact with the beer. I probably would tend to have it very much in the background with anything flavored and have it taste like a beer. I think probably the lighter beer drinking customers want the flavoring to be very much more in the foreground, but we have found that balance where the flavoring can stand out enough to be noticed and yet know this is a beer and a beer first.

John Camacho, our chef, cooks with a good bit of our beer. He's very passionate about what he does back there as well. I think his training has come through his experiences more than through a technical aspect of it, so we bounce flavors. If I have a new beer that I want an opinion on, he's the first one that I go to, and visa versa when it comes to food. We approach things the same way. We have a beer batter that's pretty standard. We also have a smoker, and we smoke with our porter and our brown ale. He makes desserts—there's a cake he makes out of porter, and there's a bread pudding he uses the beer in. He just tries to incorporate it. I really don't have to push him in any way. It's part of what he wants to do. He cooks from scratch, and he realizes that we've got a wonderful ingredient that's unique to his restaurant.

In the future I'd like to collaborate with him and do some brewmaster's dinners and have him come up with a nice five-course menu and I can pair up my beers with it. Typically that's how it goes because it takes a few weeks to prepare a beer that goes with that menu. If I know I have something that is coming out, we'll try to make the menu match up. We just try to collaborate and do whatever we can.

I'm getting out to beer shows now. My ideas about teaching people about beer are different this year than they were last year

My traditional approach is distinctive about my style of brewing, using highest quality ingredients, two-row malted barley and wheat, sticking to the Reinheitsgebot, which doesn't allow too much flavoring. Obviously, you can step outside that trying to enhance the flavor rather than to run from that. I guess I have a pretty open mind for the rest of my beer life. Up until this point I've been pretty close in the traditional. Traditional is never going to leave me. I'm going to stick with the core of that, but I'm able to incorporate some of the new things that American craft brewing has presented in the world since the early 1980s, most of it since the late 1990s. The creativity people have brought to the table—I think that a lot of that has come from the United States.

Belgian brewers started the creativity, and American brewers carried it to the next step.

What Americans have been able to do is take a style from a region of the world—pilsner, Kölsch from Germany, beers from Japan, Belgium—and mimic those styles. I think that's what happened in the earliest years. That's what I tend to still do because I'm a very traditional kind of person. But we've taken those styles and mixed and matched, taking it to another level. Not only adding the fruit flavoring as the Belgians did but just any number of things. These American IPAs were never made until Rogue started making some very crazy over the top IPAs or Stone Brewing Company or Avery Brewing in Boulder, Colorado. Those beers were 20 IBUs or something, you know, but there's a place for it. It's going to take a while before I get that extreme, that kind of creativity. It's not what's in my mind about what beer is.

Half Moon was one of the small brewing operations that received hops from Samuel Adams during the 2008 hops shortage. Templet commented:

The hops situation has been really tight for brewers all over the world, especially for those who just opened up because their supply chain is last on the list. I've been brewing for sixteen years, and I have never had a problem getting any type of hop that I wanted, but Half Moon is a one-year-old brewery, so we were able to buy supply for a year, but those hops are going to last only so far. Samuel Adams is one of the larger breweries in the United States; they're also a craft brewer. They're extremely generous to the craft brewing industry. The hops shortage doesn't only affect me. I'm sure there were many small brewers who would have had to close because of the shortage, but Sam Adams offered to sell 20,000 pounds of their own hops, two different varieties of hops that they use in their own beers, to the small brewers

that were going to have a problem if they don't have any hops. There were so many of us out there in a tight situation. I could still be making beer today if I didn't get Samuel Adams, but I couldn't promise that I'd be making beer at the end of the year if I didn't get some of these hops. I think a lot of people are in that position. There was so much response to Samuel Adams offering these hops that they had to have a lottery to select the people that needed it. Samuel Adams is taking brewers like myself on their word that they're having problems with hops. There is no way for them to come here to check in my hops storage refrigeration and see if I just wanted hops at a cheap price because I was paying exorbitant prices. The response was really overwhelming, and I'm sure many of these breweries really did need it, because he was going on good faith and was expecting the same in return. I guarantee you I needed these hops as bad as somebody else, but I didn't need as much as they were going to allow. I was asking for only what I needed until I could get another contract for hops. So I put my name in the lottery and was fortunate enough to be chosen and got my allotted hops. That goodwill that he shared is such an amazing thing because in the corporate world, these people are not sharing information and knowledge, their skills, their resources, they're in complete competition and want all of that for themselves and would be happy to see others go by the wayside. It would only benefit them. It was just such an overwhelming show of generosity. It really made me proud to be a brewer and that he is a brewer as well. Not only to receive the hops made me happy, but just that for the sixteen years that I've been brewing I've been trying to share whatever I can with the homebrewer, the professional brewer that calls or that I may need to call for help or any charity organization I might need to be a part of. It was amazing to see that type of camaraderie come together in the business world. People's financial world is so greedy. Those hops are so valuable. They could have sold them at quadruple the price they charged, and I still would have needed them and gotten them.

It was such an overwhelmingly generous thing to do that I wanted to share those hops with the local homebrew club [Howard County Homebrew Club]. On National Homebrew Club Day, May 3, 2008, I brought the club over, and we brewed a batch of wort for them. They took it and made fifteen different beers with it, adding their own hops and yeast. I was able to contribute hops that Sam Adams contributed to me. They were just thrilled. It's wonderful to see just how far those hops have spread. Even though we bought them at their cost, they put the whole program together. That took a website, people processing credit cards for payment, packaging them and shipping them out. That's a lot of time and effort to do something like that. I've made a few beers with those hops just to feature them. It makes you proud to be in this industry.

The Apple Butter ESB that I have on tap is made with 100 percent East Kent Goldings Hops [England] from Samuel Adams. I'm trying to spread them into as many of my specialty beers as I can—English variety beers.

Half Moon is participating in our first Microbrewers Festival on July 19, 2008, in Broad Ripple Village to let people know we are here. My assistant, Bryan Culbertson, is going to be there. I haven't really decided what beers he will bring, but I think the ESB, the Hazelnut, the IPA, and the wheat beer—my two most popular seasonal beers and the specials I'm most proud of.

What I expect is that we'll grab the attention of beer aficionados who know about beer but don't know about us. We're going to make the trip here to Kokomo a little easier once they know it's worthwhile.

The first year I did not do festivals because I wanted to make sure that I could represent the way that I would like. I was just playing it safe. But now I think we're ready.

When I moved here, my idea was to find things that were local to name my beers after. The only one of the six regulars I didn't name was the Pre-Prohibition Pilsner. That's the beer that the owner wanted me to make especially for the locals. It turns out they like the wheat or the IPA much better. Stoplight City Red is named after the nickname truckers all over the United States have for Kokomo because of all the stoplights they have to stop at on U.S. 31. It slows your trip down tremendously. So Stoplight City is the nickname.

Wildcat is the name of the wheat beer. Wildcat Creek runs through here. There's a Wildcat Creek Golf Course, and Kokomo High School Wildcats is the mascot name.

Old Ben Brown is named after Howard County's largest cow ever. There's a replica statue—I think it's stuffed—on display at the park downtown.

Elwood's IPA is named after Elwood Haynes of Haynes Industries. They built cars here. [In 1893, Elwood Haynes began working on a gasoline motor-driven vehicle that he called the "horseless carriage." On July 4, 1894, he traveled the streets of Kokomo in this vehicle, running at a speed of 7 mph. *Centennial History and Handbook of Indiana*, 1915.] Haynes also ran for U.S. Senate on the Prohibition ticket. He was a proponent of Prohibition, so I named one of my strongest beers after Elwood Haynes.

And then Cole Porter is named for the composer born in Peru, Indiana. The descendents of Cole Porter and a lot of the people who have worked with the Cole Porter Society are all thrilled that I named a porter after him. You never know how people will take something like that.

The Haynes international people were thrilled that they have something named after Elwood and were interested to find out he was a senator on the Prohibition ticket. I had fun with the local names. I haven't named all of my seasonals necessarily after something local, but one that I made recently was named the Kokomonster. It's a very strong ale, easy to drink, 8 percent. I don't think it fits any category except "Kokomonster." The people of Kokomo wanted that. They spoke to me, so that's what they got. I made it with sort of a cynical attitude. This honey rye will be on tap tomorrow [May 26, 2008]. It is a unique beer because when I worked for Boscos, which is a brewery in Tennessee and Arkansas, we sent many beers to the Great American Beer Festival and won many awards, and one of them was a honey rye. I wanted to make it here, but I made the recipe much different. It went over very well, but it was 7 percent alcohol, where you can't taste the alcohol. It has a nice, light, creamy texture, it's got a dry finish, well balanced, but it packs quite a punch. But people weren't tasting the alcohol, and that's what they like about it is that it packed a punch, and they were saying, "Make the rye again. When are you going to make the rye again?"

Well, anyone who has made a rye knows it's a very difficult beer to make. It's a beer in the mash tun. I don't want to continue making the honey rye over and over again. It wore me out. It's what I want to make once a year, and

they're asking for it as a constant. I've made it since, and it was just as hard the second time as it was the first time. "When are you going to make the honey rye again?" Really what I was hearing from most of these people was that they like it because it got them drunk quick—it was easy to drink. They weren't appreciating my beer the way I like them to. So I said, "I'm tired of hearing this." They want something strong that's easy to drink. They can't tell that it's strong, only that they love it. I'll make something for them. I came up with the name before I came up with the recipe. I'll make something called Kokomonster. I'll make it easy to drink. And I'll make it strong." And I did. I made it, but I wasn't planning on drinking it at all. It's not my style of beer. It actually tasted quite good. It still wasn't my style of beer because it's too strong for me, but that beer went quicker than any of the honey rye batches I've ever made. I get more questions about the Kokomonster now than I got about the honey rye, which is by design. It did exactly what I wanted it to do. But I did it with a little punch for me. It turned out well. It's just another good beer. Which is OK. [laughter] The Kokomonster has a category of its own.

You can go to any liquor store just to get drunk. I want you to have joy when you are drinking. That's the whole point with the different flavors. It's surprising that a lot of the beer aficionados that come in here thought it was pretty good. It still wasn't their favorite kind of beer, but we sold it very fast.

Chicago travel mostly uses I-69. What I notice about outside people who come here is that they are coming mostly as business travelers for Delphi or Chrysler. On weekends we get a lot of motorcyclists stopping in. There are travelers coming in from everywhere.

I've never been a web surfer to the extent where I'm going especially because some of the opinions are very skilled opinion and some are just extremely personal opinions and you have to sift through what is meaningful and what is not. That's hard to do. People have come in from this site or that site. Most of them were early on as opposed to later on. The earlier on reflect a much poorer product than the later ones, and I know that. I try to improve everything I do. I don't really keep my eye on the websites a whole lot. Just having them come and try my beer is good, and if they want to write something, that's wonderful. Somebody seeing it can say, "Oh, there's a brewery in Kokomo, I'll stop as I travel through." So they'll stop and they'll try for themselves. I know that I'm not the best brewer in the world, but everybody will find something that they like.

I guess my philosophy on life is that my personal life and my professional life are very much the same. I've always tried to reach one person at a time. I've felt that it's difficult to try to convince a large group of people or to give them information and let them take it upon themselves. It's harder for me to really get across what I feel is really necessary except on a personal level. I'm able to do that quite well. I've taught a lot of people how to make beer. I've taught a lot of homebrewers. I've worked with community organizations getting my beer out there. I try to make myself available to people that I know are interested in what I am doing in whatever way that I can. Locally, I've gone and talked to a few groups that were interested in what we are doing, just telling them about what you do. So I go and talk about the history of beer. Making beer is my life. These groups do something with that information; pass it on. I try to be an upstand-

ing citizen in whatever way that I can. It's usually not by something very extravagant. It's just connecting with people on an individual basis. It's pretty low key.

There are groups that like to come here for their meetings. There's a local bike club that likes to come once a month. We don't charge them [for a private meeting room]. They don't want to pay dues just to rent a space to meet. We're just happy that they like us, so we try to just like them back.

I feel we need to get out into the community and show that we want to help. That's how I want to do it. Not to promote John or promote Half Moon Restaurant & Brewery. But realistically I am thinking of myself and of Half Moon for how much time I can give.

Part of the big picture is to feel confident with what I have to represent with my beer and the restaurant and my philosophy. Now, after a year, I think I am ready to be out there as soon as I find time, and that will come, that will come, I know.

Interview June 25, 2008, at Half Moon Restaurant & Brewery

Brass Monkey Brewing Company

www.brassmonkeybrewing.com

ANDREW LEWIS, OWNER
AND BREWMASTER

CARRIE LEWIS, MEDIA CONTACT

Brass Monkey Brewing Company opened May 23, 2008, at Sycamore Marketplace at 115 East Sycamore Street in Kokomo, Indiana. Sycamore Mar-

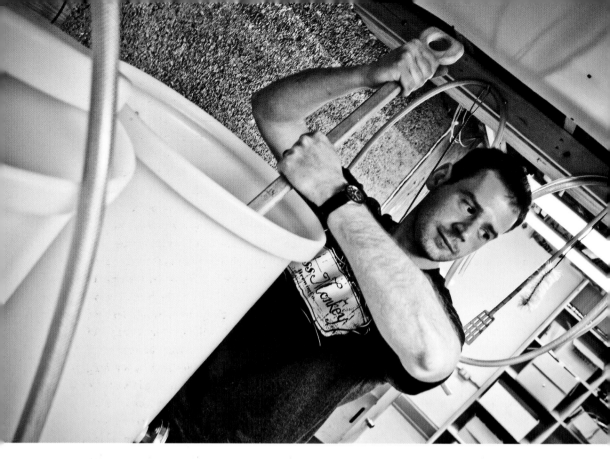

ketplace closed in November, at which time Half Moon Restaurant & Brewery put Brass Monkey on tap. Log on www.brassmonkeybrewing.com for the latest news about Brass Monkey Brewing Company finding a new location.

This oral history took place on June 16, 2008, at Sycamore Marketplace. Andrew Lewis seems to foreshadow the closing because downtown Kokomo is not "a destination."

CARRIE LEWIS Andrew started as a homebrewer in 2005, turning it into a full-blown obsession and finally a brewery of his own. He decided to turn his enthusiasm for great beer into a business in the heart of Kokomo and partnered with a local business, the Sycamore Marketplace, to make his dream a reality.

ANDREW LEWIS My equipment here is pretty much my homebrewing equipment, so basically every time I brew here, it's like homebrewing. I brew twice a day. I did two today, about 7:30 this morning and then 11:00 for the second batch.

At the opening on May 23, I was shocked because some of the stronger beers went first, the Ill Intent Imperial Stout and the Speak No Evil Belgian IPA. I only made a keg of each because I didn't think that many people would drink them here in Kokomo. So those went first and then the White Flag Belgian Style Wit and the Green Tea Pale Ale. I'd say the Green Tea is probably outselling everything else, two to one, since the opening. All of this is on tap, though I've got a batch of Green Tea Pale Ale

The Brewers

coming up I might do as a bottle release to carry out or to drink here. I bottle everything by hand; it takes so much time, so I'll do it for special occasions, I suppose, like a signature beer. My wife, Carrie, will do the labels. She does all the tap labels. She takes care of all the marketing. She's really good at it. Those were old Killian's handles that she redecorated the top of. I shouldn't say that. [Laughter] We'll scratch that one out. They've got to come from somewhere. We're recycling handles. We're very green here. We don't like wasting. [More laughter]

At the opening we were using fresh mint with beer. My main theory for that was—here at the Marketplace they have only a beer and wine list, and I feel a cocktail crowd comes in here, and they want something different, so I was trying to think of a way to make beer more visually appealing. Just unique flavors was mainly what that was about. The mint grows in my backyard. A lot of people like it, order that. I think it's catching on a little bit more, the more people see others drinking it. We can do it with any style, but we use it specifically with our stout; we'll crush fresh mint in the bottom of the pint before serving, and that's now called Green Back Stout. Another reason besides what I said about the beer-wine part is that a lot of people tend not to drink darker beers and stouts for summer, so I was kind of looking to put a twist on those to make a different summertime drink, which I think makes it a little more refreshing, a little more drinkable for warmer months.

Right now, as often as I brew. I get bored doing the same thing, so every week or every two weeks I just do something different. A seasonal beer is not often enough for me, so I plan on having something different every week, just

one keg or two kegs of a certain style. I did one I have no idea how it's going to turn out. It's got peppers and mangoes and peaches, and that'll be ready here in a couple of weeks. I was eating some salsa, and that's where I came up with the idea, you know, balance the pepper with the fruit. When I brew together a combination like that, 75–80 percent of the time it's not worth making again, but the other 20 percent of the time you have something that's different.

The hops shortage is killing me. I'm scrounging up wherever I can get them—even eBay. I didn't have my license by the time of the Samuel Adams offer, though their minimum of eighty-eight pounds would last me years. My stockpile will last only a couple of months. It only gets easier from here.

Instead of advertising we've got something new on tap, I want it to be expected that we're always going to have something new, so it's not a big deal that we have a new beer but that we *always* have something different on. That's what we want people to know—"They have something I've never had before."

Unfortunately, in downtown Kokomo we're "the destination" because not much else is going on. When somebody is coming here [Sycamore Marketplace/Brass Monkey] they're specifically coming "here" because there's not people driving by on our one-way street down here and just dropping in because they're in the area; there's no reason to be downtown at this point. It has to be a destination, or it's not going to work right now.

It's been my dream that this would spark some kind of downtown revival. I think that this gets the ball rolling. The rise in gas prices is bad timing. [Laughter] But for now I'm excited about people coming just because we're here.

I entered three beers last year [2007 as a homebrewer] in the State Fair Brewers' Cup and took a second and a third. I've got something to enter for 2008 as a professional, but because of the time of our opening it's literally going to be bottled a day before the due day [May 28]. It's going to be very young. A majority of what I brew is in the specialty category, so 80 percent of what I enter will all be in that category, so I'm competing against myself eight times over, but we'll see if that pays off.

Interview June 16, 2008, at Sycamore Marketplace

Barley Island Brewing Company

639 Conner Street
Noblesville, IN 46060
317-770-5280
www.barleyisland.com

JON W. LANG, BREWMASTER

Barley Island Restaurant & Brewhouse
701 Broad Ripple Avenue
Indianapolis, IN 46220
317-257-5600

MARK P. SCHIESS, CCP, HOMEBREWER

Barley Island head brewer Jon Lang and homebrewer Mark P. Schiess are Pro-Am brewing Mark's prize-winning Belgian Dark Strong.

MARK SCHIESS I would just like to say how accommodating Jeff and Linda Eaton [owners], Jon, and everybody here have been to go out and purchase all of these ingredients.

JON LANG These sugars bring out the dark fruit and caramel, flavors and spices. This type of beer needs sugars, and it can get expensive.

MARK Barley Island was accommodating enough to go out and purchase sixty-six pounds of this sugar.

JEFF EATON AND LINDA EATON,
OWNERS OF THE BARLEY ISLAND
BREWING COMPANY

It never wears off, winning a second GABF [bronze medal in 2008 for brewmaster Jon Lang's Beastie Barrel Stout after a silver in 2006 for Black Majic Java Stout]. We've been getting congratulations from all over. One reason to enter competitions is to get feedback from judges. Jon Lang and I look at comments, and if we agree, we adjust ingredients and process as necessary. We are constantly trying to improve our beers. If we win, it's a nice validation for our brewers, Jon and assistant brewer Mike Hess, for all that hard work. It's nice public relations for us. A contract brewer, noting our award, called and gave us an order. At an event, when we display our awards, they give us media awareness.

Two thousand eight was our second consecutive year for Pro-Am brewing. It's nice to be able to tie back to the homebrewing community, to go back to our roots. Jon and I come from homebrewing. Our partner brewers [Greg Christmas in 2007, Mark Schiess in 2008] were there on brew day, for bottling and attending GABF. It makes a nice journey. We get their feedback. It's nice harmony. We've been able to bottle each and share their experience. We've shipped some of the limited run of sixty-six cases of Mark's Belgian-style dark strong ale to our distributor, World Class Beverages.

Because I've kept my corporate day job, a lot of our work with Jon is through Linda, who sees him during the day. If he's around in the evening, we'll talk, and when we're together at beer festivals, that gives us time to talk.

Being a small brewery and restaurant gives us an active role in a small community. Beer helps people get in for events we have and for local and family celebrations. We can be a host and supply beer and food for celebrations. We're different. You can't call up a fast-food restaurant for large community celebratory events. People view a brewpub as a place to gather. We have regulars; it's more family oriented with good conversation. People are able to talk about issues of the day.

We opened Barley Island in 1999 because I like beer and brewing, and it fits with my marketing and science background. With the brewpub we've been able to build our brand, and with a ten-barrel system we're able to tweak our recipes and process. Four years after opening, we started bottling and distributing. I'm passionate about craft beer and the industry—the skills required, educating the public, and working with legislators toward what craft breweries and brewers are all about. It's intense, like running two businesses—a brewery and a brewpub—but Linda and I hire good managers and support them. We have to get involved in some issues, but to balance both sides it takes really good people to understand the direction we're going and what it's all about.

We're involved in community. We support and attend beer festivals; we donate time and product to support nonprofit organizations and to educate people about craft beer and styles. Attendance at beer festivals this year is good. Even with a down economy, we're able to grow interest in craft beer in Indiana.

Phone interview October 20, 2008

JON We're going to throw in hops in a minute. For stepping up the recipe from Mark's original 10-gallon homebrew to our 310-gallon system, we have a computer that helps us out. The big thing is that hops are more efficient in my system, so we have to back them down a little bit, but the grain scales up easily. This is my second Pro-Am. We had Greg Christmas last year making Sinister Minister. It's fun because you get to see somebody else's perspective doing the same thing that I'm doing. Even though it's in a homebrew scale, it gives me the opportunity to see different techniques, how people react to different things. It's working with another great guy—Mark and Greg— and another Belgian beer that I don't get to do too many of, so it's fun to do those and have a new recipe in the house. We wanted to brew five weeks ago, but we had a boiler issue, so we're playing catch up. This beer we'd like to age a little bit longer; it's a big beer. After we brew today, we'll get it to ferment, and once that is done, we'll let it age for a while in a cold lager tank and get it bottled up. We have until September 15. The beer will really come to life in about three months. Being such a big beer, I had to fill the mash tun twice versus once on a normal beer. We've got a lot longer day than normal, loading the mash tun with grain, unloading it twice in one day. That's probably the biggest thing. And we'll let it age a lot longer than the normal beer because of the size of it. And we're putting in the hops in big bags. This is the first time we've used whole hops versus pelletized products. That's the reason for the bags.

MARK This is great. I would like to do this for a living, but I can't afford to make such a transition at this time. This recipe is more complex than most—eleven separate malts each contribute something specific along with the Belgian candi sugar and three hop additions. The beer has turned out to be the perfect color—a dark amber cherry copper color. I have brewed this type of beer for several years, but recent brews have had carbonation problems. Jon has better control over carbonation than I have. He also has better control over yeast/fermentation temperatures, so I'm hoping this will improve the beer from last year—as this was an excellent beer three years ago when it was problem-free. It has won a few times before, so I'm really hoping for this beer to do Barley Island Brewing justice, because they are experts and I am not.

It's a little hot and a little steamy up there by the boil kettle. There are many similarities to what I do at home and what I'm doing here. There's a lot of cleaning involved. There are also many things that are different. A local cattle farmer will come and pick up these grains soon so there's no waste. He's been here twice already. So I'm getting to recycle. I'm also cleaning equipment that is a lot larger than I use. I'm getting to brew great beer. I'm happy. It's a tough beer to brew, and everyone has done an excellent job. Even with the current hops shortage, Barley Island went out and accommodated this recipe. Look at all these hops.

JON Those six bags up there is our third time putting hops in, so that's a lot of hops. Whole hops is something new for Barley Island. Without being in bags it would make a big mess.

As Mark stirs, a red light near the boil kettle comes on.

JON There's a sensor in the kettle, and if a liquid or foam gets too high, it shuts off the heat so we don't have a boil over.

MARK As a homebrewer, I have a lot of appreciation for what the professional brewers do, especially how much cleaning is required.

JON It's hard work.

MARK Knowing what these guys do, I'm trying to help out the best I can while also trying to stay out of Jon's way.

JON We have a grain hydrator that automatically mixes the water with the grain. Now we are up to adding yeast nutrient to give the yeast a head start. This is a fairly normal thing for us; I used a little more than usual because this is a bigger beer. It needs to be a little healthier. This is a coagulant—seaweed—part of it. It will grab proteins, which takes away chill haze; if you leave them in, it will shorten the life of the beer. The coagulant drops it out, so we have a clear beer, and also adds shelf life. It makes a clearer beer. We don't filter, so I use a little bit of seaweed. We brewed our normal Belgian wit, Sheet Metal Blonde, and that's the yeast we are going to use, so I had that beer make plenty of the yeast so I could have a bigger batch of yeast for Mark's beer because it is a bigger beer, a higher alcohol beer. This is the biggest beer I've made. Greg Christmas's beer was in the 7–8 percent range, I believe. We're shooting for 10 percent, so this is the highest that I've ever done. I'm not into big beers. I personally prefer a smaller beer, but this will be a good after-dinner beer.

Jon shares instructions for Mark at the boil kettle.

JON   It's fun letting somebody else do all the work, too. They enjoy it. I would have enjoyed it as a homebrewer, that's for sure.

Jon picks up a scale.

JON   I have to have some way of measuring the yeast, so I weigh it. I wanted to have yeast ready ahead of time.

MARK   I met with Jeff and Jon to discuss which yeast to use because I have used different yeast strains in the past for this recipe. This yeast strain from this company is different, but it's also recommended for this type of beer. It should complement the flavors and aroma well. I believe that Jon and I brewing this beer together will be a synergistic thing and that the beer is going to be better than if we brewed separately.

JON   As we brew we always taste and smell everything. First of all, we're using a new hops variety, so we're trying to analyze what that's bringing to the palate, trying to look into the future for what the beer is going to taste like. It'll change dramatically from what it is today. Today it is a very sweet wort—it's not fermented yet, but we are trying to get an insight on what it's going to become. When I first tasted Mark's homebrew, my thought was I can drink just a little of this because it was such a big beer, but it was an excellent flavored beer. I enjoyed it, but it was just that big. The yeast is going to give the flavor a lot of profile,

so we've got a lot of hope in the yeast right now. Beerwise, this will be a great after-dinner beer. You're going to take a bottle home to share with somebody. It's not going to be the kind of beer you're going to sit there and drink, day in, day out. That's what I'm looking for, I guess. We'll be bottling it for sale. "A good holiday beer" is one way to market it, or as a good beer to lay down for the future and save for those special occasions. A dessert-style beer, possibly pairing with chocolate mousse; a lot of people love chocolate with beer. Cheese would be good, too. I'm not a chocolate guy. A chef at Chalkie's used to cook with this type of beer.

The interview ended here but a continuing story developed; Mark sent an email detailing the adventure.

MARK   Just as you left we did have a problem—which happens in brewing. I should have expected this as all was going so well. Using whole hops, we had to bag them like large bags of tea. One of the bags broke, releasing the hops. This meant that we could not pump the beer through the chiller and into the fermentation tank. So we had to think of what to do. We could not waste all these ingredients, well-made wort, and all the time we spent with brewing twice. Jon, using his super brewing knowledge, decided to slowly pump the wort to the mash tun and use its false bottom to filter out the hops as if they were grain. We then brought the wort back and gave it a short boil, then chilled it and sent it to the tank for fermentation. This was like an Apollo 13–type save. Despite this challenge, the brew appears to be doing very well on day two. I have a five-gallon sample brewing at my house to keep me company and to also check on the brew.

Yes, I was a little nervous brewing and using someone else's equipment and their time. I have to say again how much I appreciated this opportunity at Barley Island.

I originally brewed this beer as "Monkey Dunk" four years ago. I took it to two meetings/parties, and ten gallons were quickly gone. Everyone wanted more. I adjusted the recipe and changed the name to "St. Indianus" to represent its abbey style and its origination. It was a good beer, but I had carbonation problems with samples for the State Fair. It did OK and won, which is required for the Pro-Am, but it was not the beer it had been. So brewing this brew at Barley Island gives me an opportunity to improve. I met with Jeff Eaton and Jon Lang with samples that were a little young; however, they demonstrated the dried fruit and plum esters of this style and its phenolic spice. Jeff gave it the thumbs up, and we planned on brewing in a few months. Due to some unexpected delays, we are late by a couple of months, so Jon and I worked hard that day to catch up. If all goes well, we will brew again for bottling and distribution of "Single White Friar" as a "reserve" Belgian Dark Strong.

I am just a homebrewer with an appreciation for good beer. I usually brew in small batches of five gallons, but I try to brew a large variety of styles each year. Brewing small allows for experimentation, and if you have an off brew, it's no big loss. I also can do odd brews with, for example, peppers, sweet potatoes, melon, spices, adjuncts, and other ingredients that are not usually present in commercial beer. I did this especially years ago when I first started brewing.

My great-great-uncle, George Ringler, owned a brewery, and my great-grandfather owned a saloon and market that was St. Louis's largest in the nineteenth century. I am told that it was the stopping place for travelers and pioneers to get their sundries and have a few beers before heading "west." My father enjoyed his beer, as influenced by his great-uncle and his travels in Europe. He also made wine for our family until the big wine explosion of 1968, when my mother put a stop to his vintner activities. I think this family influence resulted in my zest and love of brewing and beer.

Decades ago, I used to make wine in college and helped brew a beer in Ohio in 1983. However, I did not start homebrewing routinely until seven years ago. I had a local beer club, CIBAS, Central Indiana Beer Appreciation Society, and many of its members were homebrewers. These members steered me to Anita at Great Fermentations, who helped me get started with brewing. At the same time I was a frequent patron of the old Chalkie's Billiards Bar. Belgian beers were a focus there. I now wanted to make these beers for myself.

I work long, varying, and stressful hours in a hospital. Homebrewing provides me with relaxation and stress relief. Homebrewing also allows me to use skills I have gathered from other jobs I have had in the past. It is a good blend of art and science.

I belong to three homebrew clubs: the FBI (Foam Blowers of Indiana), the THC (Tippecanoe Homebrewers Circle), and the BHJ (Bloomington Hop Jockeys). These people and most of the others I have met through brewing are some of the nicest, smartest, and most interesting people I have encountered. Wherever I travel, I try to enjoy a brewpub and meet the brewer(s). They are always proud of their profession and the brews. I have learned a lot just by talking with brew people.

The more I learn and study about brewing, the more I realize what I do not know and need to study more. I have spent the last several years studying "beer color" and its relation to malt components. This turns out to be more complex than I wanted to know. I doubt this project will ever be finished.

Jon: We bottle and keg our menu of beers and distribute statewide. Jeff and Linda Eaton opened the brewpub in 1999. It's reported that in the 1860s a Joseph Xauer owned a brewery on Conner Street.

I had been a homebrewer for ten years before my family relocated to Noblesville from Minnesota in 2000, and the opportunity came to switch from working as a certified hydraulic mechanic to serving as assistant brewer to D. J. McCallister at Barley Island. In no time I was named brewmaster, with Mike Hess as my assistant. A lot of trials and errors are done as a homebrewer. I do a lot of reading about brewing, but I learned to drink good beer when I went to Germany as a student. "Be as natural as you can" became my philosophy.

My preference is a smoother palate with not much carbon dioxide for less bloating and unfiltered brews. For the first year and a half, I kept recipes consistent for the consumers. After that, I started developing my own recipes. I'm a beer drinker who likes variety. People love to come in and drink something new. Barley Island's Flat Top Wheat is a crossover from bottle to tap to get customers into the brewpub. Dirty Helen Brown Ale is our number one best seller on tap and in bottles. It's an easy drink with sweeter maltier brew, medium hop bitterness, and copper penny in color. Its name came from a legendary tavern owner who supposedly could outswear anybody in town.

Barley Island's beers all have historic connotations based on research by a Noblesville resident. We have a "waste-not" philosophy, so our spent grain goes to an angus farmer in Noblesville.

We call Barley Island Brewing Company "Home of the Fifth Basic Food Group." We also make root beer to serve on premises at the bar and in the restaurant.

Interview August 12, 2008, at Barley Island Brewing Company

GREG CHRISTMAS, HOMEBREWER

Greg Christmas, a Purdue University graduate in engineering, is a multiple-award winner for his homebrews and a certified beer judge on the national level. In 2007 he undertook a new challenge—team up with Noblesville–based Barley Island Brewing Company brewer Jon Lang to enter a unique beer in the 2007 Great American Beer Festival Professional-Amateur Division competition [Pro-Am]. While Sinister Minister won first at the 2007 Indiana State Fair competition, the richly smooth Belgian black beer didn't place in the national top three awards. Nevertheless, the experience had a profound effect on Greg's future.

Greg was born in Lafayette, where his father was a student at Purdue. The family moved to Vincennes and then to South America in 1969 when Greg was 7½.

Jeff Eaton had high hopes for Sinister Minister at the 2007 Great American Beer Festival [GABF]. Pub customers were drinking it faster than anyone expected. It was pretty popular on tap at Barley Island. They had to stop serving so there would be enough to bring to the competition. I hope Barley Island will brew it again for the pub, even if they don't continue to bottle it for home use.

Jeff and Jon wanted to do a Belgian. I had two inspirations to do something different, Brugge in Broad Ripple and New Belgium in Colorado. [Brugge Black and New Belgium 1554 Brussels-Style Black Ale. During the nineteenth century, traditional Belgian black beer was replaced by blond beers and went out of production.]

Routinely, you expect to find Belgian dubbels and tripels. Everyone does them as homebrewers. So when Jeff said, "Let's develop a recipe," the pressure was on. I had to win at the state or regional level to be eligible for the GABF Pro-Am. When we were talking about a beer, we wanted something that was different, that would stand out. Jeff had talked with Ted Miller. Ted gave us an idea of what he was doing, and it put us on track.

I came up with a recipe for a Belgian black. I used sinamar, made in Bamberg, Germany. I had heard of coloring malts—I bought a small amount—like for a schwarzbier, which is a dark pilsner. I had grains that I took the husk off to get a dark color without bitterness.

For the first pass, I fermented half the batch with one strain of yeast and half the batch with another strain of yeast.

People were coming in from Wisconsin to visit Barley Island to talk about distributing there. We all tasted one batch and tasted the other. Then we blended 50/50. Everyone tasted that, and we all agreed that the sum was better than the parts. So that's how we brewed with two yeasts.

In the process of moving from homebrewing to pub brewing, we made a lot of modifications. Things that I can do as a homebrewer

are time-consuming and not practical for a brewpub. I was able to ferment in two batches and then combine the two for the best tasting brew. Their equipment isn't designed for that kind of process. They didn't have the capacity to brew in two batches. But I was afraid that one yeast would take over if we brewed both together, so I made adjustments. It turned out one of the yeasts I used is a strain that Barley Island uses all of the time, so they only had to bring in one different strain. In any case, when you scale up, there are adjustments. It was a cooperative effort.

I made a second batch after the tasting, using grains and hops that Barley Island has in stock so they wouldn't have to bring in even more ingredients that were special. You have to draw the line to make a joint enterprise palatable. However, they did get coloring malt from Germany and Belgian candi sugar.

We brewed with the two yeasts together, and it was fine.

What got me started homebrewing was picking up a student newspaper at Purdue and coming across an ad: "Learn how to brew beer."

I looked at my buddy. He looked at me. We said, "Wow," so we marched down there. We tasted. "It tastes like Beck's dark," my buddy and I concluded. Beck's was the upscale beer at that time. It was around 1982.

The guy who ran the ad is still active in the Lafayette area—Richard Fudge. At the time he was my younger brother's English teacher. He's from England. You couldn't get craft beer, so he was making his own beer.

We went and listened to him. It was information overload. We got all the ingredients. The notes said to boil it. But the pot we had was way too small. It boiled over. We also missed the "boil for one hour" part. We dumped the underboiled concoction into a five-gallon plastic bucket on top of cold water. We didn't use a sanitized spoon for the yeast. All no-nos. It was putrid. My first foray discouraged me. That's just chapter 1 of all my failures.

My friend went on, and he made a beer that was actually good.

I've since learned valuable points about yeast management. It needs to be the first thing you think about, not the last.

At work, we had a student who was struggling with tasks. He told me about the great beer he makes, so this really got me motivated. I thought, "If he can make great beer, I should at least try."

I went to Easley Winery in Indianapolis and talked to Mrs. Easley, and she gave me tons of advice about brewing beer.

I was there getting ingredients. I'm asking about grain. I bought grain and hops for the first time. Mrs. Easley said I needed a grinder or I could use a rolling pin to crush the malted grain. A grinder cost thirty-five dollars. I used a rolling pin. I mashed and mashed. I bought a bigger pot. Well, to make a good stout, you need a good crush. I did not have a good crush. When I dumped out the mash in my backyard, the ducks came and ate it all up. There was that much whole grain. So I bought a hand crank grinder, and I'd crank and crank.

As I went along, I figured out what I was doing wrong. There was no formal way to learn homebrewing. It was all informal networking that I didn't know about. But one day Mrs. Easley said, "You ought to talk to them." I called. Paul Edwards called back.

I was always a beer guy. When I saw the ad to learn how to make beer, back in 1982, it was part of learning how to do it, but also part of

the mystique coming at us from beer ads on TV. "Fire-brewed Stroh's!" I was wondering, "What is this stuff?" All that fascination, buzz words and terms.

Brewing—it's part of my family, my heritage. My mom was the eldest of thirteen. Her dad was a southern Indiana coal miner. My father was one of six. People raised their own food, made their own jelly, canned. I'd watch my grandmother butcher and pluck a chicken. She knew I was fascinated, and she would sit me there and I'd watch with my mouth open. We made candy. We learned from family. It was making something from scratch.

One year when I won best of show at the Indiana State Fair, I realized by then it's the end of the day. Your entry has to stand out to be remembered.

One of the things that got me into Belgians is that there was a college liquor store with competitive prices. My friend and I saw the biggest bottle of beer on display for four dollars. Back then you could almost buy a twelve-pack for four dollars. We wondered, "What is this?"

My friend said, "I've got two bucks."

I said, "I've got two bucks."

It was Chimay Rouge, with a cork. We tasted that beer, and it took our breath away. The flavor explosion! I got hooked. At 7½ percent today it's middle of the road. Back then we were drinking 4 percent.

Had I known then what I know now, I could have saved some of the liquid for yeast! I can remember years later I was reading Michael Jackson's descriptions of his first drink of Belgian. He had the same experience. It was overpowering, dynamic. It is a great beer.

I keep some notes. Some guys have walls like Walden Pond. Some have a scientific approach. I feel it's three-legged—you have to have all three. One third is recipe, one third is technique, and one third is yeast management and fermentation.

If someone asks for a recipe, I give it to him or her. My nature as a person is that I'm not meticulous about taking notes. The process part is all from memory. If I deviate, I make notes. I rarely make the same recipe twice. I try to analyze what I have done before. I'm always making changes and experimenting. I'm looking for balance. I don't push the envelope. It's the way I brew.

Belgians have a complexity, yet they are simple. You think, "It's so simple it can't be right." I've done a lot of research. The Belgian process and yeast are dramatically different from German, etc., brews. I gravitate to the Belgian beers, but I also enjoy other beers. Taste evolves. Bock is almost too sweet for me now. Homebrews of English milds have great balance.

The great American craft beer movement in the last ten years exploded. Brewers pushed the envelope, developed new styles. I understand what the Belgians are trying to say when they object to American brewers calling it a Belgian-style beer. I think a better way is Belgian-inspired. It's not to steal, but to give credit. We went to Bruges in Belgium a few years ago. It was late afternoon on a weekday. We went to a pub, and it was packed. It's part of their culture to talk to you. A man pointed to someone and said, "He's the brewmaster." He introduced us and we talked. It's part of the culture.

People who inspired me are Fritz Maytag, Michael Jackson, the founders of Sierra Nevada, Jeff Lebesch, who started New Belgium, John Hill, who opened Broad Ripple Brewpub in 1990 as Indiana's first. That was something. I didn't know what a brewpub was. In 1990 I was at an intermediate level. Being able to come to the Broad Ripple Brewpub got me thinking, "This is the next notch up. Have a fresh beer served the way it was intended."

While I was at the GABF in 2007, I was talking to my friend who had recently moved there [Colorado]. When his wife didn't have a job when they moved, he saw it as an opportunity to do what she really wanted to do. He got me thinking, and that's when I saw this opportunity to work with Dogfish Head. They're growing so fast they need someone who can move right in. When I read their ad, I thought, "With my engineering background, they're talking about me."

I won't be brewing for them. I'll be associated with new equipment and maintaining existing equipment seeking efficiency for their operation.

Interview January 30, 2008, Broad Ripple Brewpub

Greg moved to Delaware to work with Dogfish Head in February 2008. He continues to homebrew and to win awards. He continues his membership in the Indianapolis-based Foam Blowers of Indiana Homebrew Club.

Rock Bottom Restaurant & Brewery Downtown

10 West Washington Street
Indianapolis, IN 46204
317-681-8180
www.rockbottom.com

JERRY SUTHERLIN, BREWMASTER

indianapolis@rockbottom.com

Tanya Cornett was one of the first brewers I worked with when I was at the Oaken Barrel. Around 1996, they acquired a production brewery in addition to the brewpub in Greenwood. They took over the lease of Indianapolis Brewing Company and purchased the brewing equipment, and I went over to the East Side Brewery—the production brewery—to work on the distribution side, and Tanya was at the Brewpub in Greenwood because she was coming up from Columbus. I was doing the bottling product and kegs for distribution. That was fun. Tanya was definitely into it then. I'm not surprised how well she has done.

I got into brewing because I was bar tending and waiting on tables at the Oaken Barrel. I was going to school, not really knowing what I was going to do. I was jumping around at school [changing majors]. What's funny is that when I heard they were opening up a brewpub in Greenwood, I was one of the first to say, "They are not going to make it." [Laughter] Was that around 1994? A year later, when I got tired of working at corporate restaurants, I went on board with the Oaken Barrel, serving and then bar tending and I really got into the beer part, so I started helping out with the distribution. I would deliver kegs to restaurants and bars a couple of days a week with the O. B. delivery van. So naturally I had to clean those kegs and fill those kegs; then I had to clean those tanks that I filled those kegs from. It was different from anything I had done before, but I really enjoyed the whole atmosphere, so I just backed my way into the brew house and started brewing and was at the Oaken Barrel for quite a while. More than anything it was sampling the product and appreciating it and wanting to know more.

After Oaken Barrel I had a small stint at The Ram. I worked with Dave Colt for five or six months. I got there late July or early August—was that 2004 or 2005? At the time The Ram was definitely opening up another restaurant [Fishers]. They expanded the brewery by four tanks. I had had some experience at the Oaken Barrel, tearing down the production brewery they got rid of and pulling out the old and putting in a new brew house at the brewpub. The Ram was actually looking at opening a new brewpub somewhere else in the area, so I signed on to go there, but they never did do that. I came to The Ram a week or two before the new equipment came down to help brew a fair amount of beer because they would be down for a full week or two. Then I helped put the equipment in, and I was getting ready for the Fishers store to open when I got the Rock Bottom job. So I left the week Ram opened the Fishers store, since they didn't really need me that much. That's when I headed out to Colorado to get the training for Rock Bottom.

When I was hired on, the downtown Indy Rock Bottom was getting into their tenth year, so the core beers were set. I was told that with the normal flight of beers, "Here's the recipes. You can tweak a little, but don't go too crazy." I didn't do too much to them, but I tweaked all of them just a little except for Brickway Brown Ale—that's a good recipe. So we have four

beers that are going to be the same at all times, at this point, and we have a seasonal wheat, and we can throw any wheat style in there. I generally make it a lighter wheat style because I tried darker wheat styles, I tried a weizenbock, and a dunkelweizen. I think it's just the look—people don't go for it much. So most of the time it is a hefeweizen. I like it. That's my favorite wheat style. And then there's the stout, which I change with every batch. I don't know how many at last count I've brewed over the last three and a half years, but those two rotate.

Within our region—there are five or six regions within Rock Bottom, ours is the Midwest region—we set a schedule of tapping dates. Liz Laughlin at Rock Bottom College Park and I will sometimes do the same style.

Especially being in the same city, it's cost-effective to use the same yeast. We set that for the year, and since we have eight taps, there's definitely one extra tap to play with. So it's really anything I want. If it's not a seasonal, I may do something I've been wanting to do for a while. But I've also split up two extra lines so I can have as many as ten different styles on at a time. That's kind of the fun part. I think the last time I checked recipes, I had sixty-seven over the last three and a half years. Some of them may not have made it to the tap. [Laughter] I was just tinkering. This company gives you a lot of freedom. It's nice to have the backing of thirty-four other Rock Bottom brewers you can call—which happens around town as well. There's a lot of support, and then you get a lot of freedom. You check a recipe with your senior brewer, which is the regional brewer, and they might say, "Well, you've got 'this' in there, what do you think about 'this'?" I've always had a good relationship with those guys.

At The Ram they have their corporate recipes for their main beers that are the same throughout the country, and that was good. I think that makes you a better brewer if you have to make an exact beer. Ram brewers send their samples in to be analyzed, and you get feedback. Dave Colt always created his own specialty beers. But all in all, I like the freedom here better.

With the Fire Chief Ale, basically we can do anything we want. They just say, "Make a red beer." Everyone throughout the country takes a quarter from every pint and donates it to a local fire charity. Our charity is Survive Alive, a child fire safety awareness program. When I came on three and a half years ago, Rock Bottoms had raised over a million dollars for fire departments. We each do different things. It's February for most of the country, but we do ours during April because of the big international fire convention that meets annually in downtown Indianapolis. Each day during that week a different department comes in, they guest bar tend, pass a boot around, and sell T-shirts to raise money for their own projects.

Our company has a division called Rock Bottom Foundation, which handles all of the community charity work. This summer we're sponsoring the Second Annual Brewmasters Golf Tournament to raise money to go for something we call "Miracle on Washington Street." On Christmas Day we bring in needy families and give them a nice sit-down Christmas dinner, give them gifts and necessities. We

reach out to shelters and missions in the inner city, but we're not going to turn away anyone who comes to the door. We've been doing about 400 the last couple of years.

There are two ways to look at the Brewers of Indiana Guild ReplicAle event. One way is that a vendor is donating ingredients, so we get to make a free beer [to serve at the annual July Microbrew Festival at Opti Park in Broad Ripple with income going to Lymphoma/Leukemia research and the Optimist Club]. The other way is to see how brewers can take the same recipe and make it their way. You're not going to get a completely different beer, but I've never tried one yet from different brewers that tastes the same. Dave Colt gives us the recipe, and he says he usually tries to throw a little twist in there, something slightly different. Obviously the water chemistry for each brewer is going to be different, as is how we are going to hop the beer, so he basically said, "Use your yeast, use this percentage of this malt, this malt and this malt, and use this hops any way you like." We are getting all the malt donated as well as getting a great price on hops from Brewers Supply Group. No one is going to give away hops at this point. ReplicAle is how you find out how different brewers do things. It's fun, especially for the people who go to the Festival to experience that. Other states do a ReplicAle, but everyone does it differently. I'll probably brew closer to the July date because of the logistics of tank space, but I could brew it and tap it whenever I want. Dave sets the rules for getting it to the Festival for people to try and compare, but otherwise it's up to the brewer.

Our mug club is set up a little different than most. Usually there is a fee involved. Ours is more a frequent flyer program. It's free, and you're getting five ounces more beer for a penny more over the pint cost. In Indiana you have to charge more for a larger glass. You also get pint points when you bring your card in, and you save to earn gifts. There are nice prizes. After 120 pints you get your name on a keg, and people get really excited about that. We send emails out for what is going on; we do one tapping a month, and I'll buy the beer for a half hour and put a nice appetizer out. We hope people will enjoy that and come back.

Quarterly we do a Brewmaster's Dinner where our executive chef, Victor Garcia, prepares four dishes for four beers. Our company does a pretty good job making sure that there's pairings and cooking with beer. Almost all of our recipes have some beer in the ingredients. Happy hours are illegal in Indiana for alcoholic beverages, but we have specials for food.

Going back and talking about connections between brewers, I worked with quite a few brewers at Oaken Barrel. Among many others, I worked with Ken Price at Oaken Barrel and at The Ram with Dave Colt. If you're smart, that's where you learn, working with different people. And there's the circle that goes around. I used to work with Dave Colt, and Clay Robinson brewed here at Rock Bottom, and then Clay went to The Ram, and when Clay took off, Jon Simmons, my assistant, took Clay's position, and now that Dave started Sun King, Jon took over for Dave, and Adrian Ball, who worked with Omar [Castrellon at Alcatraz] and then was my assistant, is going to be helping Jon out at The Ram. I think that doing that [working with different people] makes you a better brewer. Everyone has their own style of brewing. I've been lucky working with a lot of people. Ken Price at Oaken Barrel really helped me turn into a better brewer. I think before that point I could brew anything, perform any task, but I wasn't thinking about it. Ken's a real intellectual; he puts a lot of thought into everything. He set me on the path of theory, helped me out a lot in thinking about what I was doing. I could have gone into any brewery and made a beer, but I wasn't necessarily at the top of my game. I learned a lot as well from Dave Colt. I was only there for "a minute" [half a year] [Laughter], but I learned some of the ways he did things and I worked with a lot of good brewers during Rock Bottom training, and I can call them up at a moment's notice. I started with Brook Belli, who was the original brewer at Oaken Barrel. I learned a lot from him. Anyone you work with you should learn something, good or bad. If it's bad, learn what not to do or what not to be.

In our [craft brewing] community, we're unique in that we all support each other. People are kind of surprised by that. If you really look into the craft brewing market, most people still haven't tried a good craft beer, so you're hoping that it's going to be a good one when people try their first. As far as the craft beer market in Indiana, probably ten years back when I was with Oaken Barrel our section of the [overall beer] market was probably 0.2 percent, and in the last year or so I've heard it's 2 percent, so it's a little bigger at this point. It's pretty good growth. It's not Portland, Oregon, where it's 52 percent, but Indiana is getting there. It's getting better with the Hoosier Beer Geek blog. Those guys really get around. They are great ambassadors. In the last year nationally, craft beer is the only segment that is growing.

Interview May 29, 2009, at Rock Bottom Downtown

Rock Bottom Restaurant & Brewery College Park

2801 Lake Circle Drive
Indianapolis, IN 46268
317-471-8840
www.rockbottom.com

LIZ LAUGHLIN, BREWMASTER

I had two older brothers, so I had some beer before I was 21 and that was, as I remember, Pete's Wicked Ale and Red Hook. Those were the craft brewers growing up. Of course, we had the yellow fizzy stuff, but, yes, craft beer was "wow, beer with flavor." I went to college in Oregon, which is the Mecca of craft brewing. When I got there as a freshman, I realized, "Wow, this is a whole world out there I never knew." You'd go to a store and see hundreds of different bottles, sort of like a little kid in a candy store. How I got into craft brewing: I was tinkering around in my brother's garage one day and found a couple of carboys [secondary fermenters] and Charlie Papazian's *The Complete Joy of Home Brewing*. The book was kind of moldy and stuck together. I was peeling the pages apart and laughing at the pictures of the '70s people, so I went home and read that book and fell absolutely in love with making beer. So it went from there making flavorful recipes that I had in a store that I wanted to mimic or I liked something about a couple of different beers and wanted to create my own of different flavors that I had tasted. I went to the University of Oregon, which is in Eugene. I was going from Massachusetts, where I basically knew two craft brews. I don't really remember Sam Adams. Pete's Wicked Ale is what I remember the most. Being in Oregon would have been in the mid-1990s, when I truly learned about craft beer.

I was born in Cape Cod. The path to professional brewing started with homebrewing, probably during my sophomore year in my house with extract brewing. It got boring after I did five, ten batches, something like that and got into all-grain. I love hands-on. I love building. I love being creative. I'm very artistic, very scientific oriented, so homebrewing and all-grain brewing fit my two favorite things—building a brewery and then creating a recipe. And I'm into cleanliness. I did all-grain for about six years through college and a little bit after, built a few different types of breweries, had it all outdoors, had sinks, refrigerators—everything outside or in sheds, not in the house—the house is for cooking, not making beer. I was learning about yeast, which fascinated me. I graduated with an environmental studies degree. I had no idea what I wanted to do, but I knew that I loved this. I have lots of hobbies—gardening, always building stuff around the house, carpentry, painting—so I never thought I would have a profession. I thought I would be one of those people who do seasonal work, travel doing seasonal work, and figure it out. I wasn't looking for a career. I jumped around a little bit and said, "All right, I haven't done anything I really want to do. Why don't I move back to Eugene, where there are five breweries?"

At the time I was working in a winery doing crush bottling, so that was cool. But I didn't have much to write on my resume except for homebrewing. How many homebrewers want to be professional brewers? Everybody! So the brewers almost laughed when I walked in: "Hey, I've been homebrewing this long. Can I wash kegs for free or I'll do whatever." And it was like, "No, for liability reasons," or "We're not hiring," or "Sheesh, a woman." All sorts of

different responses, except from two fellows. They definitely befriended me and kept me under their wings. I'd go in a few times a month and walk into the brewery and keep asking questions. One fellow told me if I wanted to better myself, I should start building my resume and take the BJCP, Beer Judging Certification Program, and join the homebrew club, and keep entering beers in the homebrew competitions. So I did all that for eight months; passed the BJCP with flying colors. I worked at the winery, but I studied for three months. It was the hardest test I've taken in my life. I went away for the summer, and one of my buddies hired somebody else while I was gone. I came back and got hired eight months later by Steelhead Brewing Company in Eugene.

So finally, yes, I've got my foot in the door because it's a difficult industry to get in. But number two, in a small town, number three in Oregon, because there are so many home-brewers and so many beer geeks who want to be brewing and waiting to get their foot in the door because they hate their corporate job or whatever. I felt I was extremely lucky, but I was also dedicated and very persistent in trying to get into the door. So that's how I began the professional brewing. I worked at Steelhead for two years as assistant brewer and felt I had gained what I could get out of that particular brewery, so I started exploring some other options in Portland. I knew a lot of the guys up there and really befriended Van Havig at Rock Bottom. I kept asking questions about the job and about the company. Everything he described about the company was very appealing. So I kept giving him phone calls. He turns over brewers pretty frequently. He trains them, and then they go off to a new brewery. He said one of the downfalls of this position is that if you want to stay in Portland, we're going to train you and ship you out. I said, "I'm ready for anything. I want to be a head brewer by the time I am 30." At that time I was 28 or 29. I worked with Van Havig for a year, and they said, "Hey, there's an opening at the College Park location in Indiana." And I said, "Where is Indiana?" [Laughter] I knew it was somewhere in the middle. I'm from the East Coast, living on the West Coast, so I was ready. I didn't want to leave Portland, but I was ready to go, ready to start my own brewery and have all of those different responsibilities. So here I am two years later. Van is the senior brewer of our company, but, hey, Van is our man. I still call him if I have major questions. He's a great mentor; a very knowledgeable guy about anything, not just beer.

Any Rock Bottom you go to, just like any brewery, you are going to have something light, something red, something brown, and something dark, something hoppy or malty, and something in between. Any brewery you are going to, you are going to have that kind of selection. Any Rock Bottom you go to, will have color differentiation and different styles. The unique thing about our chain company is that I get to make my own flagship recipes—and, yes, they are the same. I'm not going to change a flagship recipe. It's a flagship. But they are my recipes, and if you go downtown Indianapolis to Rock Bottom, to Jerry Sutherlin's place, his flagship pale ale might be more hoppy than mine or might be more bitter than mine. His red ale might be more red in color than mine, or my brown might be more chocolaty. Yes, they are going to be the same similar style, but it's different recipes, and I think that's what is extremely unique for a chain. On top of our six flagships we always have two seasonals on tap for whatever the season is. This month [October] it's a pumpkin ale. The people here are really catching on to the IPAs and are begging for and loving more and more hops, so I've been trying to keep an IPA on. Coming to Indiana, I was scared because all my friends were making fun of me, saying, "You're not going to find any good beer" or "You can't even buy cold beer in Indiana." Oh, man, I didn't know if it was true or not, so I got here wondering, "Is anyone going to like hoppy beers?" Coming from the Northwest, that's what we love. When I arrived in December 2006, the number one selling beer was Rock Bottom's Circle City Light—basic beer, even though I love this beer and think it's an awesome recipe. [It was the 2006 gold medal winner at the Indiana State Fair Brewers' Cup competition.] But now the best seller is the Double Barrel Pale Ale, which makes me so excited. People are graduating in their taste. They are coming here for flavor, not just the yellow and fizzy. Mostly who comes here are the neighborhood regulars.

For seasonals, it's an interesting predicament. How do I play it out? Do I make the beers I want to make, or do I make the beers that most of the clients want, and thus it's going to sell? I could make an IPA every time, and it's going to sell, and they are going to be happy. But I'm not much educating them or giving them a variety to choose from. Most of the people would drink an IPA, but the other folks out there will try something else. Like I'll have an altbier, and they'll say, "A German alt? I've never had that. I'll try that." Or right now in the fermenter I have a wheat wine. A lot of people will say, "A wheat wine? Is that a wine?" No, it's like a barley wine, only it's made with wheat. So I think that will be a real mind-blower, serving it at the bar in a snifter or something fancy, and some guy looks over and says, "What's that guy drinking in a snifter? That looks awfully fancy." Something like that gets them excited about something new. But sometimes it doesn't work, and I think, "Well, that's how it's going to be." I made one of my favorite beers. It's a cream ale, and I put it on nitro. It was amazing. It was like a Boddingtons-style beer [founded 1778 in Manchester, England, taken over by Whitbread in 1989]. This was like a year and a half ago, and it didn't sell. People heard the words "cream" and "on nitro" and got freaked out. So I took it off nitro, carbonated it, and sold it as a golden ale, and it flew out the door. Same beer. So that was an experience where my favorite beer didn't work. A year from now it might work. Boddingtons is catching on more and more. I think it is sort of hit and miss, but I will continue making different styles to slowly educate people. When I got here, they were only drinking the pale ale, and now they're all begging for

an IPA, so that's just two years. People rarely are drinking the red anymore. They love the brown now. So they're changing. I've seen the change with certain regulars; they'll say, "Did you change the recipe of this pale ale?" "No, I haven't changed it at all." "Well, I don't think it's as hoppy or as bitter as it was." I'm like, "It's your palate. I'm telling you, it's your palate."

We're also bringing them along with beer and food. On the door of Rock Bottoms are the names of the manager, head brewer, and executive chef as a team. We have a brewer's dinner quarterly. That's an extra special time that we get together and I'll make special beers for the food recipes, or we'll pair the appetizer, soup, salad, and entrée, with the specialty beers that I have. So we'll play this back and forth. This one [October 2008] was fun. We knew the pumpkin ale was coming out, and Rachel Ralston, our *sous chef,* made this delicious ginger snap crust pumpkin cheesecake, but she didn't put any spices in the cheesecake, so the little bit of spice that I had in the pumpkin ale really brought the pumpkin flavor out of the cheesecake, and it was the most amazing dessert pair I've had in a long time. So it's special to get together and find those creations and educate people about different flavors in food and beer. We have a lot of regulars who like to come to the brewer's events. We usually have around forty people, which is a nice size, enough to speak to everyone and not so big as to get overwhelming. It's nice, too, because people meet different folks. We'll set it up in a horseshoe shape, and you just come in and sit, and you end up talking to whoever you are sitting next to. I met two wonderful people at this last one. I met them once at a tapping. I sat in the last empty seat, and it happened to be next to them, and we stayed for about an hour and a half after the dinner just chatting.

So you're able to make great friends, and that is what it's all about—sitting down, sharing food, a meal, and meeting great people. Unfortunately, the monthly tappings are the same date as Downtown, because I think we would get some overlap if they weren't.

I am actually the third brewer here. Brian Boyer filled in until Iain Wilson could get his green card and come over from England. He stayed for a year, and I've been here two years. People don't really have the palate until you've had good stuff.

I would say I was spoiled rotten in Eugene. We had about five breweries in town when I was brewing. Three of us were very close within walking distance. We were all good friends. So the six of us [three head brewers, three assistant brewers] hung out at work, after work. We used to wear the white jumpsuits, and while the mash was resting, we'd go over to someone's brewery and have a pint, and then we'd play Frisbee together, go golfing together. So I was spoiled because we hung out brewing, after brewing.

It's not my style or my taste, but a lot of people want fruit beer here, so I make kegs of fruit beer, but I stay pretty strict to the guidelines. I really understand all the ingredients I'm using [for brewing]. I can make a recipe in my head and know what it will taste like in the end. It's craft and artistry.

A unique aspect is that I'm a woman brewer. Eileen Martin is another brewer down at Upland. Belinda Short is an assistant brewer with Omar Castrellon at Alcatraz. I would like to keep promoting women to try different beers. If someone comes in and says, "I want to try a beer, but I don't really like beer that much," I always give them the brown or the red. I ask, "Do you like coffee or chocolate?" If they say

yes, I will give them the brown, and when they say, "I don't like the dark stuff," I say, "Just sip it. Have a few small sips and try to enjoy it and see what you think." And then it's like, "Wow." It's mind blowing. Or I'll give them something I have on tap that has clove flavors, to associate it with something. If you give them just a light lager, they can't associate it with anything but beer. But they can associate these other flavors with something that they either like or don't like. So I think promoting women to drinking flavorful beer is something worthwhile. Also getting women to brew beer, get back to our roots. It's interesting that it's such a male-dominated industry; everyone thinks you need to be this big beefy guy to lift all this heavy stuff. Actually I think I have an advantage being small. I can jump in and out of stuff, get under stuff, get behind stuff, get into all the nooks and crannies to clean where other folks can't quite get under or get in. Fifty pounds—no one should be lifting anything heavier than that, no one should be lifting a full keg. So go, girl, step out, get into the industry. It's happening. I can see it happening, and I think it will continue to keep happening.

Here we do twelve barrels at a time. I do have the capacity for twenty-four, but this brewery is way oversized for this restaurant. People come in and see the capacity and ask, "How do you get through all that beer?" I say, "We don't. I do half batches to keep it fresh, keep it moving." But it's big and beautiful, and I love it. We don't do bottling. We do growlers, kegs. Bottling is a whole other piece. It has never been part of our mission, and I don't think it ever will be. That's not to say Jerry or I wouldn't do specialty stuff, do a saison or bottle some barrel-aged stuff and make a nice label and sell it out of the restaurant. I have not done that yet, but that's not to say we won't do that—have brewmaster's specials. That would be fun, and it's not that hard. Spend a day filling 100 bottles and that's it, and you sell them for what they're worth—specialty bottle buying. I think that's another thing we're starting to catch on to. We think people will spend fifteen dollars on a bottle of wine, but they won't spend fifteen dollars on a bottle of beer. But I think we are starting to catch on that people will. We're starting to be seen as a specialty product.

Tanya Cornett worked at Oaken Barrel. She's at Bend Brewery right now. She's one of my friends from Oregon. When I told her I was coming to Indiana, she told me to go check out Oaken Barrel. She worked with Jerry Sutherlin. It's such a small world. She's the first woman to win the Champion Brewmaster Cup, awarded at the 2008 Brewers Association World Beer Cup in San Diego; Small Brewer of the Year 2008 at GABF, gold medal for IPA this year, double IPA one year. She's awesome; she's great.

Teri Fahrendorf is one of the more famous women in the industry just because she has been brewing for so long. She's been in the industry for like fifteen years. She created the Pink Boots Society, which is female brewers, cellar men or women in the labs, trying to get us all together. Even finding these women helps us. They had their first meeting at the 2008 World Beer Cup and then at GABF.

I'm using head brewer instead of brewster. I was getting a lot of kidding, so "head brewer" is what I sign on the growler. Well, winning 2008 GABF large brewery of the year as a Rock Bottom team says something about the company putting together a team and sharing the honors; it's getting something right when

company brewers win four gold, a silver, and a bronze at GABF.

Interview October 17, 2008, at Rock Bottom College Park

Ram Restaurant & Brewery

140 South Illinois Street
Indianapolis, IN 46204
317-955-9900
www.theram.com

Ram Restaurant
12750 Parkside Drive
Fishers, IN 46038
317-596-0079

JON SIMMONS, HEAD BREWER

jsimmons@theram.com

DAVE COLT, FORMER HEAD BREWER

On May 1, 2009, Dave Colt, The Ram's head brewer, left to open Sun King Brewing Company with his former assistant, Clay Robinson. Jon Simmons, moved into the head brewer position to brew for the Downtown and Fishers locations.

On May 14, 2009, Simmons was at the Open House event for Sun King Brewing Company, along with other Indiana craft brewers who brought kegs and bottles of their brews to toast another Indiana brewery.

COLT There definitely is camaraderie among us all. There isn't any brewer, Downtown especially, that I couldn't call on a moment's notice and have them help me with whatever problem there is—Jerry Sutherlin, Omar Castrellon, the fellows down at Oaken Barrel—anybody really. The camaraderie is fantastic. I am grateful we have such a connection that we can help each other out. There's

transparency with things that are going on. We can go over to Rock Bottom where Jerry's got a milk stout on right now, and I can ask, "How did you make this?" and he'll tell me. I'm not going to duplicate what he's done. We each try to help prop each other up and make the best beers we can possibly make.

SIMMONS The reaction to me being named head brewer now at The Ram has been great, especially with the Downtown guys I've gotten to know really well. I worked for Jerry for a couple of years. He got me started in this about three years ago [2006] and introduced me to Dave and Clay and Omar. Jerry took me on and taught me a few things. I came to The Ram last year, in July [2008], when Clay left.

COLT Jon's training for The Ram started even before he came to work here because Jerry would bring him in to try our beers as opposed to what Jerry had on and would bring him across the street for what Omar had going on. And there's the BS sessions where we all get together at one person's pub and we're talking about what we are tasting in different beers, what beers are out there in the market that we like, so we're educating each other. It's a continuous cycle of doing that. So Jon was familiar with our beer. The basic difference between The Ram and Rock Bottom is some of our procedures and applications, but the end product turns out well any way you look at it.

My recipes belong to The Ram. Jon may look at my recipes and get some ideas, but he's going to be his own brewer, so he's going to have his own recipes. There may be nods to things I've done in the past, or by the calendar you'll see beers that are familiar, but the thing about being a really good brewer is being able to replicate flawlessly the standard recipes we have [The Ram's flagship beers].

SIMMONS Next year I'll put a little spin on them [the seasonals], I'm sure.

COLT The maibock is a seasonal all Rams put out around the same time, so you'll always see a maibock without me being here. The double rye I just made is my last special beer at The Ram. I'm a hophead, and I hadn't really gone out into the hophead arena, so I wanted to close the door but not shut it with this beer. This recipe now belongs to The Ram. Jon has already made a seasonal beer, the Irish dry stout that was really fantastic; a very creamy beer into the Guinness, Beamish arena is where it was at just smack dab.

SIMMONS The Mug Club was really great with a lot of handshakes, pats on the back [at the tapping for St. Patrick's Day]. "Welcome," "We're behind you," "We support you." They welcomed me in as Dave's assistant nine months ago when they also told Clay, "Great job," when he left. It was the same thing last Thursday [April 16, 2009] when they thanked Dave for a great job and welcomed me aboard.

I'm asked a lot what got me into brewing. Well, I was waiting tables at Rock Bottom. It was my first brewery experience, and I really appreciated what those guys did but didn't really understand it, didn't really know a lot about beer, but I put in some time there working in the restaurant. When Jerry came over [as Rock Bottom Downtown head brewer], he said he could use a little help, so I said I would give it a shot, and here I am. Just started from the beginning, no prior knowledge of beer making whatsoever. Jerry took a chance on me and got me going.

COLT Without sounding glib, I've always liked beer ever since I wasn't supposed to have it and I was "stealing" sips from various beers my stepdad purchased and a lot of it was Hamm's, Stroh's, Carling Black Label—the classic, quintessential American lagers. He'd always get the Stroh's bock beer and told me that's when they clean the vats out, when they have that particular beer, and as a kid, sure, that made absolute sense. But then I thought, who would want to drink that? That would just be horrendous. If they're only cleaning those vats once a year, you're taking a chance.

I'm from South Bend. I graduated from high school in 1984. Brewpubs didn't exist at that point. We lived really close to Notre Dame, so it wasn't hard to convince a college student that if you get a case of beer for me, I will buy you a six-pack. College students jumped at that chance, so we were getting mixed six-packs of Augsburger, all kinds of strange things. I should have known then this is where I'd end up.

There are a lot of water issues here in Indianapolis that made the beer salty when I opened this store with The Ram, so we had a lot of hurdles when we first sent our beers out to the West for all The Ram brewers out that way. The reviews they sent back weren't scathing. They were honest and to the point. I don't know nearly as much as John [Hill] did [about water]; I hope one day to have half as much information as he has. We started attacking the situation, called the water company, and they said, "Well, if you're downtown, your water comes from four different aquifers, and they change randomly, depending on availability and stuff like that."

So we were dealing with an unknown water source that changes every day as opposed to being out around or closer to the edge of the doughnut, and you know where your v is coming from is secure, and you have a known commodity. Water is one of those things we all take for granted, but 90 percent of beer is water, so if you have crappy water, you are going to have a crappy beer, and there really are no two ways about it.

There are, at last count, 70-some categories of beer, and some of them have subcategories, so we are approaching 100 different guidelines. Water has to be adjusted.

SIMMONS I'm kind of new to the game, but I've had some great teachers along the way. Jerry Sutherlin broke me in and was very patient. Clay Robinson promised me Dave wasn't going to be a yeller and a screamer, and so Dave definitely polished me, because we worked together more consistently than I worked with Jerry at Rock Bottom. I've worked in the brewery a lot more here and learned a lot. Well, I've been told a lot, instructed about many things, hopefully I've retained some of it. A year ago I was moving beer around to pubs and restaurants around the state working for Cavalier [Distributing Company], and Rock Bottom gave me a couple of days at their brewery to hang on to what was kind of a dream that I wasn't sure was worth pursuing, and then Dave got me down here and welcomed me aboard. Nine months ago, I was overwhelmed in here. Three and half years ago I came down here with Jerry to visit with Dave and Clay as a first step to being on the staff at Rock Bottom and just listened to a conversation between the three of them and probably understood every third word. [Laughter] It was like listening to a foreign language. So they taught me all the long words.

COLT Spelling all the yeasts is what spell check is for!

SIMMONS Dave actually got me on board at Cavalier. I worked with them for about a year. I was needing some part-time work. I wanted to work in the brewery at Rock Bottom, and Mat Gerdenich was gracious enough to put me on his Cavalier staff. It was an opportunity to meet all kinds of people outside of Indianapolis who are involved in beer. The Cavalier staff is very knowledgeable about beer, so I learned a lot from them, what they are expecting out of a beer, if a beer met their expectations or not. I put in my time doing that and then came here to The Ram. I'm a young guy, and I've still got a lot of strength in my back. Hopefully it will hold out. [Laughter]

COLT I started as a bartender at Circle V when it opened up, and much like the way Jon started, I kind of pestered V [Mark Vojnovich] a little bit. "Hey, I've always loved beer, and I'd like to come back one day and see how that happens." That was April 1996, and I haven't really looked back since. At the time we had Circle V, Alcatraz was the first brewpub downtown, and then Rock Bottom and Oaken Barrel; of course, Broad Ripple was the very first.

The annual Brewers of Indiana Guild ReplicAle event will go with me to Sun King, and it will continue to be a feature of the Indiana Microbrewers Festival held every July.

My recipes while working for The Ram belong to The Ram. The cool factor for me would be if we get beer up and rolling at Sun King and then Jon sends some of my beers in along with his beers to the 2009 Indiana State Fair Craft Brewer Competition. Then I could possibly win in the Indiana Brewers' Cup with two different companies. [Laughter]

Interview April 24, 2009, at The Ram Downtown

The sordid tale for my second Pro-Am brewing starts from last year, when I called Anita Johnson at Great Fermentations. She was enthusiastic about Michael Pearson as an excellent homebrewer. She also thought our personalities would match. She was right on both. We brewed an imperial IPA and sent it to the Great American Beer Festival [GABF]. It got a positive reaction from the judges. With their critique, it made it to the medal round. I think we did an accurate representation of the recipe. It sold out at both stores [downtown Indianapolis and Fishers Rams].

Well, what a difference a year makes. In light of the hops crisis, to brew with Mike again, I gave him a list of hops I have. A lot of hops he uses are the same. I picked his altbier to brew with him. He comes in when he can during the process.

For me it's taking care to be precise with his recipe scaling up from 10 gallons to 10 barrels. That's 310 gallons. You can't just multiply by 31. Each ingredient percentage is worked out. You tweak to make it come out precisely color wise. You adjust hops to the IPU's utilization of the Ram brewing system.

Because of circumstances, our brew won't get aged as long as it would in Germany. It has to be ready for samples to send out in September [2008]. When the beer shows up for the first round of judging in Denver, it needs to be in peak condition. It can age for use at The Rams. We will be making a full batch commercial size on tap. We do not bottle for commercial use. We will have a public party for Michael Pearson's altbier in September for him to celebrate with his wife and MECA Homebrew Club members and his friends and the general public.

It's a very comfortable relationship. Michael is a passionate homebrewer. My question about Pro-Am brewing is "Why wouldn't you?" On the practical level, it's a good marketing strategy, but what the heck, it's fun, except for the bottling [of the samples to send to GABF]. We don't have a bottling operation at The Ram. What we brew here is sent in kegs for The Ram in Fishers and served on tap.

Last year Clay Robinson and I were bottling, and Michael said, "You make that look easy." If you're into the brewing, you know who the brewers and the bottling people are just by how they behave. Brewers tend to move more slowly. Bottlers are always on the run, rushing to get back to the bottling machine. When I worked at Circle V, getting all the beer into the bottles was a challenge. For the brewer, the transfer to the kegs is an art.

Anything made by humans is art. Some we exalt, some not. I'm a graduate of Hanover College. I started at Circle V Brewing Company (1996–2001), founded by Mark Vojnovich and Curt Grelle, and earned my credentials through the old-fashioned Guild System, learning as I was doing. Like any chef, it's combining biology and chemistry to combine the basic ingredients in slightly different ways to create distinctive brews that will be appealing to beer drinkers who want a better quality than a mass-produced beverage. There are two types of barley. Mega brewers use the less expensive six-row. Brewpub and microbrewers use the more expensive, richer tasting two-row variety. Even though The Ram is part of a microbrewing class of beers and customers expect the regulars [flagship beers] to taste here as they do elsewhere, I'm free to be creative with specials, as is every other local brewer. The downtown Ram brews for both locations.

I'm proud to be a brewer in Indiana and tell people, "Drink Indiana Beer." We're not a bunch of hacks from backwoods. We make some of the finest beer in the United States.

We're pretty damn lucky to have the home-brewers and professional brewers working together to bring out the best. When we go to GABF, we are making Indiana beer known.

Telephone interview August 2008

Sun King Brewing Company

135 North College Avenue
Indianapolis, IN 46202
317-602-3702
www.sunkingbrewing.com

CLAY ROBINSON, PRESIDENT/BREWER

[see Clay's story in the Indiana Craft Beer Roundtable, pages 13–23]

DAVE COLT, VICE PRESIDENT/
BREWER/OWNER

dave@sunkingbrewing.com
[see Dave's story in Ram Restaurant & Brewery, pages 83–88]

In the change now to Sun King, Clay and I basically are taking the brewery out of the pub setting, and we are going to make it accessible to everybody. We're going to do much the same things that we have done together at The Ram and Clay did previously at Rock Bottom when he was assistant brewer there. We're going to be "in your face" at the bar. We're going to sell kegs to bars and restaurants, so we are going to do quality education for their sales staffs; we are going to be out and about, doing lots of tastings and tappings at various locations that will have our product on tap. Lucky for me, I have Clay to be out there to be the front man. We work in concert together very well, so it will be more of the same of what we've done.

People can stop by our shop. We'll have tasting room hours, not until midnight, but you can come by, chat us up, tour our new equipment, and while you're visiting Sun King Brewery, get a keg to go.

We won't bottle or can right away. It will probably be six months or so before we package. Clay and others associated with us at Sun King are at the Brewers Conference right now, so they're looking into different systems. You will probably see us can as opposed to bottling. If you can and bottle at the same time, people are going to choose bottles. But in all the research I've done, taste test after taste test reports you can tell no difference, or in fact it really can be a better tasting product. Guinness proved it, and that's huge right there. So people are seeing craft beer cans already in the market. It's green, and it's more economically sound. You get a shipment of cans and how much does that weigh opposed to the same amount of bottles. For receiving shipments of can pallets, we have full doors that open to the dock, so we're set up at Sun King.

Our building is in the historic Cole Noble Neighborhood. The building is brick; it is absolutely an outstanding building, not very pretty to look at out front, very plain-jane, but we have plans to make it more inviting. We're working with Matty Bennett, owner of Sequences Design, to do design work for us. How

many restaurants has he had his hand in that are outstanding now? He's pretty keen about this project.

We plan to have a relationship with Easley Winery. Joan Easley absolutely was and is at the forefront of Indiana's craft brewing. All the heavy-hitters in the homebrew world as far as Indiana is concerned owe a great debt to her. Every time I've talked with the "old-timers," the guys who have been around the block, who started Foam Blowers, got it from her. We've gone across the street and said, "Hi, we're going to be over here," and they seemed pretty all right with that. We also expect to have a pretty heavy presence in the surrounding neighborhoods—downtown Indianapolis, Mass Avenue and Fountain Square—simply due to

the fact that Clay and I know a lot of people, and those people have been kind enough to say they will support us, and they expect us to make good beer. Hopefully we will handle that end of the bargain because they said, "Sure, we'll give you a try and see what you've got."

By mid-June 2009 we'll have beer in the market. A lot of it depended on the application for our federal brewers license being approved before we can file the state documents. It's a process that takes up to ninety days from filing the federal application. We've done everything we can to make it easy for the folks in Cincinnati to take care of it [regional office for the Federal Alcohol, Tobacco, and Firearms Commission].

When we go into packaging, that will be another whole hurdle of approvals.

We're standing on the shoulders of John Hill. It's a sweeter path for us because others have made that trail. They have my thanks and undying gratitude. Because of them I can realize a dream of mine a lot sooner than if I were out there swashing through a wilderness. We owe debts to those who came before us. Michael Jackson did more for beer in America than most anybody, except for Charlie Papazian.

Interview April 24, 2009, at The Ram Downtown

Alcatraz Brewing Company

Circle Centre Mall
49 W. Maryland Street
Indianapolis, IN 46204
317-488-1230
www.alcatraz.com

BELINDA SHORT, ASSISTANT
BREWER (2008–2009)

At Alcatraz, sharing the bock currently on tap.

This bock is one of my favorite beers. It's the one that is selling best besides light and wheat. I'm pretty sure no one else in the area is making any, so that has a little to do with it, but it's a very good beer. It's not quite as heavy as stout or porter, but it has a good body.

This is how I came to be working with Omar Castrellon at Alcatraz. I did some homebrewing with a boyfriend. We had gone to Great Fermentations, got a kit there, did a few brews, and we were constantly going to breweries. We made friends with a lot of the brewers in the area. I ended up needing a job because I had some hours cut in my other job. I was looking for a completely different job that would make a little bit more money, but the jobs I found didn't pay very well.

My boss at my other job said, "Why don't you get a job in a brewery? You would be great at that."

I said, "Well, the thing I noticed about the breweries around here, if you want to get a job in one, you have to know somebody. Everybody knows each other."

He said, "Well, don't you know all those people?"

And I said, "I do, I guess."

So I called Anita Johnson at Great Fermentations, and I asked if she had heard of anybody needing help. She said Omar was looking for someone. So I got my resume to him, and he hired me. That was a year ago.

The first thing Omar taught me was how to clean beer lines. The second thing he taught me was how to clean the fermenter. Then how to clean serving tanks and clean kegs and fill kegs. Now I pretty much do every brew with him. When the mash is in, I come in and look at his recipe and get the hops and the yeast ready and go through the whole procedure of getting everything ready for the brew.

We don't get into new recipes because of the fact that we have what we have, so we have to work with that. We don't have a whole lot of creative license right now. We've talked about doing some casks, and I'm a real big fan of cider and some Belgian styles. We've talked about a barley wine, which I keep pushing. We've only got five fermenters, so it makes it hard. We definitely talk about different recipes.

As for my future, I'm hoping to either work with someone who has his or her own brewery or possibly have my own.

I got into homebrewing because I had been drinking craft beer for a while. The first craft beer that I had was at The Ram. I really like wheat, and then one day I was introduced to Hopslam [Bell's], and I fell in love with centennial hops and hoppy beers, double IPAs. I just really started getting into the different complexities of beers and really, really liking them. It still happens now when I try new beers. A couple years ago when I started drinking barley wine I found that I absolutely adore barley wines. The thing for me, which everybody else tells me happens, is that I built up the passion just from being around the people who have the passion and I absorb information.

About my adventures working with Omar, I would say the first day I had to clean a fermenter I hadn't really gotten to know Omar yet, and I couldn't tell if he had a dry sense of humor or if he was being serious. Sometimes still I can't tell. He told me to take a hose from the bottom as we were emptying out the fermenter, the beer that was at the bottom, and he said, "Now this is going to explode."

I thought, surely it's not going to explode, and if it did that, we wouldn't do it this way. And sure enough, it went up and back down and all over me and all over the place. I thought, why did he do that? He never told me why he did that. Did he do it to be funny, or did he do it to make me figure out a way to not have that happen again? I don't do it the same way that he does, but that never happened again. I had no reason to believe that it was true about exploding; it's not that I didn't believe him, but I also thought he was messing with me. And then I thought maybe he's just testing me and trying to see if I can put up with him.

I do a lot of cleaning. Probably 80 percent of what I do is cleaning.

Being able to do the brewery stuff makes me feel good to go home and be tired and feel like I actually did something that day as opposed to standing around and trying to help people. I don't tell a lot of people that I work in a brewery, because there is this stigma that I can get them free beer that isn't necessarily true. But I have noticed that some people really love beer. It's nice to be a part of something that people really appreciate.

I thought about all those things—the visual art that goes with brewing, labels, tap pulls. Obviously, I haven't taken Omar's class to get into the business part. I feel there is a reason he doesn't teach me the same way he teaches his class because he's teaching that as a theory class. What I'm learning from him are practical things that I need to know, a step at a time, and I have to be able to remember them at a moment's notice while I'm already covering an important chore.

I've noticed that in brewing, like in cooking, it's gotten to be a strange role reversal. It used to be that women brewed and cooked, and now it's men. I get the question a lot. "What is it like being a female in the brewing industry?" So I tell people, "I was never a man in the brewing industry, so I don't have any idea what that should be like."

When I go to festivals, there are so many younger people trying really good beer. I see them all over. Maybe they don't quite understand what they are drinking, but when they get older, they will find the craft beer market.

Interview May 22, 2009, at Alcatraz Brewing Company

The Brewers

Broad Ripple Brewpub

842 East 65th Street
Indianapolis, IN 46220
317-253-2739
www.broadripplebrewpub.com

KEVIN MATALUCCI, BREWMASTER

[see Kevin's story as part of the Indiana
Craft Beer Roundtable, pages 13–23]

AARON EVILSIZOR, HOMEBREWER

AARON I took today off from work to partner with brewmaster Kevin Matalucci.

KEVIN We are brewing the biggest beer yet made at Broad Ripple Brewpub. Big in the sense of taste because Aaron's 2008 Indiana State Fair "best of show" Russian imperial stout has an alcohol level of 10 percent with a full rainbow of hues from first sip to final swallow. We will allow the brew to age until late February, and we'll serve it on tap paired with a menu of appetizers, entrees of winter fare, and rich desserts and for BRBP regulars and new customers to enjoy by itself during an evening of spirited conversation. It all makes the extra amounts of malts and hops and longer brewing time worthwhile.

AARON The original homebrew recipe took me fourteen hours to complete on my ten-gallon-system. It was my wife's birthday.

I was supposed to take her out. We had pizza at home.

KEVIN I usually can get in and out in six-plus hours for the 4–7 percent range of recipes I usually brew at BRBP. This will take longer because of the quantity of grain. The process of brewing is like making drip coffee. The mash tun for this beer is so full of grain you have to wait for the liquid to drain, and you have to keep stirring so all the liquid is in constant contact with all the grains to capture all the flavors. Aaron's recipe is wonderfully complex and will be deceptively easy to drink at 10 percent. You want to drink it slowly. The deep fruit flavors—plum, raisins, cherry—come from the malts and the esters produced during fermentation due to the English ale yeast Aaron has chosen.

AARON What might sound like an oxymoron—English ale yeast for Russian imperial stout—is actually an enticing bit of history that fits into my penchant for reading and research and my own palate for beers with rich complexity developed during a longer fermentation process. I've always enjoyed Russian imperial stout at microbrewers festivals, so I thought I'd try one and see how it turned out. This is the first time I've brewed this recipe. I entered it in the 2007 State Fair Brewers' Cup, but it was still too fresh; it had stronger alcohol notes and didn't have deep fruit flavors. It didn't win, but in 2008 I entered the same recipe aged in bottles in my basement. This time it took "best of show."

KEVIN A year's aging makes a big difference in a big beer, and even five more years of aging in the bottle should make Aaron's brew even more complex and worthy.

AARON I'm just happy to be brewing together, not rushing the process, yet eagerly looking forward to late February 2009 and the tapping. My brother-in-law got me a brewing kit for Christmas two years ago, and my homebrewing just took off from there.

KEVIN Our regulars are quite excited by Aaron's beer. I'm excited, even though this is the seventh year I've brewed an Indiana State Fair "best of show" at BRBP.

AARON People are fascinated by big beers. Everybody gets a little something different when they taste this recipe. I'm excited about the sharing with so many more people.

Interview November 10, 2008, at Broad Ripple Brewpub

THOMAS WALLBANK, HOMEBREWER

At the 2008 American Homebrewers Association [AHA] National Homebrew Competition, Thomas Wallbank won gold for his Düsseldorf Altbier, besting 149 other entries in Amber Hybrid Beer.

My girlfriend (now wife) bought me a simple beer-making kit for my birthday in about 1995. That first batch turned out quite good, and I've stuck with the hobby due to the fascinating combination of science, art, history, and challenge of getting wild animals (yeast) to do what I want them to do. In the mid-1990s, there were a few online resources that inspired me to switch from extract to all-grain brewing after just three or four batches. My main influence has been the daily edition of the *Homebrew Digest* and its very knowledgeable participants. The professional diversity (bakers, refrigeration repairmen, food scientists, chemists, metal/welding experts, professional brewers, etc.) of participants results in a great exchange of ideas as well as good practical advice. In print, Ray Daniels's great book, *Designing Great Beers,* was a big influence. In the world of craft beer and styles, Michael Jackson has influenced everyone.

Given family and other interests that compete for my time, I utilize processes and equipment that allow me to brew an all-grain batch of beer quickly (4–5 hours vs. 6–7, which seems typical for homebrewers). My batch sizes are relatively small at 5–8 gallons. This allows more iteration of recipes and processes. Automation of temperature control makes my brew day easier and aids in consistency and control. Before brewing a new style, I'll put considerable time into researching both style guidelines and history of the beer style to determine my target. I'll then put time into determining the most appropriate ingredients, processes, and yeast strains that will allow me to hit that target. This range of options gives homebrewers a unique advantage over professional brewers.

I joined the FBI less than two years ago [2006]. Before that I had very little in-person interaction with other brewers, and I now realize I should have joined a long time ago! Firsthand tasting and discussing with other brewers are invaluable in improving one's beer. The shared interest and camaraderie are great. Ron Smith has been a major factor in inspiring the club and making it attractive to a wider group of homebrewers. There are three monthly meetings, each with a unique focus and appeal (social, technical [CIA], and brewpub visit/tour).

With a young family, my main challenge is time (for brewing, judging, research, travel).

The other (in a more lighthearted tone) is matching supply with demand—I always seem to have either too much beer produced or not enough! I probably get the most enjoyment from the challenge of putting together the brewing equipment—stainless steel, pumps, valves, electronics, water, CO_2 regulators, etc.—and getting it to all work together. I'm constantly changing my brewery's setup. Producing beer, judging, etc, are almost secondary. Travel has been one of the most rewarding aspects of my brewing interests. Düsseldorf Altbier has very limited availability outside of Düsseldorf, Germany. Having made the effort to travel there and sample most of the commercial examples helped and inspired me to brew the beer that took the gold. At work I've come across several other homebrewers, and having this common interest, like any other, aids in forming good working relationships. Since becoming an active FBI member, I've enjoyed meeting other Indy area brewers (often out of state), sharing information about the club, and encouraging them to join us. Sharing in the planning and work of the club's recent activities creates a sense of ownership and belonging. The FBI's great "club night booth" at the American Homebrewers Association 2008 convention in Cincinnati and being voted as having the "best beers" really reinforced this. Here's Ron Smith's summary:

"At the legendary Club Night, we had a great presentation with about twelve of us decked out in the FBI black suits, hats, and shades. Uniforms, and six of the spouses making quite the memorable impression in their racy FBI Prisoner outfits. We had twenty-four kegs on tap all at the same time [reminiscent of the HBO series 24], including six historic recipes from once outlawed beers (which was our theme). The lineup and overall quality of our beer not only had a packed house of perhaps 1,000 people coming back again and again for more, but we were voted the Club with the Best Beer! This was out of forty-two clubs in attendance from all over the country. This was an incredible surprise and an awesome honor!"

The AHA's National Homebrew Competition is the largest beer competition in the world (professional or amateur). This year there were nearly 6,000 entries, and to win one of the twenty-three first place (gold) medals is really very exciting! Homebrewers produce much beer that is arguably as good as or better than commercial product, and I feel honored to have had a beer be singled out from this field of many great beers.

Telephone and email interviews July 11, 2008

Brugge Brasserie

1011a East Westfield Boulevard
Indianapolis, IN 46220
317-255-0978
www.bruggebrasserie.com

Brugge Brasserie Production Facility
401–402 South 9th Street
Terre Haute, IN 47807
812-234-2800

TED MILLER, OWNER AND BREWMASTER

MICAH WEICHERT, BREWERY MANAGER
AND HEAD BREWER (2007–2009)

TED MILLER I'd like to spend the next several years really trying to build a Brugge brand. We've got the Tripel de Ripple, which is gaining serious momentum, but I think we have at least four or five brews that could really drive us over the next five years. My ultimate goal is for the Terre Haute Brewery to brew enough beer to maintain its own profitability and grow, so I can go build a brewery on a horse farm where I can play with micro-flora and wood. We do some barrel aging now (Diamond Kings—'09 looks, or I guess smells, rather promising), but I'd like to have a whole bunch more brews on oak. All of us in Indiana are going to play a role in growing the craft beer category. Right now, Brugge is unique in that we do Belgians almost exclusively, and this has turned some people on to our craft. The market here is probably too small for that, though, so we are looking at a line of American craft beers in traditional packaging. Probably in the "robust and completely insane" mold, but still a broader market than the Belgians. What I envision for the present and future is a whole bunch of hard work! As for the present, although beer is somewhat recession resistant, I think we'll see a pretty big spike in 2010 if economists are correct in estimating that we'll pull out of this current slump by q4 or q1 2010. For the distant future, I think Indiana will eventually catch up to states like Oregon when they finally plateau. Craft beer now accounts for 25 percent of supermarket beer sales by dollar volume in Oregon against a national average of 6.9 percent. Indiana is at about 1 percent. We have some extremely talented brewers here; we just need to learn how to get those awesome products off of the shelves and into the hands of the consumers. New consumers. We have the enthusiasts in the category already. In fact, they are our biggest assets because they have this tremendous passion for our craft and love to talk about it.

Email interview May 28, 2009

MICAH WEICHERT I was at 23rd Street Brewery in Lawrence, Kansas, before coming here.

I've been brewing eight or nine years now professionally. I was happy in Lawrence, and things were going really well. Sales were constantly increasing, distribution was increasing and doubling, and I won a couple of medals at the Great American Beer Festival—a bronze medal for a Belgian new style pilsner, a silver medal for an Irish style red ale.

I met Ted and Shannon Miller about three years ago at the Great American Beer Festival. Their booth was just a little down from ours. I liked their beer, and we became friends. Then at the craft brewer conference last year in Austin, they offered me the job here to run the brewery. I decided the next best thing to owning my own place was working for somebody that I really respected. I think that's a lot of the problem with brewers and their relationships to owners or upper management. We brewers are particular about the way things should be done.

I love Ted's beer. I really fell in love with the look, the marketing, which is probably the most important thing. In selling beer it's what you look like, what's your logo, what's your marketing approach. A good beer industry person can look at an approach to marketing and can tell without even tasting the beer if it's going to be successful. I loved the name, I loved the look, the flower, the chalice, and the beer is fantastic. I could tell it is going to be successful. It's a great time to get involved in the Belgian beer movement; it's been on the rise and the new craze the last couple of years. It's like a whole new world of beers and one I never really knew much about.

Prior to working for Brugge, I really only brewed a couple of Belgians. I never really got into the big hops movement. How much hops can you put in a single batch of beer? Belgian beer is a bit of an acquired taste. So the market-

ing, the beer, the look, and Ted and Shannon, and then on top of that, I was very impressed with the history of beer in Terre Haute, with the brewery dating back to 1836. Places like this are untapped cultural bits of brewing history that people in Indiana don't even know that much about. I thought, there can't be too many places like this left. The history is almost like a dream—to find a place like this that you can revive and make something new out of.

Terre Haute has obviously been in a depression, a recession, for the last fifteen years or more, but they are coming out of that, and there's a lot of new building going on. There's progress, but the general attitude of people is no pride. There's so little pride here in their community, and to be able to bring something to a place like this, to bring something to a community that kind of lost its heritage is a great thing. It's worth more than your paycheck. The brewing heritage here has been lost, and Mike Rowe has done a great thing. He is the one who really dug it up and resurrected it and took it as far as he could. And then chance has it that we came in, and now we're doing our part. After we're gone to do something else, hopefully someone else will come in and keep that going. It's obvious that people here want that, and they need that cultural pride and heritage to be revived and to have something to be proud of because they're not really proud of the penitentiary or the car factory or the paper plant or the things that give a funny odor to the town. But the odor of boiling hops and malted barley is something that's nice and adds a nice feel to the area. The revival of the brewing culture here—reportedly, at one time twenty breweries of all different sizes were operating all at the same time—that was a big selling point.

I was born in Topeka, Kansas. I'm German by descent—a little Irish, a little Scottish, and a little Native American, but mostly German. My father, Ivan Weichert, was stationed in Germany in the late 1960s and early 1970s right near the Czech Republic. He can speak Russian, German, Japanese, and all sorts of languages. He's a translator in the Army. Both my parents were Air Force brats and moved all over the world with their families. My dad, from living in Germany and Czech Republic, gained his own appreciation for pilsners. Pilsner Urquell, besides my own beer, is probably his favorite beer. He was really the first influence for "This is what beer is supposed to taste like. This is what good beer is."

When I started experimenting with beer in high school, all the kids were drinking Budweiser Light and all the domestic American beer, but I didn't care for it. It didn't really have good flavor. At some point someone introduced me to what at that time was craft beer.

There was a brewery that opened up in town, so I started learning about the craft beer culture and about the microbrewery world and finding flavors like porters and stouts. I worked as a busboy in the brewery in Topeka, but only for a couple of weeks because the person who hired me wasn't supposed to be hiring anybody new. When upper management found out, they had to fire me, so I thought, "Well, that's a short career in the brewery business." But I met some people who were homebrewing, and I started experimenting with homebrewing, but I never got that far into homebrewing that I could make anything good consistently.

I had a friend who worked at the Pony Express Brewery in Kansas City. He knew I was looking for a job and that I had at least some

The Brewers

idea of the brewing experience. So he said, "Do you want to work at the brewery and we'll train you professionally?" And I said, "Are you kidding? Should I come in today?" I went in the next day, and they hired me. My first boss was Stacey Kanes, and he still works in Kansas City, now with the Ameristar brewpub. He wanted to hire somebody without a lot of experience and without bad habits. He wanted somebody to train from scratch. I was a sponge just waiting to absorb the beer culture.

That was really nice having my first job in a microbrewery. A lot of people in the industry started out in a brewpub. Maybe they washed dishes or waited tables or bar tended then acquired the assistant brewer's position, and then maybe, if they were fortunate enough, got the head brewer's job in a brewpub. I felt really fortunate to get into a microbrewery setting right off the bat where I was not only able to brew the beer, transfer the beer, filter the beer, do the bottling and the kegging and warehouse management and all the stuff that comes with the microbrewery. We were making 5,000 barrels a year with just three guys in a huge warehouse in a random place in Kansas.

I had friends who lived in Hawaii, and I went to visit them a lot. While I was working at Pony Express, I was visiting, and like the second day there my good friend said, "Why don't you just go over to the Kona Brewing Company and get the head brewer's job." "Yeah, like that's going to happen," I said. "I'm just going to walk in there, and they'll give it to me." Sure enough, a week later we went in there, and one of the owners had flown in from Seattle, and he offered me the head brewer's job right there. I said, "Are you serious?" and he said, "Can you start tomorrow?" and I said, "I work

in a brewery in Kansas. I'm going to have to go home and settle things up there and come back, but I'd love to." My boss somehow knew that was going to happen. When I was preparing to go on vacation he said, "Make sure you come back, OK?" Sure enough, when I came back, I said, "Sorry, but I got an opportunity of a lifetime here to run a brewery in Hawaii." It sounds pretty amazing, but it wasn't all it was cracked up to be.

Business in Hawaii doesn't really run like business in the rest of the world or mainland United States. My boiler went down, and it took a week to get a boiler technician over from Oahu, and two weeks to get a part in, and another week for him to come back. For one month I wasn't able to do anything. At the other brewpub on the island, Maui Brewpub, their boiler had completely shut down. So they stopped paying their brewer for about a month or so, and this is a guy who had moved his wife and two kids down from Alaska. They didn't want to spend money on a new boiler, so they said, "We're not going to pay you anymore." And that was it. After they were out of commission for about two months, they came to me and said, "Would you make some beer for us?" I said, "I'm not sure after what just happened." But the other brewer said he wouldn't hold it against me, so for a while I was running the only two breweries on the island.

My fiancée was in school back in Kansas, so I got really lonely out there. It was situated with these plantation cottages and these coconut groves. It was a really beautiful place, and there were honeymooners there. It drove me totally crazy, because the woman I love was 6,000 miles away. I was traveling back to Kansas to spend about a month, and I was in the air when the 9/11 attacks happened. I was supposed to have a short layover in L.A. and then fly to Denver and then to Kansas City. When I booked the flight, I had asked if I had to get off the plane when I got to Los Angeles, switch planes or anything, and the clerk said, "No, it's just going to be a refueling stop, and then you'll be on your way. You won't have to de-board the plane."

When we got to L.A., they said everybody had to get off the plane for special cleaning, so I'm thinking some situation happened. We got into the terminal, and everybody was crowding around the televisions. Nobody could believe what was happening. The only thing I could think was is this the beginning of Armageddon? I'm not supposed to be in Los Angeles when Armageddon hits. I want to be out in the country, someplace besides a major city. So they closed LAX. I went back to the terminal to board the plane. I'm thinking, I need to get home to Kansas. They said, "No, the airport is closed. Everyone just go home." And I said, "That's what I'm trying to do, just go home to Kansas." And they said, "Nobody's getting on this plane. Everyone just go home." And they came on the speakers and announced, "LAX is officially closed. Everyone must leave the airport." There's thousands of people trying to get their baggage and get outside the airport and trying to figure out what's going on. I had one friend in Los Angeles, and she came and picked me up, and four days later I think I got the last rental car in all of California and drove back to Kansas almost nonstop.

So after that happened, Hawaii didn't really appeal to me because I didn't want to get stuck out there if something else happened and be away from my family and my fiancée. So to make a long story longer, I was planning to leave Hawaii and go back to Kansas.

Pony Express had closed down and was reopening with new investors, and they asked me to come back and work for them. So I did, and I worked with them for another year and a half. Things went pretty well, and then they were going through some management and investor changes. The brewery was going in a direction that my brewing staff and I didn't want to go, so we all made a mass exit. Then 75th Street Brewery in Kansas City was opening a satellite location, and I ended up going to work for them. I had only been brewing for about a month or so and things were great with them, a well-run company but a corporate company that didn't really appeal to me. They had seven area restaurants and a couple of breweries. They had their hand and money in just about every brewery that had opened. At one time they had money in Pony Express, which I didn't know at the time. They were just a large company with a lot of upper management. I had five or six bosses I had to answer to, which I didn't like, and they brought in a new general manager at one point, and he really was a big part of turning that place around, so we were making good money and making profits every week. We liked the direction he was going, so he decided to buy the brewery out from the parent company, Kansas City Hops. Between him and me and another manager we basically made it into our brewery, and we enjoyed that, and then the job popped open at Brugge, and I decided to make that change.

Great beer is such a blessed job. All the people in the industry are good people, and there is so much more camaraderie than there is competition, and everybody takes care of one another. Most of us are not getting rich off of it or making huge salaries, but I'm able to support my family and offer a good quality of life to them.

The Brewers

After being in the business for probably two years, I started realizing I'm at the point where I either go back to the kitchen or landscaping, which I had done before, or I make a career out of brewing. I was already a professional brewer, but I had to take that next step. Being of German descent, it felt like it was of my birthright to make beer. And I've never really been out of it. When my father tells people, "My son is a brewer, and it's really good," part of him might be living vicariously through me and just that he is appreciative of a good beer. The Czech Republic–style Pilsner that I won the bronze medal with I named Papa's Pils after my dad. I had my son at that point, so it was like the new papa and the old papa, but I named the beer after him because it was his favorite beer, his style of pilsner, and the first year we entered the competition, we won the bronze medal with it, which was a proud moment and is even now.

Early on, when I was brewing professionally, my brother was a recovering alcoholic and drug abuser. I was having a moral dilemma thinking, "Am I being a cause of the problem?" I tried to understand the traditional role of brewpubs, which has been to bring people of a community together and to promote responsible drinking and not drinking with driving. I realized that while you can't make anyone else's choices for them, you have to try to lead by example, try to be a good influence. Most breweries and brewpubs donate their time and brews for community events and for fund-raisers for organizations that are helping people.

First coming to Indiana I didn't know they had so many breweries. I didn't know the Brewers Guild was as organized as it is and that the brewing community is so strong. I didn't expect it to be. Having lived in other parts of the country, nobody was talking much about Indiana. At first I was a little standoffish; this is a pretty tight little brewery family in Indiana, but the more I looked at it, I could see it's nicely knit. I've been here a year now, and I feel I've been accepted.

The thing that makes a great brewer is the lack of ego. We all make good beer. The common goal is to keep improving, to accept comments and to learn from experiences—good and bad. In small craft breweries, everything is challenging. You have to go to a brewery and work with what they have. That's why most brewers are renaissance jack-of-all-trades types of guys and gals. We have to learn all areas of the industry, including equipment and machinery.

Bottling the Brugge beers, going from brews made on a ten-barrel system served on tap to a product that is on the shelf, we didn't really tone down, but we made them a little more "user-friendly." When Ted Miller originally made the Black, he had all kinds of coffee and chocolate, so we had to make it more feasible and functional in a bottling setting. We bounce ideas off each other: what we taste in the beer, what we think might be the caliber of a certain flavor, whether we want to add or change anything. We have to make changes gradually. Ted has been willing to hear what I want to say and, of course, vice versa. Ted is willing to teach but also willing to learn.

Interview August 26, 2008, at Brugge Production Facility in Terre Haute

MICHAEL S. ROWE IS A TOUR GUIDE
OF THE HISTORIC DOWNTOWN TERRE
HAUTE BREWING DISTRICT.

The Terre Haute Brewery started in the building where M. Moggers Restaurant & Pub is now at 9th and Poplar. The Brewery extended all the way down to where you see the white clay building. That was the bottling plant. The stable, which housed more than fifty-five Clydesdale and Belgian horses, was the other side of what is now the CVS drugstore. The horses delivered beer. All of this parking lot down to here was a five-story brewing complex. They were the seventh largest brewer in the United States 100 years ago.

[According to the 1915 *Centennial History and Handbook of Indiana,* Terre Haute "has the largest distillery in the United States with a daily capacity of 60,000 gallons and over 400,000 barrels of beer are made here annually. Its glass factories make on an average over 500,000 bottles daily" (433).]

Before refrigeration they had to have cellars for the beer. We have blueprints from 1905 that indicate these parking lots were nothing but cellars; 64 feet wide by up to 120 feet deep with 20-foot ceiling. It's all still here. We thought it would be great to access this sometime. We know exactly how to get in. It's just trying to figure the permit process. The two-story building down there with the beer sign out front, the first floor used to be a little bar and they ran [a pipe] from here across the street underground. They didn't even have taps, they just had like a meter, like a water meter, and they charged that way. The bar was privately owned. See the windows on the second floor? It was a brothel. [Laughter] There was like five little rooms up there. There was one bathroom and a shower. Each little room had just a little hand sink. The walls are still there. The guys who used to work [at the brewery] used to get paid on Friday afternoon, go across the street, beer was served from right underground, and if they wanted to they'd go upstairs. At the time the brewery employed over 900 people. Part of the union contract allowed them to drink on the job. They had twenty-two tickets issued and they would be drinking all day on the job and then go across the street. The interesting thing about that place, too, the brewery wanted the city to recognize in a big way what it contributed to the economy, so they consciously paid the brewery workers in silver dollars. Now, there were 900 employees paid in silver dollars, which created a nuisance for the whole town. The story I heard, when the old guy died and they liquidated the tavern and someone else got it and they were remodeling, they located a couple of sacks of silver dollars stuck in the wall. They probably went into the remodeling [payments].

When CVS was putting a new building on five years ago, I got to know the project manager really well. We were excavating the old brewery here, and he wanted to get an idea of what he was dealing with structurally. They moved the site three times. They couldn't get to the bottom. There was a basement 12 feet, a cellar below that 20 feet, and so they kept moving the site. When they were over here they found an exit in the cellar that went back to the stables just like Italian castles. The old lighting is still on the walls; the plaster and brick are intact. It's pretty fascinating. The initial brewery started in 1837. At that time the Wabash and Erie Canal went down 9th ½ Street. There's an old cellar here that exited down at the canal dock where they transported beer by wagon or canal boat. There's a bittersweet story that kind of reflects things that happened all around the Midwest.

It's a long story. The building we are sitting in now, M. Moggers, 904 Poplar, is where all of this started. My forebears had primarily been in apartments, housing, real estate, and we bought this building. It was condemned for demolition in 1990 by the city. I actually had to get it stopped when the crew was on the way. The city called them back. We bought the building to renovate it and adapt it for rentals. When we bought it and had gone through it, I started researching and learned in 1974 it had a grain business in this property, and I thought if it goes back that far, maybe there's an earlier issue, so I started researching earlier through the city directory and the historical society and found all this documentation from 1862 advertising Bleemal's Brewery on the Wabash & Erie Canal, near the Poplar Canal. This piqued my interest, and as it turned out, just at the corner of the building, which is 9th ½ Street, is the canal bed, the largest manmade waterway in the United States, through and right up to the brewery. As we started to re-model, we found a number of artifacts, sales receipts from the Prohibition where Ernest Bleemal [Flour & Feed] was selling grain to the Terre Haute Brewing Company for what we assume was a nonalcoholic beverage. Out of curiosity we started excavating a portion of the canal and found remnants of what was originally used as coolers at the canal dock for beer; we found old cellars, the old brewery. Early on I called this my biggest life distraction. As one thing led to another, I didn't have the heart to cover up all of this history, all of this place.

My earliest documentation of this building is as Terre Haute Brewery in 1837. An old document states—the United States was in a state of panic similar to the stock market crash of '29—that there were several firms that put out notes to bail out Terre Haute, which was filing for bankruptcy. One of them was Terra Haute Brewery, so up until we ceased production last spring [2007] we were the second oldest active brewery in the United States, which is pretty remarkable.

This restaurant was used as the Terre Haute Brewing Company garage 100 years ago. This was open all the way to the front at Poplar. I first came in here and framed all this, put the bar in; all of this I built, recycling material from other buildings that were being torn down. I managed to duplicate stain and shel-lac that would have been used 100 years ago to give it that old look. We got our brewery open in 1995, and by November 2000 we had actually made it to the old brewery, which is here. We dug it out by hand, finding the old cellar, actually launching the brewery here, but we couldn't keep up. We had 100-gallon-a-week capacity and were selling about three times that, so that's what spurred me to buy the building across the street. Shortly after 9/11 we purchased a brewery on the East Coast and brought the operation here and put it in the building across the street and then went into production for CV [Champagne Velvet beer]. That is the current events story.

I've always been fascinated with the leg-acy of this entire district, which was an early German immigrant district. It's an amazing heritage they brought here. I've got the origi-nal recipes for Champagne Velvet of 1901 with the brewer's name, Walter Braun. I met his de-scendants. He didn't speak English. They were very successful even 100 years ago. The brewery imported him from Germany and brought him to Terre Haute. He lived right across the street. As head brewer he brought all his recipes. It's just amazing, that whole legacy. To think 100 years ago a railroad spur came up here and trucks trucked beer to twenty-one states.

When we started this reclamation, Terre Haute did not think of saving much. It was a cottage industry for demolition. I had to have several meetings with the city to convince them we shouldn't bulldoze this. Once we did this, I saw the pride in people's heritage. There is more to a city than a strip mall. Once people recognize that they have a rich heritage and they can connect to something that is worthwhile, they take pride in it. That is something we connected with. We opened this place first, in 1995, then took the old Stables building. It's really gorgeous. It's an old Victorian stables that was destined for demolition. There was a grocery chain that was going to use the old buildings as a distribution site and raze the stables, so we had to save all the buildings. In doing so, I think people recognized there is a connection with the past. There is something to be said for that.

I used to do tours for students and teachers at Indiana State University and others to see the evidence of the canal docks, evidence of the underground, and they'd start going out to the river bed and get all excited about shards and pottery, real artifacts that are here. They'd get excited and then go back to their routine lives and busy schedules and nothing really happened. We found some amazing artifacts. There is an old beer cooler along the dock. During the Civil War they paid the brewers in coins; we found a leather pouch in one of the brick walls. I was involved in throwing sand with a shovel, and these coins separated. There'd be like a 1852 and the newest coins were like 1864. When we got it cleaned out, we noticed the brick out to the wall. We pulled the brick out and noticed there was another bag of coins, another cluster of coins, inside the wall.

We had the next door building all full of artifacts. I have a collection of Champagne Velvet that spans 120 years. Before Champagne Velvet, they called it Terre Haute Beer. I have signs from that period. I hauled fifteen truckloads of Champagne Velvet and Terre Haute Brewing memorabilia and put it in storage. We had a whole display for years that was part of the tour.

I would like to see that legacy continued. I consciously retained the trademark Champagne Velvet, which is a registered trademark we bought from Pabst Brewing Company [which had acquired the trademark]. I would like to see the collection end up where we display it with the recipes.

I was born and raised here. I have family that goes back three generations. One side were German immigrants—Schomer—which is pretty German. I have photographs of Willy Schomer when he was seventeen; he worked here. The Terre Haute Brewery in the abstract leased this property in 1905. My grandmother said he worked in this building. In the pictures they looked like kids holding Terre Haute Brewing Company amber bottles. That was part of the display. I had no idea, coming into buying this building, that there was a tie, that he actually worked where we are sitting. So there was a tie 100 years ago.

I graduated from Indiana State University. Sociology was my major; I could have minored in psychology, but I took social science, which has been helpful. I started reclamation in 1990. It's surprising the number of *Trib-Star* articles written over the period of time that started in February 1990.

We haven't done tours for over a year. We were on the curriculum of schools. I would change content with the age of the people on the tour. For the kids it would be about the Civil War; for adults it would be about beer. We have a lot of visuals—the old brewery below, the canal dock. We would start outside and show where the canal was, talk about the buildings, the overall complex, and work our way into the brewery and end up across the street with the current brewery and top it off with beer or root beer.

It seemed like a natural progression—I see it as the biggest distraction in my life, but it was one of those things—to find all the CV stuff, doing the tours, doing the two restaurants, and then have the brewmasters book walk in the front door.

People in the community knew I collected this stuff, so I had a guy walk in who said in his basement he had a book that had something to do with beer, would I give him twenty bucks. At the time I thought I was giving him too much money, so I didn't even get his name and gave him twenty dollars and I'm thinking, "I've just thrown away twenty bucks, but he might come back with a CV cold top can or a Champagne Velvet sign." So he left, and I'm flipping through the book, and inside is a handwritten recipe for Champagne Velvet beer for 1901. On the backside it has a letterhead of the brewery at that time. On the front of the book is "Walter Braun," who is well documented as the brewmaster. He was actually assistant brewmaster at that time. Once we found the recipe, we had a guy come in who was a microbiologist who had been with Eli Lilly; he had been making beer in his garage. I gave him a copy of the recipe, and we spent a year working on the recipe, and then we set up a brewery downstairs. His name was Ted Herrera. At the time I met him, he was working for a local pharmaceutical company, Schering Plough. Based on Walter Braun's recipe, we launched CV in 2000.

There was never an end to it. It was like opening a door and there was more stuff. It isn't over yet. That is my biggest concern. I really would like it to survive.

Mike Rowe was born on December 4, 1933—the very day that the repeal of Prohibition went into effect.

See also:
www.cvbeer.com
www.brewersofindianaguild.com/History/
http://specials.tribstar.com/terrahautestop40/stories/CV.html

Oral history interview August 26, 2008, Terre Haute

Oaken Barrel
Brewing Company

50 North Airport Parkway, Suite L
Greenwood, IN 46143
317-888-7642
www.oakenbarrel.com

KWANG CASEY, FOUNDING CO-OWNER

kwang@oakenbarrel.com

MARK M. HAVENS, HEAD BREWER

GERALD "JERRY" JACKOMIS, HOMEBREWER

KWANG KASEY I used to run Broad Ripple Steakhouse. I worked there from 1990 until June 1994, when Oaken Barrel opened. I got interested in microbrewing through the Broad Ripple Brewpub. A friend of mine, Ted Miller, was a brewer there, and now he owns his own brewpub in Broad Ripple, Brugge. We call John Hill "the mayor of Broad Ripple" because of all the people he started in brewing. My chef, Mark Pfeffer, came from Broad Ripple Steak House.

My founding co-partner, Bill Fulton, and I grew up on the south side together. He and I went to school just down the street from each other. We're the same age. He went to high school with my wife, so we all knew each other through college, and we all had the same background. He met our first brewmaster, Brook Belli. They were living in Atlanta at the time.

Bill and Brook considered opening a brewpub in Atlanta, but Atlanta hadn't passed the law yet that you could brew beer and serve it on the premises. So Bill decided to look around here. We got together and had a casual conversation. Young guy's dream, "I want to open a restaurant or brewpub." We had lunch at Red

The Brewers

Lobster, and the ball started rolling, and six months later we got serious, put the finances together, and pursued real estate properties. It's like a ball rolling downhill. Once you start going and you see your dream develop, you say, "Wow, it's really going to happen."

We chose this south side location because Bill and I grew up down here. It took us about six months to get everything together with construction. And it still was tough for us because engineers, property tax, zoning commission, they didn't know anything about brewpubs. The Bureau of Alcohol, Tobacco, and Firearms back then didn't know all the rules. They were slow. Now you can apply for a license and get a permit in two weeks. Then my building inspector didn't know what to expect. He told me, "I don't know about firewalls in a brewery, what temperature it has to be, what the fire rating has to be."

We opened fourteen years ago, so we were among the forerunners. We built the business from the ground up. The building was a day care center. We jokingly say we went from day care to night care.

Jerry Jackomis arrives and is introduced. He took third place with his pale ale in the 2008 Indiana State Fair Brewers' Cup, the first competition he entered after homebrewing for seven years.

KWANG I need to introduce you to my brewmaster, Mark Havens. Two and a half years ago, Mark was a homebrewer, and he came here as what I called "a keg washer," working part-time. He honed his skills a little more, and then he became assistant brewer under Ken Price, and when Ken left, Jeff Helms became head brewer. When Jeff left, I was hesitant about Mark at first. We had a reputation to uphold. Most breweries will hire someone with more experience, but I love enthusiastic people. Mark came to me. "Give me a chance. I'll prove it to you. If I can't, we'll hire somebody else. The thing I have is if I don't know, I'll ask somebody." And he did. He called Ken many times. "Am I paying the right price for the grain?" His enthusiasm made up for experience, and his passion for beer makes up for any lack of skill. To go from assistant brewer to brewer of the year in less than a year is quite an honor. There he is, the brewer of the year!

Mark Havens enters from the brewery.

KWANG We were talking about starting Oaken Barrel with my former partner, Bill Fulton. I consider him the most intelligent person I've ever met. We were both smart kids, but I always took the shortcut and got away with it, but Bill was smart and crossed the T's and dotted the I's. That's why we got along so well. He was the behind-the-scenes guy. No one knew who my partner was. They'd ask, "Who is that guy?" and I'd say, "He's the brains behind the operation, the guy who pulled the three of us together and kept us together. He's the reason we're here today. He's the brainchild behind the whole thing. He kept the wheels turning." The restaurant business, on some days you ask, "Why am I doing this?" He made us see why we were doing this. He could see two or three years down the road, "This is where we want to be." The first year we were open, he showed me a paper. "In ten years we want to be here." He inspired and laid it out for me. He had a vision, and we're right along that. Brook left about 2003. He had some health issues.

Assistant brewer Andrew Castner enters from the brew house.

JERRY I drank my share of nasty beer in college. I always liked beer. It took me a little while to figure out there's more than the big three out there. As I started messing around more and more out there, I thought this is a neat thing to get into [craft brewed beer]. The nice thing about [craft brewed] beer is that I tend to get full before I get drunk, so it got to be safe, and I kept trying more and more. A friend of mine had gotten into homebrewing, and he talked to me about it. I had never considered it. I have a brother who was making wine at the time, and I thought that was interesting, although I'm not a wine drinker. My friend got me into it, showing me the nuts and bolts. It was mainly extract brewing. I don't think he's brewing any more. I haven't seen him in several years. I just picked up and went. I still brew mostly extract, although I do a lot of partial mash. I've got six-year-old twins, so I don't have a lot of time to do full all-grain batches.

KWANG We do small batches of different beers to test which gets positive response. In the fall and winter this past year, Mark and Andrew did small-batch beers.

MARK We did six beers, three full kegs at a time.

KWANG They did a coffee stout that flew out of here. We don't know what response we'll get.

JERRY I did a chocolate milk stout last year, just a small batch. Absolutely horrible. [Laughter] But I stuck it aside, and every once in a while, I throw one in the fridge. It's getting a little better. It's almost a year old now.

KWANG Brook Belli's philosophy: If it's not good at first, let it sit a little bit, and if you keep everything clean and keep tasting, it can turn out to be an OK brew. When he made a fruit beer, Razz-Wheat, he had to refine the technique several times.

JERRY I entered a pale ale for the 2008 Brewers' Cup because it's one of my favorites. I like British ales, although I'm getting into the American hops in the last couple of years, and now with the hops shortage they [American hops] seem to be a little more available, so I'm starting to do a little bit more American. The ales that I like are bitters and pale ales like Bass. When I start thinking about pale ale, it's always like that ale. I've worked my way to the Fullers and everything else. So I felt I had a handle on that. I don't remember which hops I used, but I think I overdid it, because it has an abrupt finish where in most of the other ones it broadens out a little bit. I didn't nail as much of the fruitiness that I thought I would. I think I fermented it a little cool.

What's nice, it came in under 5 percent alcohol, so it's a drinkable beer, very distinctive hoppiness, a lot of alcohol. My current favorite commercial is Arrogant Bastard, and that's got a little catch in it right at the top, and I like that. It's not something to drink all night. Oaken Barrel Gnaw Bone is very good.

KWANG That's my favorite beer to drink. Once in a while I like IPAs.

JERRY You don't want to drink IPA all day long. The others I like are porters and stouts, but not all the time, and I don't know enough people who like stouts to keep five gallons of it at a time. I drink a lot of porters. The other entry that I had was a bourbon barrel porter.

The Brewers

It's a brown porter that actually is secondaried with American oak chips soaked in bourbon for several months. It came out really well. I didn't expect it to win, but I wanted to hear what other people would say about it.

MARK Have you gotten feedback yet?

JERRY No.

MARK They got a lot more entries this year.

KWANG Who won homebrewer of the year?

MARK Mike Pearson. He's with MECA. MECA is the homebrew club that comes in every Friday.

KWANG I call them the bucket crew. They turn the buckets upside down and sit in the brewery, drinking beer. Friday, on the way home, tell your wife you're going to be a little late. [Laughter]

JERRY What time do you guys meet?

MARK From 2:30 until whenever our wives call and say "Hey, get home." [Laughter]

KWANG It's getting bigger. It started out with four guys.

MARK Now it's eight. It's a good resource for us. They have really good palates.

KWANG We ask them, "What do you think?"

MARK It's like immediate feedback from judges because they judge commercial beers, different categories in the commercial beers, and we had two stewards over there [2008 Brewers' Cup]. They bring their brews to share. Some will be bottles. Some will be keg conditioning. So feel free to come on in. It's a lot of fun.

JERRY I usually do half a batch in a party pig and half in bottles. By the time I finish the bottles, the pig is usually three to four weeks out. It's been sitting for a while. It's interesting to see the difference. That's one of the things I like. Once I've bottled something, it's one beer a week until I like it.

KWANG It's what we do here. It's how Mark started his career. Brook was a civil engineer. He worked at it [brewing] until he was good at it. He went to brewing school; he took it seriously. Our wives wonder about us.

JERRY My wife wonders sometimes, too.

MARK Mine was, "Quit your job to do what?"

KWANG I did that when I opened Oaken Barrel. I was 29. I look back now, and I look at my friends, and I see they're miserable. They don't have hair left, hardly smile. I'm laughing every day. My wife says, "You never grow up." She jokingly says, "This is your big club house, and everybody comes to play."

JERRY If you can make a living off this.

MARK [speaking to Jerry] Do you plan on going into all-grain?

JERRY I have a friend that I brew with. I don't belong to a club. We do this on our own. Between the two of us, we're starting to gather up materials and put stuff together. He's retired, so he has time, and he goes around and will pick up a couple of kegs. We're doing the plumbing. By the end of this year we'll have everything together.

MARK Will you do larger batches?

JERRY We're probably going to do ten- or fifteen-gallon batches and start getting a little bit more into kegging.

KWANG Are you getting into Belgian beers at all?

JERRY Occasionally. I did a Belgian dubbel about a year and a half ago that I did a secondary with sour cherries. It wasn't to make a kriek, but it came out about 9 percent alcohol, and I've been slowly drinking it. We had some friends coming from Denmark, and I wanted to have something that was a little bit different to give to them. So we did that, and I let it sit for four months before they came, and I stuck the rest of it in the closet. I might have one left, or I might have had the last one this weekend.

MARK If you have one left and want to share it with us, I'm definitely game. [Laughter]

JERRY One bottle, if it's still left . . .

MARK The homebrewers bring just one or two bottles, and we share. When it was just four—we're getting a little bit less each now with eight. A few sips is all we need. That's what judges have to make their judgment on.

KWANG I told Mark next time we go to Denver for the Great American Beer Festival, there's a homebrewing division, Pro-Am, we might enter. The rule is you have to brew a full batch to bring. Mark is a new father, so he won't go this year, but next time.

MARK What we'll probably do if we decide to brew Pro-Am is get some judges in so that way there's no bias and we make sure it's at the top of the game.

KWANG A competition brings out the best in us. You can make a beer, and you can find touches to make it even better every day. I have restaurant customers who notice a little change in flavor. They'll say, "Hey, why is this beer different?" I say, "We're trying to make it better." "Well, I liked it better the other way." I have to explain, "It's better beer. Just because it's not what you're accustomed to doesn't make it not better."

MARK Our beer is not the same consistency every time. Part is that we're not like the big guys with top-of-the-line equipment. Over there they just push a button to make sure everything is the same.

KWANG I tell people we're still homebrewers. It's just a little bit bigger.

JERRY This is my first competition. I did it mainly for the feedback. After a certain period of time you think, my friends, I'm giving them free alcohol, so they're always going to like it. But I really want to see what other people who know [the style] think about it. And that to me is the biggest value of it. I make the same kind of beer all of the time, and I never make the same one twice. You change something, even if it's just a little timing or your hops have a different value, or something like that.

MARK I say I don't want to do it the same way because I just had it that way. I want to try something different. I did enjoy winning brewer of the year. Deep down in my heart when I took over, my number one goal was to try to get our sales back up throughout the state. My second goal was definitely to make us the brewery of the year, to excel. That's why I came up with the small batch series, trying all the different beers, trying to do as many as I could, and whichever ones I thought warranted entering, then I would enter it. Last year we didn't win, and that was frustrating, because I still talk with Ken every week, and he says, "Mark, you've got to get it back. You've got to get it back." He's just an endless supply of brewing knowledge. This is his fourth brewery that he's been at, so he's seen so many different things in his time, so he's saying, "Try this, try that." I did the same recipe that we did last year that didn't win, but I tweaked and brewed with a little more care this year.

KWANG And you did win.

JERRY Besides making a beer you like, you also have to consider the commercial viability for what the market wants and that type of thing.

MECA HOMEBREW CLUB, SHELBYVILLE AND INDIANAPOLIS

Founded in 2007 by Bill Ballinger, Mike Pearson, Brian Pickerill, and Bill Staashelm. The new members are Keith Baute, John Showalter, Sean Reeves, and Jim Matt.

BRIAN PICKERILL We just thought it would be fun to brew together, and Bill Ballinger invited us to his brew barn. We didn't set out to start a club at all; we just started brewing because we thought it would be fun. We were right about that. We all started brewing on our own, though we talked about it a lot before we ever got together to brew simultaneously.

Most of us brew our own separate batches, but it's a lot more interesting when someone else is there brewing another beer at the same time. John and Keith brew as a team. The rest of us brew our own batches, but almost always at Bill Ballinger's because he has the fantastic brew barn, though we have also brewed at my place and at Bill Staashelm's.

Mostly it's just fun to brew, talk, and sample each other's beers on brew day. We also share what we might be out of (or forgot to bring), and we give each other advice and kid around a bit. The club's main goal is to make world-class craft beer.

Bill Staashelm and Brian Pickerill have been friends since high school and started brewing in 1994. Back then we didn't brew that much, and although we got together for brewing once or twice, we weren't both brewing, but one would visit while the other was brewing. Bill Ballinger and Bill Staashelm became brothers-in-law in the '90s and BB started extract brewing.

The three B's first got together to brew at Ballinger's brew barn in spring of 2005. We all brewed extract that day because the Bills had not started all-grain yet, and I didn't think I should try it "over the road." We won some ribbons at the 2005 Indiana State Fair. Then in fall of 2005, we got together to brew all-grain [AG] for the first time together. The Bills got new ten-gallon mash tuns that day. I brought the mash tuns and the grain and walked them through the process that first time. (I have been brewing AG since about 1997.) I think the next time we brewed, Mike was there. Mike and Bill work together, and I had talked about it at work a bit.

As for me, I like a lot of different styles. I don't really have one favorite beer, but some of my favorites are weizen, Belgian golden strong, English ales, and stouts, classic American pilsner, American pale ale, and American wheat. I like to brew different beers. I like to brew whatever I feel like having around for the next couple of months (or longer in the case of the "big" beers).

JIM MATT I used to be a total "hop head" (loving the hoppy beers), but since taking a class on how to judge beers (the Beer Judge Certification Program, BJCP), I have come to appreciate all beer styles for what they are. I am still very passionate about hoppy American IPAs (India pale ales) and Belgian-style beers. But I love a well-made Bohemian or German pilsner! I'd also like to add that most of the MECA members have had some exposure to the Beer Judge Certification Program, and a few members have even taken this comprehensive exam in order to become better brewers.

BRIAN I can't tell you how much the new guys bring to the club. Jim the Belgian expert, John and Keith are winning all kinds of AHA awards—really incredible, and now we have Sean, who I still haven't brewed with, but he brings a lot with English styles and in a lot of other areas as well.

The MECA Brewers are the reigning Indiana Homebrew Club of the Year 2007 as determined by the Indiana Brewers' Cup rules. Their beers have won recognition in local, regional, and national competitions (e.g., some MECA brews have placed in the National Homebrew Competition).

JIM I first had heard about the MECA guys through Anita Johnson, owner of Great Fermentations, a homebrew and home wine making supply shop. Since I am a bit of a loner, I had wanted to enter my beers in the Brewers' Cup on my own and see how things settled out. There was a table of very passionate, excited guys right next to my table at the awards summary. Sure enough, it was the MECA Brewers, and I thought to myself after all of the awards were given, "That is the winning team. I want to join them." I first brewed with them in August 2007 at Bill Ballinger's barn. I have since learned so much more about brewing and am looking forward to the future!

BRIAN Ballinger won best of show in 2007; that one beer (Serenity Now) counts the most toward the homebrew club of the year. Also, I think he won the most ribbons, but Mike was very close or perhaps won more than Bill (not counting BOS, which of course only one person can win). The beers we won with are on the State Fair website and too many to list here from memory. My awards were only two—first place for Classic American Pilsner and first place for English Pale Ale.

JIM Two first places are nothing to sneeze at. Way to go, Brian!

BRIAN Jim Matt was not an official member of MECA at that time, but he won three ribbons (two second place and a third) for three of the five beers that he entered.

The link to the Brewers' Cup awards:
www.brewerscup.org/2007HBWinners.htm
http://hbd.org/indiana/
Pictures from our first brew day after the Brewers' Cup in 2007, taken by Jim Matt:
www.flickr.com/photos/77954922@N00/sets/72157601828559741/detail/

Email interviews March and April 2008 with Brian Pickerill and Jim Matt

MARK You're absolutely right. I don't enjoy raspberry. I do like Razz-Wheat. That's the beer that pays the bills.

KWANG John Hill is the grandfather of brewpubs in Indiana. Broad Ripple Brewpub does their style of beer. They are good at what they do. I tell people we like to experiment with a lot of beers, and getting back "brewer of the year" again, it validates us that you can make a variety of good beers. Mark does a good job of blending every style. We see ourselves as more in the forefront of other brewers or other brewpubs that focus on their style of beer. When Ken first came here, I wasn't that much into Belgian beers. He broadened my horizons. He did a saison and a line that was hard to do. Some brewpubs may not want to do them. They don't want to pour their money down the drain. But Ken opened up our taste buds.

MARK Ken told me, "You're not going to knock it out of the ballpark every time. You're not going to hit a home run every time." That's really hard for me. I want to. As homebrewers you want to make an award-winning beer every single time. It might be the best beer you ever made, but not according to somebody else.

JERRY I try to brew what I like.

KWANG We do what we know we're good at. If our people appreciate it, that's all that's possible. We don't do light-style beer. Some people ask, "Why don't you brew a light stout, a really mild, light alcohol?" If they want that kind of beer, and they're coming to a brewpub, they're missing the whole point. Mark called me while I was on vacation. He said, "Hey, we won." And I did a cartwheel. I was vacationing with a friend from New York. He's a big beer drinker, so we went out and celebrated. He was so happy for me. He was like, "I remember when we were in college we were trying different beers, we were drinking just domestic, we were drinking all these different beers."

JERRY In our neighborhood, the kids all play. I live on a cul-de-sac. We close up the cul-de-sac. The parents all sit outside drinking and watching the kids. On ninety degree days, I'll pour some Coors Light. But when I come in and I'm having dinner, I'll have something more substantial. It all has its purpose.

MARK This weekend I tried something different—a lager from Coney Island Brewing Company.

KWANG [speaking to Jerry] I've got a question for you, speaking as a businessman. A while ago I was talking with a friend, Greg Emig [Lafayette Brewing Company], about an idea, but ten years ago I didn't think Indianapolis was ready for it. Now there are so many homebrewers, maybe Indianapolis is ready for a U-Brew. It seems there are people like you—you have twins, you're busy, you don't want to get a bigger system, you don't want to tie up your house, your wife will yell at you if you take up half the basement. So I thought of opening something where a homebrewer can come to make a beer. Cleveland has a U-Brew, and they are so busy you are six months out to get a spot to brew. Talking with homebrewers, I say, "Your next step is all-grain," and they say, "I don't have the space. I don't have the time." At U-Brew, people rent the space, and we provide the equipment, the grain, and the storage; we help out.

MARK Don't make this too well known. We don't want anyone to steal our idea. Being a commercial brewer, I have access to and know where a lot of materials are at. At a U-Brew, six or seven are brewing at the same time. I can help them out with different styles, help with bottling, labels.

KWANG I get a lot of offers from realtors to move, but my landlord, who loves beer, says, "Don't move."

JERRY Greenwood needs you. This is the only thing like this down here.

KWANG I know the guys from Mad Anthony in Fort Wayne, Blaine and Todd. Their sister worked for me when I first opened. They were managing someplace, and they came in here and they looked at each other and they said, "Why can't we do it?" I heard them talking about it so I said, "Quit talking about it. Do it." They were talking about it for years. Finally they said, "You're right." They decided on the Fort Wayne area. I got inspired by John Hill—not so much by John Hill personally but by the guys working at Broad Ripple Brewpub, seeing Greg [Emig] and Ted [Miller] drinking beer together. Ted being a big sports fan, Broad Ripple Brewpub had only one TV, and Ted is saying I want TVs everywhere and I'm like, "Do it!" And now Ted's got TVs everywhere [in Brugge Brasserie].

JERRY I just found out about this stuff [winning in Brewers' Cup] two hours ago, so I haven't had much time to think about it.

KWANG On your day off, come in here and hang out with the guys, watch them brew. We'll put you to work.

MARK We've always got something to do.

KWANG Do it on a cool day. Don't do it on a hot summer day.

MARK Let me know about helping with the hops shortage. I can get them at a cheaper price. I don't want it generally known, and I don't mean to put Anita [Great Fermentations] out of business.

JERRY If there's a certain type of hops that I want and Anita doesn't have it, I go on the internet. Today it's a crapshoot. But when it works, it works.

MARK We can help with what you need, an ounce or two—28 grams that's probably what I accidentally spill. [Laughter]

KWANG Little people like us, who used to be homebrewers, we help. If guys need bottles—

MARK Even caps. We try to make it easier for everybody.

JERRY I messed around with making wine. When I talk with people making wine, everyone's got their little secret; I talk to a boatload of homebrewers and everyone wants to give you tips. I go to Broad Ripple Brewpub and Great Fermentations, and everyone has something for you. There are no secrets. If you want to brew saison, it's "Here's how I did it. These are the hops. This is how long I set it." People will pull out their notes and tell you.

KWANG Mark gives help to a brewer who walks in here. Brook helped everyone. Omar, when he first came as the brewer at Alcatraz, he used come down here and live here. [Laughter]

JERRY That's another thing especially at the brewpubs. It seems like liquor stores will cut each other's throats. Brewpubs are all in competition, but everybody is working together and everybody seems to know everybody and go to each other's release parties.

KWANG Every brewer who has worked for me has been named brewer of the year, except for the brewer right between. Mark joked with me. He said, "Hey, I won. I'm the only brewer at work who is brewer of the year." We had a brewer working under Brook, Tanya Cornett. She moved out to Oregon and became brewer of the year.

MARK At Bend Brewing Company.

KWANG I was so happy for her winning awards. I tell people the story of my kitchen manager. When he was nineteen years old, a typical teenager, he had no direction for his life. He got in trouble with the law. I called a good friend of mine, an attorney. I told him, "I'm trying to help this kid out." I told him the situation. He said, "Let me meet the kid." He met him and he said, "I'll take on the case." We go up before the judge and we're asking for leniency. Out of all the judges, we got the toughest judge. He looks at me and he asks, "Why do you care about this kid? He's nineteen years old? He's only worked for you for nine months."

I said, "You know, Judge, you hear how in life somebody made an impact. I feel like a calling that I could change his life. I think that if we give him a break, he'll turn his life around. He'll change his life."

The attorney turned to the judge. "I took this case for nothing. That's how much I believe in Kwang and this kid. I met this kid, and I think we could really make a difference."

The Brewers

The judge looked at me and he said, "I had a person like that." For some reason, he brought the three of us together in that room, and he said, "I'll give that kid a break."

For thirteen years now, he hasn't touched alcohol. He has changed. He is my kitchen manager. He wasn't just working in a restaurant as a job. He took on a career path. He looks to me as an older brother.

People come together for a reason. I tell people, "That's what I gave back to him." When I first met Mark, when he came by, he was working in a jail, but he wanted to be working in a brewery. Mark has a degree in criminal justice. Ten months ago, when I gave him the opportunity to be head brewer, I was losing sleep over it a little bit. I had applications from experienced brewers from other breweries, but I thought about it and something in my head told me, "Give this kid a chance. If it doesn't work out, you can always make a change." In my life I've taken a lot of chances. You've got to go with your instinct. I did, and when he called me about the Brewers' Cup, I was happy, but not for myself. I was so happy for him. I made the right choice. I knew that six months into his job, because he really cares. He talks to me every day about how to save by having grain delivery every other month instead of once a month. It saves a couple hundred dollars. It adds up. That's money for the restaurant. Mark says, "The more money I save, the more money the restaurant makes."

Channel 13 called for an interview about the cost of hops, and I said we're doing things to cut corners so we don't pass on the increased cost to customers. We did not raise our beer prices here.

Razz-Wheat is Brook's creation. I tasted the beer before we opened the restaurant.

Talk about unique beers. I'm not a fruit beer drinker. I was a wine drinker, and I could appreciate all the flavors behind it, but I didn't realize all the complexities of making that beer. We did it as a seasonal beer originally, but my people tasted it, people who had never had it before, and they said, "Wow."

When we started going into the distribution side of the business, we used to distribute ourselves, and Razz-Wheat used to sell right out the door. Most bar managers, restaurants, they didn't want to talk to us. But when they heard raspberry beer, they'd try it and see how good it is. Then they became more aware of different beers and tasted it, and they'd come back to ours. "There's no comparison." The difference is that we use real raspberries instead of extract. Costwise, it's four times as much to use real raspberries. Razz-Wheat has become the staple of this place. I say I'm with Oaken Barrel, and people say, "Oh, you're the guy who makes raspberry beer." I say, "I make other beers, too. We make many beers."

Mark says it's not his favorite beer, but he knows it pays our bills. We now distribute with World Class Beverages. That's Jim Schembre. He wishes this state was more like Colorado or California, but we'll get there. Indiana is not so much behind times as "we take our time." We're more cautious. We don't follow trends or fads. Indiana is coming around to microbreweries. Microbreweries went through some tough times around 2000. It shook out the "wannabees." The places that made good beer, they survived. We see a lot of the chain brewpubs that opened up on the coattails of the trend, but they didn't make good beer.

It was our dream to be on the distribution side. When the people in the original Indianapolis Brewing Company were ready to retire, they said, "We don't want to give this all up. We want somebody to carry on the tradition." So we bought the brewing operation in 1995. The cost of energy started going up. The utilities were higher than our rent. It was too big for us at the time. Thirteen years later, yes, if we still had the facility, it would be great. But we were brewing as much here as we were brewing there. We had to let the space go. Now we fight for space every day. When Mark has to bottle, we have to take half the brewery out. It's twice the work.

We capitalized on the IBC image of "Miss Liberty" on top of the monument. Our former graphic designer, Rob Skorjanc, redid the old artwork. Rob is very talented. He grew up with Bill, and he went to school with my wife and me. We used to run around together. He came to work with us. He bought into our dream and worked with us for ten years.

People try our beers outside of the restaurant. Say somebody from the north side of Indianapolis or southern Indiana buys one of our beers in a bottle shop, they try the Razz-Wheat, and they ask, "Hey, where's this brewery located?" They're told, "Greenwood, and they have a restaurant, too." Then people say, "Oh, that's great. I'll make the trip." So they come with the wife and kids or by themselves, and they have dinner, and they order different varieties of beers we have on tap all of the time. Once I get them in here, they become regulars.

I was told a long time ago by one of my former restaurant managers, "Treat your customers like you would treat your mom and dad." I follow that advice. A couple comes here from Ohio. They come once a month. I tell them don't just come here. Make a weekend of it. Go to Broad Ripple and enjoy more. The beer brings them here; the service brings

them back. I try to match food that goes well with beer. I didn't want the standard pub fare, but you've still got to do some pub food, yet I wanted to go a little bit beyond that. When I first opened, I was strapped for staff. But my chef, Mark Pfeffer, used to work at the Broad Ripple Steak House, and he came here to work with me. I call him the godfather of pizza in Indianapolis. He opened Bazbeaux, Some Guys. We've been working together for eighteen years. He grew up in Broad Ripple.

I think it is the people who work for me that make our operation unique. I have an outstanding wait staff. I have waitresses who have been here ten, fourteen years. They've been with me through tough times. They talk with the new staff coming in, tell them about the time when all that people knew was Bud Light. Now people know what they want when they come in. The waitress who was here since day one will tell you how I went to every table to try to explain, "You have to try this beer," and spread the gospel of beer literally at every table, and I talked with my kitchen staff to try to imagine foods that go with beer and to have the patience to believe that this will take off. They stuck with it. We were unique in that we had a vision and we didn't stray from it. We didn't change it to try to accommodate the mainstream restaurant bar or the brewpub. We stayed with our vision and built a loyal local following, like John Hill, who stuck with English-style beer and generated a loyal following. It's the people. You will never generate that in a corporate restaurant. We treat customers like family. When they're happy, we're happy with them. When something bad happens, we feel the pain as well. When a company closes down the street, we think of what people are going to do for jobs. They tell

The Brewers

us their bad stories and their good stories. We care about the baseball teams. We make toasts for our families when there is a death. We feel like we are part of the community, and they treat us the same way.

Something I noticed when I went west and went to a brewpub. They made five beers of their own, and they had twenty beers on tap, beers from other breweries in the state. When we change our tapping system to a standard, I'd like to put in taps from other brewpubs for my regulars. Maybe they don't get up to Broad Ripple. The brewing industry in Indiana is growing, and we are getting more publicity. I'd like to see it catch like a wildfire. Jim Schembre from World Class is frustrated because in other states, you see microbrew beer taps in ballparks. You go to Indianapolis, you can't get good beer everywhere. For all the beer drinkers' sake in Indiana, I'd like to see it mushroom.

MARK It took other places awhile to get going. We're just slower than other places. I just hope we move forward.

Interview July 21, 2008, at the Oaken Barrel

TONY MACKLIN, HOMEBREWER

FRANK FELICÉ, PHD, HOMEBREWER

Homebrewers Frank Felicé and Tony Macklin are musicians. They brew as a team and have won three Indiana State Fair Brewers' Cup awards together: Dead Man's Chest Ale—a brown ale with rum—red ribbon 2006; Ex-Pat Amber—an American brown ale—blue ribbon 2006; and March Time Special—English special bitter—red ribbon 2008.

FRANK AND TONY (VIA EMAIL) The composer Guillaume de Machaut wrote, "Music is a science that would have us laugh and sing and dance." We like to think that beer makes this easier to accomplish.

FRANK I had wanted to brew ever since I lived in Portland, Oregon, where I really started to drink homebrews by a number of folks that I knew out there (and one of my best friends from there became a homebrewer shortly after I left). After I reconnected with Tony in Indianapolis, I found out he was brewing with another friend, and I asked to tag along for a portion of the process (bottling) and loved it. Shortly afterwards, my wife gave me a starting kit for my birthday in 2002, and off I went. After a couple of solo brewing experiences, I found out that Tony's brewing partner had moved to Minneapolis, so he and I started brewing together in 2003, which was great! As you know, he's a great guy in every sense of the word, so having some time with him to hang out, catch up, and solve all of the world's problems while brewing is wonderful.

TONY I had also tried to brew once on my own, and it turned out awful.

FRANK At this point we're trying lots of things. Recently we brewed an IPA because we hadn't done one before this. Also, when given a kit recipe or something that's pretty standard, we'll try and "kit bash" it, adding some supplementary ingredients (honey, rum, spices, lemons) to see how it will turn out. Dead Man's Chest Ale and the coffee-hazelnut stout Brown Eyed Girl turned out better than we could have ever expected. The lemon wheat beer, well, it finally mellowed into something oddly drinkable, but it was a great liquid to poach fish in.

TONY We're becoming known for "adding booze to our beer"—a great experiment to see how flavors complement and change over time.

FRANK The most fun I have with brewing is the alchemic process What is this yeast going to do? How will it ferment? What do these hops taste like? How will the beer change over three months? Six months? It's a living thing.

TONY Both of us like cooking and experimenting with recipes, so brewing is an extension of feeding that creative urge.

FRANK The most challenging parts about homebrewing are space, gear, and sanitation. Since we brew in our kitchens, it's hard to set up and tear down before, during, and after the brewing process. (And I'm paranoid about sanitation. I think I'd hose the whole room down if I could.) It's also difficult to do good straining of the wort. It's messy. We'd also like a way to chill the wort more efficiently. (At my place, I can't attach a wort chiller.)

TONY I agree with the sanitation issue. Also, given the increasing availability of ingredients and information on brewing, anyone can make a decent, drinkable beer. But the challenge is in making a great beer, and even more in repeating it. We have become more efficient in straining and cooling the hot wort as it is transferred into the fermenter. We've also done more with "dry-hopping"—adding hops to the primary and/or secondary fermenters. Buddy brewing is going to be harder [after Tony moves away]. I hope that we can still do a couple of batches together a year under our "Dr. Frank n' Tony's Monstrously Good Brew" label while bringing new friends into our dual-state homebrewing family.

FRANK Both of us know how to do the whole process, so we'll take turns on each of the steps sometimes I'll buy the ingredients, and we'll brew at Tony's. He'll get water and start it to heat. I'll dump grains into the bag. He'll pour the beer we're drinking that day. We'll both gaze longingly into the brew kettle at the "tea." He'll stir as I pour extract, and we'll both time. When hops are added, whoever is closest will add them. We usually alternate, especially when we get to straining, pitching the yeast, measuring, and bottling.

TONY Frank brings the thoughtful discipline to the creative process, while I'm more apt to experiment and modify along the way without planning. We've had success with both approaches.

FRANK For me, the only reason to compete is to get the feedback from the judges. Medals and ribbons are okay, but I'd rather brew and share and receive feedback so I can continue to improve as a brewer.

TONY Agreed. It helps to get specific feedback from both the discerning palates of friends and the certified judges at a competition. Plus, my dad loves to tell his drinking buddies that his son brews award-winning beer.

FRANK Friends and colleagues end up with most of what I brew. It's hard to drink that much beer quickly so that we can brew again. Two things come to mind about homebrewing. If you want good beer, you really can't do too poorly by what you've brewed yourself, especially if you live in a small town where a great selection of beer is hard to come by. In a larger city, you can obtain good microbrews (hooray for the folks at Brugge, The Ram, and the Brewpub), but I lived for too long in smaller, out-of-the way places where it's hard to find such things. The other aspect is one of craft. I like making things, and this is another avenue to do just that. I like beer. Why not make my own? (I'll learn to make wine as well someday and then perhaps whiskey.)

TONY It is the safest way to combine interests in chemistry, drinking, and playing with boiling hot liquids. I'd only add that we give our big kudos to the growing number of excellent Indiana-based breweries. They provide homebrewers like us with great inspiration and high standards to meet.

FRANK Comparing music with brewing—they each have their own styles and genre, and to make them correctly, you must become intimate with their strengths, weaknesses, and compatibility with other "like" items, like food pairings and band mates. For me, it's another way of exercising my creative spirit.

TONY Beer and music are highly individualized tastes. In both, some people are passionate ambassadors of a niche, some like sampler platters of styles, and others will take whatever generic crap is fed to them. At some point, Frank and I need to invent the iPod shuffle version of a keg to serve them all.

FRANK Brews besides my own do I most favor, in no particular order:

Black Butte Porter (preferably on tap), Deschutes Brewing Company, Bend, Oregon
Ruby (a wheat ale, with a faint aftertaste of raspberries—it's not a fruit beer), McMenniman's Pub, Portland, Oregon
Thomas Hardy Ale, O'Hanlon's Brewing Company (high alcohol and hops)
Indiana Amber, Oaken Barrel, Greenwood, Indiana
Caramel Porter, Saranac Brewing Company, Saranac, New York
Moose Drool, Big Sky Brewing, Missoula, Montana
Buttface Amber, Ram, Indianapolis (and other places)

TONY My tastes in music and beer go in two- or three-month phases. Right now I'm into creamy British ales like Boddingtons and Adams Broadside. Saranac's Caramel Porter is an amazing fall/winter beer—something we need to reverse engineer, since it's hard to find west of Pittsburgh. And, most of all, Guinness is my Scooby Snack—wave it in front of me, and I'll do anything.

FRANK Tony moved to Pittsburgh in the summer of 2008. I am going to miss brewing with him a lot, but hopefully we can hook up when either of us is in the other's location.

Phone and email interview August 22, 2007; update emails summer 2008

Upland Brewing Company

350 W. 11th St.
Bloomington, IN 47404
812-33-2337
www.uplandbeer.com

Upland Tasting Room
4842 North College Avenue
Indianapolis, IN 46205
317-602-3931

CALEB STATON, HEAD BREWER

SCOTT JOHNSON, MARKETING AND
PUBLIC RELATIONS DIRECTOR

EILEEN MARTIN, BREWSTER

CALEB STATON I'm from Muncie, Indiana. So I'm a Hoosier-born brewer.

Upland is the largest selling brewer in Indiana. We just turned ten [in 2008]. Last year [2007] we had a 50 percent capacity increase in our brewery and we're looking to launch sales in Louisville this year to keep up [sales reach]. We'd like to grow to put another tank in. As you grow you get to a more profitable production level. Our restaurant is very successful, but we're still trying to get to where our packaged beer is profitable. With our Dragonfly IPA we only put a dollar in our pocket for every case that we sell. It's just not a very good margin.

Last year [2007] we brewed 5,100 barrels after a two-year stretch of 4,200 barrels. We couldn't do any more than that. The recent increase in price for ingredients kind of stagnated growth. We haven't lost, but we haven't grown our capacity. The top of the pot probably would be 7,600 barrels. If I add an additional tank, we can get up to 9,000. I'll need two more after that to get to a 13,000-barrel brewery without new construction to the building. It's our four-year plan. We do all our production right here. We bottle about a million bottles a year right here on site.

The Upland Wheat is about 65–70 percent of what we brew a year, so it's definitely our frontrunner flagship beer. It's the best selling beer that's brewed in the state of Indiana, so we do very well with it. Our IPA is second, and after that our other year-round brews and we do our seasonals. What we sell in the restaurant is pretty close to what gets sold wholesale. The Wheat—we go through about a keg a day at the restaurant here. The IPA is the second biggest selling tap. Then our Pale Ale, Amber, and Porter are pretty close to what gets sold in the restaurant and packaged. But certain seasonals, when we put those on, that stuff flies through the restaurant, but it may take a little longer to introduce a new seasonal into the market and to get it to sell at a routine level in Indiana.

We distribute in every county in Indiana. Louisville is our first across the border. We are in the middle of talking. It's a courtship kind of thing where you want to get linked with the right distributor out of the gate. Once you sign that agreement with them, your brand is their property in whatever area they are distributing, so the only way to get out of that is if they give unsatisfactory service. The only way for us to switch to another distributor is if, after

we sign the agreement, they are willing to sell to another distributor. There have been a lot of classic feuds with craft brewers. That's the issue Bell's got into in Chicago and Brooklyn [Brewing] got into early on. If you're not on good terms with your distributor, you could void it [the contract], but it's actually not until five years later that the contract could cease. They actually hold the ropes.

I was homebrewing in my basement shortly after I graduated from college. I did that for several years. My job previous to working here at Upland, I was managing a drive-in movie theater, so I wasn't doing much with my college degree at that point. Though I've always had fun jobs, I decided to do something with my degree, and I liked brewing. I understood it, so that's what prompted me to research schools, and I ended up in UC Davis, their master brewers program. I took that course, got an internship at Berkley at Trumer [Brauerei], where all they brew is a pilsner. They're part of a large brewing corporation here in the United States. I was looking while I was interning for positions primarily focusing on the Midwest and Indiana, where we have a lot of catching up to do as far as what's happening in the state of Oregon and out west, so I wanted to come back and bring good beer with me.

There was another UC graduate working at Upland, Andrew St. Lawrence. They actually on their website had a chimpanzee posted as their cellar man—just a picture of an ape. So I emailed them back and said, "If you're sick of that knuckle-dragging chimpanzee and you guys need another brewer, I'm definitely looking at that." I did get an email after that—and the job. It's part of the weird humor that goes around this brewery.

We originally brewed lambic in 2006—to age a year—we launched last year [2007].

We brewed in 2006 when we were hitting the ceiling on capacity. The tanks were full, so we made a style that is aged in oaken barrels. It was an experiment to expand production. It might not have worked out. I tried to follow everything. I had researched how they do the style in Belgium, and I tried to get as authentic as you can in the United States. I think we did everything right. Every bottle sold soon after we released it. We got a lambic blend with wild yeast and lacto bacillus. It's got some ingredients you normally don't want to get anywhere near your breweries. We got our fresh fruit from the Huber Orchards in Starlight, Indiana. They grow a lot of fruit there. They're also making wines and spirits down there. We've got an arrangement with them for fruit, which is their blackberries, strawberries, blueberries, and raspberries, and we are going to get peaches for the round we are doing this year. The cherries and kiwis we had to get through one of the local produce guys. I don't know if a kiwi fruited lambic has been done before, so I want to see what happens. It might be a waste of fruit but we'll see. It's very interesting at this point.

Our customers drank it all. They're my best and worst critics—the five guys at the end of the bar that day. The brewpub serves as our pilot. Any new batch of beer we are going to do, this allows you to test it out. It's kind of our test market. Typically, they are not going to be as harsh on you as the guy who picked it up off the shelves. Any time we launch a new beer here, it causes excitement. They like to see what we are doing. It's general interest; our change in tap handles here. I've put 100 pounds of kiwi in the bunghole one at a time. I froze them previously overnight and let them thaw out to break the cell walls down. It took me about an hour to get all the fruit in the barrel. It's a very labor-intensive kind of brewing. A good rule of thumb is about 100 pounds of fruit for a barrel—sixty gallons, about a pound and a half of fruit per gallon. I think we're kicking up the blueberry a little this year [2008]. We want it to shine through a little bit more so we're going up to 125 pounds on that. There's a little bit of tweaking here and there, but not a whole lot. We pretty much hit it out of the park in the first try. We use three-year-old hops, not for bitterness but to try to get the preservative quality. We don't add sugar; it ferments on the sugar that's in the fruit itself. It ends up being a nice traditional dry, wild beer. We use Oliver [Winery] wine barrels. They are neutral, but after a year you do get a little oak one way or the other. We cleaned our barrels very well after the first round, so we're reusing them. The first year we had four oak barrels. We've added twenty more of them. So we're looking down the road. It's getting like whiskey production. You've got to think beyond the typical brewing to two years ahead for the next round.

Experimenting with different recipes is what brewing is all about. You've got to make some mistakes sometimes. I tend to think I don't make very many, but we'll see; it's near to me, it's what's fun. A lot of that is processing, like "Why don't I do this this way?" It's part of working around things. How can you most efficiently make quality beer? Innovating all the time. I think our first round of saison that we did we were a little heavy-handed on the amount of spices we put into it, so we had what I would have called a green saison which we ended up blending down with our Upland Wheat to reduce the spice character. One of the spices is star anise, which is drastically licorice. It was so glaring that we just had to

Ron Smith's Castle Rock Irish Red Ale was distributed to select stores, pubs, and restaurants throughout Indiana following its release at Kahn's Fine Wines and Spirits on January 30, 2006. Upland Brewing Company of Bloomington bottled Ron's recipe after it beat out dozens of entries to win the 2005 Indiana Ultimate Beer Geek Challenge. Conducted by World Class Beverages from 2004 through 2007, the award also recognized the contributions homebrewers were making to the craft beer industry. Each year a specific style was designated for entrants who had to follow the guidelines established by the Beer Judge Certification Program. Style #9D Irish Red Ale, the 2005 Challenge, was judged prior to the July 2005 Indiana State Fair Brewers' Cup Awards.

A Purdue engineering graduate, Ron also holds an MBA from IU Kelley School of Business and serves on its board of visitors. He has been homebrewing since 1991. His awards include best of show in the 1999 Indiana State Fair and a coveted gold medal in the 2000 National AHA (American Homebrewers Association). Ron is a longtime member of Foam Blowers of Indiana. He is a certified craft beer judge and teacher for judge certification. For the general public, Ron teaches a series of classes titled "MBA: Master of Beer Appreciation." In 2007 he was selected president of the Foam Blowers of Indiana Homebrew Club, the year he convened the first annual Indiana Homebrew Club Day "Brew-B-Q."

I have a ten-gallon, all-grain tower system that is a permanent setup in my garage. I have a dedicated drain and hot and cold water lines running to the brewery area. I serve all my beer on tap in small kegs. I use the same ingredients, processes, computer software, et cetera, that the micros and brewpubs use.

Most people are pretty amazed by all of this once they realize how professional it is, but I am only one of many that take brewing to this level these days. The Ultimate Beer Geek Challenge is an incredible award for a homebrewer to win. Having your brew bottled and distributed statewide is an experience I will long remember.

The changes in homebrewing since 1990, when I started, are that more people are doing it, excellent ingredients including pure liquid yeast strains are readily available, and the equipment has improved, with a more efficient and effective device for everything. Also, the general public is more educated on better beers, so the hobby is more accepted and people don't fear what we make, like it is some sort of witch's concoction. All of this has led to many brewers making truly excellent beers.

In addition to being more flavorful and complex, craft beer tends to be higher in alcohol than most domestic beer, so more mature beer drinkers have learned how to appreciate the quality rather than the quantity.

Molasses adds a complexity and depth to the flavor of Castle Rock Irish Red Ale. It adds a toffee and rich caramel character to the malty sweet component of the beer. The yeast strain is where a great deal of the flavor of a beer comes from. The yeast I used for the brown (Wyeast 1028) finishes drier, has a harder, more minerally profile. The yeast I used for the red (Wyeast 1318) creates a softer, more balanced character and finishes a bit sweeter. Thus, using the same wort (unfermented beer) but different yeasts can create a very different beer.

The style guidelines for an English brown mild and an Irish red are similar, but brown mild calls for molasses. Changing the yeast with the brown mild turned it into a better Irish red than the Irish red I had brewed specifically for the competition, so I entered the brown mild as a red, and it won. That's why this red has molasses in it. I probably never would have thought to put molasses in a red, but I think my future red recipes have changed. The moral to this story is never decide what your beer style is until you've finished it and tasted it.

When I brew, I start with ten-gallon, all-grain batches that I split into two five-gallon batches in order to experiment with different yeasts, dry-hopping, and other conditioning variables, while remaining true to the requisites of the specific style.

The explosion of craft beers and breweries has settled down, so the successful micros and brewpubs are now less focused on survival and making a beer for the broader masses and more focused on differentiation and making new and different beers. One of the directions that the craft brewing industry has been going in is the creation of new "big beers"—that is high gravity, high alcohol beers. One of the first big beers was an imperial stout. The name "imperial" applies to any new or out-of-category big beer. Now beers like imperial IPAs, imperial reds, are becoming common. These awesome big beers are usually "sippers," and they can get quite expensive, so a big bottle is more like buying wine. Homebrewing has come a long way from its roots, and many, many homebrewers are making beer that is as good or better than the microbreweries and brewpubs.

Interview January 23, 2006, at Ron Smith's home-brewing operation, and June 2008 via email

blend it down a little bit, get it to be more palatable. Part of it is just a lesson on how you spice a beer in appropriate amounts.

We do have a good beer archive, but it's not for anything we are going to sell. Part of it is you have only just so much space. I do have some 2005 Winter Warmer. It's really just for samples, for a rare occasion when the brewers get together to see how it is after a long time.

Upland started bottling about six months after they opened [1998]. I think the structure of the business was to be a packaging brewery out of the gate. The restaurant was really more to serve as just part of the marketing. I don't think they ever thought it would be as successful a restaurant as it is here. The restaurant growth didn't happen until after I got here four years ago. The growth curve on the restaurant has been excellent. I wish the brewery followed it identically. Part of it is that Bloomington is moving down this way. We're becoming more of a known location than they were when they opened.

I would say that Bloomington itself is kind of an anomaly. To have two breweries in a town of this size in Indiana is pretty impressive. We've been around over a decade. Bloomington appreciates local quality goods that are handmade, whether it's a chair or a guy that fixes foreign cars in his backyard. It's just that type of community here. Half the beer we sell is sold right here in Monroe County. We can see our market from our rooftop. It's a nice way to be. People around town who go to restaurants and bars know that so many of our beers are on tap. For our retail market, it's nice to gauge what's going to work elsewhere in the state.

SCOTT JOHNSON There's something here at the brewpub that we don't have anywhere

The Brewers

else. Caleb and his staff use our customers as testers with a small batch [of a new brew] to see how it sells. One of the beers we did last year is a schwarzbier that got a lot of praise here at the brewery so it's probably a beer that will end up growing over time. We know that by how well it did here at our brewpub. It reached even other bars in town by word-of-mouth. People wanted it; bartenders wanted it.

In terms of national press, it's our brewers going to places like the Great American Beer Festival with good beer for its competition every two years. Upland has won several awards over the last few competitions. It gives us national recognition. Also, Playboy magazine did an article on us last year. It was a national story on breweries. That's huge for us. A few months after that, we were getting all sorts of email and calls from all over the country trying to get our beer. They end up coming here and taking it home in their [car] trunk. Playboy picked up on our Bad Elmer Porter. He was kind of a mysterious Indiana Guy, edgy, and he appealed to the kind of writers they have. I'm not sure how they came upon us. I assumed it was some graduate from IU who is working there.

Another piece of national recognition is with our lambics. For some reason people found some of the beer geek websites like BeerAdvocate.com and Ratebeer.com that really loved them. The people who rate beer like to trade so someone from here will ship our lambic to California; in return they'll ship something from their area to the people here. People have rated our lambics from all over the country even though we sold them only in Bloomington and mostly through here. They may have had them at Kahn's [Fine Wines & Spirits, Indianapolis] for a short period of time. On the websites, now our lambics are rated outstanding. We hear from people worldwide. Someone who lives in Spain loves Belgian lambics. He said he is planning on coming to Indiana. He seems to be interested in coming here for our lambics. I think Three Floyds is working on a lambic, at least a kriek.

CALEB For some reason, when you look at the ratings of beer, our lambics are in the top twenty. We did no advertising except that when we released the lambics we did a reservation where you could reserve four bottles. We did only a small batch so one person had a max of buying six bottles. Our Schwarzbier did really well. I'm excited to launch it this year. We've got it to where we want it to be. We're pleased with our saison. The Preservation Pilsner is the newest to be draught.

SCOTT We're more than happy to donate to philanthropic events. They can overwhelm you if you're not careful, so we try to pick mostly local or Indiana organizations. We give to Habitat [for Humanity] all of the time. They'll raise money on it by themselves. They do with it whatever they do. When the Habitat for Humanity throws a party for their workers, they'll serve our beers. They'll have a good time. That spreads the word for us. We're not really a cash rich company. We make beer, so that's what we donate. Some of our festivals here are for direct benefit; they are fundraisers for Exotic Animal Center or Sycamore Land Trust.

We're going to get some figures hopefully this fall from internship students in SPEA, the School of Public and Environmental Affairs. They are going to look at the philanthropic impact, how much we do.

CALEB There's always something going on. Nothing really major that shakes the company or where we need to rethink our business plans. Our menu always has been good, but we've gotten better. I've looked at the first menus. We've gone from the staple burrito to the buffalo burger now. Ryan Harvey, our restaurant manager, saved a lot of menus.

There are a lot of aches and pains starting a business. It's only made us stronger as a business. I'm kind of a kid at heart, and I think that we look for that in most people we hire. I'm the youngest of the brew team, but both Eileen Martin and Mike Lahti are very creative on top of being focused on what they are doing. We all have fun. The job can be very stressful, and part of it is working as a team, and if everyone can pat each other on the back and have a pint, that's the key element to keeping the ship running smooth here, it's having fun. It doesn't have to be stressful. I think it's pretty interesting to have the owner 38, I'm 29, the restaurant manager is 24, and Scott is 25. Doug Dayhoff, the principal owner, brings a kind of liveliness and fresh ideas. We're attached to the place. We're attached to the beer. We all want the company to grow, and if we do, it will put more money in our pocket, but we all realize that is not going to happen if the beer is not the best all of the time. It's kind of a cyclical thing. We brew the beer that we drink, and we drink the beer that we brew.

I think stretching the palate with the Schwarzbier is part of the youthfulness thing. I wanted the art for it to contain a black panther—Black Panther Schwarz is the name I had in my head. Bloomington itself has this local legend about a black cat that supposedly roams around Monroe County. It's like a local bogeyman sort of thing. It's been in the *Herald-Times:* "Black panther spotted again." It's kind of fun, so we got the label made up with this nice picture of a panther on it. I remember that our past brewer, David Sipple, had worked for the [Exotic] Feline Rescue Center, so I gave

the EFRC a call and I said, "We're going to throw this festival, and we'd like for you to be involved. Whatever involvement you want to bring along, that's great. We're just looking to have this be a fund-raiser for you. There's a big cat picture on the label." They ended up bringing a full-grown leopard onto the patio. They went overboard on what I expected, that sort of fun stuff. Navi, the black leopard they did bring, was not real happy. She was really nervous. She is real young. The second Schwarz-Tag is coming up. We try to make it close to Halloween, the last Saturday in October. This year they are going to bring one that is more suited to crowds.

scott The article that ended up in *USA Today* about that event wasn't the most positive. They ended up saying we had a caged animal. They missed the philanthropic angle. They didn't talk about that at all.

We'll see [Bloomington Brewing Company brewer] Floyd Rosenbaum in here maybe every other week. He just comes in, has a pint, checks up on what's going on. We just had a big kickball tournament last week during the tenth anniversary [May 27–June 7, 2008], Upland versus BBC, Oliver Winery showed. With all the brewers in Indiana there's a general sense of brotherhood, sisterhood, family. Everybody assisting each other, we're not competitive; we're all scrambling to get a bite out of the market. We're oversaturated with the American light lagers. Still in Indiana, where craft beer is less than 2 percent of the entire beer market, so we've got to grow.

Having two craft breweries in Bloomington is a good thing for growing the craft beer market. Students being here for four years, they're going to get introduced to either one of us. We're definitely better than the other regular stuff that's out there, so they get exposed and they spread the word to wherever they go, "Hey, Bloomington's got good beer . . ." I don't know if there's an Upland Wheat keg on a back porch [for a student party]. Most likely not, but some students are picking it up in another way. I do several beer dinners a year, whether it's in Indianapolis or Muncie. A lot of that is education or marketing. Omar Castrellon at Alcatraz has a beer class at Indiana University Purdue University in Indianapolis. I went up and spoke at that class for one session. Festivals are a great way. Being a brewer is about educating people about better beer, beer style guidance. There's so much ground to catch up. It's a big uphill climb, and we're still able to reach only a small audience to try to convert mega brew consumers to at least try something made locally, which would seem pretty obvious, but for some reason it's a hard sell. I do as much of it as I can, but I also have to brew beer.

You've got to get the beer in their hands. Caleb and Eileen try to get out as much as they can to where people are drinking beer and talking with them.

CALEB Upland Wheat is a very successful crossover beer for our distributors and retailers. It's talking to them [customers at a bar where there's a choice of mega brews and microbrews], "Would you like to try something else?"

Interview June 11, 2008, at Upland Brewing Company

CALEB STATON, HEAD BREWER

Upland Brewing Company Brewer altered its schedule to brew and bottle Ron Smith's award-winning Castle Rock Irish Red Ale.

Ron's Irish Red Ale has a characteristic that makes it stand out. My theory is that the molasses stabilizes the color and the head. He created a recipe that is easy to translate from 10 gallons to 1,000. The one challenge was the molasses. We had to find thirty jars of the same brand to keep it consistent. The groceries in Bloomington wanted to know what on earth we were doing. Well, I got back with the jars, opened one, and turned it over. Whoa, nothing was flowing out. I started laughing. We had to figure out how to get molasses out of the jars pretty fast. The other challenge was getting the label OK'd. We referred to it as "Castle Rock's sticky journey through the hallways of the Alcohol, Tobacco, and Tax Bureau." They had a hard time with molasses in an Irish red. They insisted we specifically list molasses on the label.

When we put the pull from Ron's operation side-by-side with what Upland made, and the two look alike and taste alike, we know we've done it.

To make Ron's beer a regular for Upland, it would have to prove to be commercially viable. Then we would decide if it's year-round or seasonal. People would have to ask for it. Upland tries to look for that "new thing." Our market is for the mature beer drinker. There are a lot of good beers out there. We invite people to start finding them.

Oral history interview January 30, 2006, Kahn's Fine Wines & Spirits, Indianapolis

EILEEN MARTIN I started craft brewing at the Silo Brew Pub, Louisville's first brewpub, in August 1992 with David Pierce when things did not work out with his original assistant. I saw it as a great opportunity to get into brewing professionally. Little did I know that I would fall in love with the art and would acquire a true passion for it.

After being at the Silo as an assistant for a year. I took over as head brewer when David Pierce left to open the Bluegrass Brewing Company (BBC in Louisville). I then did brewery installations and start-ups for Diversified Metal Engineering (DME) Brewing Services out of Prince Edward Island, Canada.

I went to work for a local pet store before being offered the Beer Buyers position at the brand-new Party Source Retail store (now Liquor Barn). My next job was working for Beer House Distributors—we specialized in microbrews and imports—out of Newport, Kentucky, as their sales rep for the Louisville area. I then went to Browning's, where I helped fill out all of the ATF [Alcohol, Tobacco & Firearms] paperwork, found and helped install the brewing equipment, and designed all of the recipes. I was there for a little over two years before they let me go (a blessing in disguise). With no other brewing jobs in the area available, I worked as a manager at a Bluegrass Brewing Company satellite location before deciding that I was not happy doing what I was doing. I knew that I wanted to get back into the brewing industry, and to do so I was going to have to relocate. That is what brought me here to Bloomington and Upland.

Adventures would be the pleasure of meeting other brewers/brewsters, visiting their facilities, and hearing their stories. Brewery owners and supplier representatives are on that list as well. Most everyone in this industry is willing to lend a hand, share tips and information when it is needed, and that is such a great thing.

As far as misadventures go, what saddens me most is having worked for brewery owners who are in the business for all of the wrong reasons. The ones that have no real knowledge of beer or the business, but just see it as a money maker; owners who believe that a brewing degree is worth more than years of experience.

I prefer "brewster," since it pertains to the female brewer. Brewmaster is too masculine. I have always been a "true to style" brewster by following the guidelines for color, bitterness, alcohol, etc. This has gained me a lot of respect from my fellow homebrewers and brewers alike. All of the beers that I produced at Browning's were my recipes. My beginning recipes were adjusted only slightly to achieve what I was looking for. I believe that simplicity is the best policy for me. It is a job, but it also has to be fun and not so serious/scientific.

I tend to think that I make pretty good lagers, which are to me harder to produce consistently/correctly. I also feel that brewing a beer to style is more challenging than making a lot of the newer styles of beer that have come along in recent years. Bigger isn't always better. I like to think that I have proven myself in my work ethic. I started out in the cellar only to move to the brew house six months after I was hired. I work well with others who work as hard as I do, and not so well with those that don't. As far as working individually, I can get much more accomplished and stay focused on what I am doing.

As to who mentored and influenced me: Dave Pierce, for giving my first brewing job;

my parents, Tom and Rita Martin, for teaching me to work hard and making me believe that I could go anywhere and do anything that I set my mind out to do. Teri Fahrendorf, a former brewster from the West Coast who has been at it longer than I have and whom I've had the pleasure of meeting and getting to know; she truly was/is an inspiration to me.

As to changes in craft brewing I have observed, there are so many more resources and so much more information available since I began almost sixteen years ago. New beer styles are being created all of the time, and this just continues to grow. Education about good beer is being taught these days, which makes one appreciate craft brews a little more.

I was born [in 1966] and raised in Louisville, Kentucky, and have five brothers (four older, one younger), and two older sisters. My parents and all but one of my siblings are still there now. I have never been married and do not have any children.

A boyfriend in the late 1980s started homebrewing. I didn't care at all for homebrew at first, but I soon acquired a taste for it and better beer. That was when I got into homebrewing and encouraged other fellow females to do so. I still love to homebrew when I get the chance. My boyfriend of four years, Dale, is my rock who supports me in everything that I do. He and our dog, Caesar, moved to Bloomington with me when I decided to relocate. Brewing is truly a passion for me. It's something that I love to do and I put my heart and soul into.

Telephone and email interview

Bloomington Brewing Company

Lennie's Restaurant, Brewpub
1795 East 10th Street
Bloomington, IN 47408
812-323-2112
812-339-2256
www.bloomington.com

JEFF MEASE, OWNER

jm@bloomington.com

FLOYD ROSENBAUM, HEAD BREWER

frosenbaum@bloomington.com

ROSENBAUM This was the first year for us growing hops. I harvested several pounds this year, and hopefully in about three years they'll actually mature out to produce a lot more. Fall 2008 we brewed a small batch with homegrown hops, dry-hopped with Cascade, all from the farm. We dried the hops. In the fall we cut the vines clear to the ground and used some organic mulch. For the first year I was pleased that they all came up and none of them died. I was glad to let them grow real wild. Normally, when they come up, you clip them, so in 2009 there will be some pruning.

There was no mold. It looked liked there could be some, but just at the end of the season. When you look at plants that have powdery mildew, you can see it. I planted marigolds, so as far as insects, I really didn't have any problems.

Of course, the garden was full of tomatoes, pumpkins, watermelon, muskmelons, corn, and beans. Tomatoes are outliving everything, and they are still producing. We haven't dug up the potatoes yet. This is my part-time avocation. This has nothing to do with the BBC farm. This is ours. We put it in at our own ex-

pense and labor. Grab a tomato off the vine and enjoy it.

For the commercially purchased hops in 2007, I looked at the hops crops and the market and basically determined we should buy three or four boxes in advance of everything. We did get low, but we didn't get to a point of panic. The brewing industry itself helped out anybody. If you said you were in a tight pinch, you got help.

MEASE That's what's special about an industry like brewing. We help each other out. I've come to really appreciate that about the beer industry.

ROSENBAUM Sam Adams was on top of it.

MEASE They actually sold the hops to the other breweries at the price they paid for them, which at the time was $5.75 a pound when they could have sold at $35.00 a pound. They only asked that out of respect for the industry to not buy them for $5.75 a pound and resell them for $25.00. Two main styles were available for what the brewing industry normally uses. They put names in a hat. It worked out really well. Breweries got through this little stage [hop crisis of 2008]. The Brewers Association and others helped out to the point where small brewers were able to maintain.

ROSENBAUM Like others I cut back. We didn't do as many IPAs, but as far as flagship beers we have on tap, we were able to do them. It may not have been all that bad, since it gave us a chance to experiment a little bit and come up with new things.

MEASE We didn't grow all that much farm produce in 2008 to supply all our restaurant needs but did more for 2009. We do better in my garden across the street. In this space [Rosenbaum's private garden] close to the black walnut tree, the plants don't do as well.

The Brewers

Plants just do not do well under black walnut trees. So welcome to the farming. There's lots to learn.

In 2009 we put in 50 more hops plants. I imagine we'll put in 100 next year and just feel our way through. Best not to go too crazy; see how location works and how variety works. The farm at this point is experimental. It takes a lot of work. I think it will be awhile before we have so much of a hops crop for it to be intense. I'm sure we will find the [physical] help we need from our regular staff.

We bought this farm because we knew we wanted to expand the brewery, to let the Bloomington Brewing Company grow. We have been making as much beer as we can make for a number of years. As we looked around at the different ways to expand, I settled on the idea of a farmstead brewery like what you find in Europe. I don't know if there is any model for it in the United States. There are a few in Canada. It's not going to be a huge brewery, but it is going to be significantly bigger than what we have now. Part of what we want to do is provide an experience for people to get out of town, to come out into the country and enjoy it. We want to be part of our communities' lives and be a respite for travelers. A lot of our [Indiana] breweries now are in old buildings that are redeveloped, and that's a great way to have another experience. Bloomington is not so big, and since Upland has already done the downtown old building redevelopment model, we really didn't think it was the best thing for everybody to do that again, so we decided to do something completely different.

I grew up in the country, and I've always wanted to get back to that. I've loved gardening since I was a child. My grandmother got me a subscription to *Organic Gardening* magazine when I was nine or ten, and I can remember poring over the Burpee seed catalog in February and planning my garden. Floyd likes to garden as well, and he's got quite a green thumb. He also loves the country, so it was a good fit for him to live in the old farmhouse here. The farm has plenty of room, and in terms of the variety of agricultural possibilities, it's nearly unlimited. That can actually be a little bit daunting sometimes. We've got pigs and quail, chickens and water buffalo. We picked a bunch of wild grapes last year and made jelly. We didn't get much, but the flavor was just phenomenal. It would have been too expensive to sell, so we had to give it away. So growing grapes is something we'd like to do along with fruit trees. Spring 2009 was fruit tree year to put in plums, cherries—things that would work for beer.

The important thing is you have to take the long view. I suppose it could happen fast if you had unlimited funds, but I think it's better this way. Somehow life to me is fuller when we allow it to develop organically rather than trying to force it in a moment. Instead, to let the ground speak to you about what we want to do together.

[Looking out from the garden] Here we're going to build a lake at the bottom of this gulch. We're going to clear trees out and put in a lake. In the higher valley up there we're going to dam that off and put in a smaller pond, so we'll have one that's about forty feet higher than the other. We might even be able to play with a little micro hydropower off of that, or at the very least there is potential to create some beautiful water features that add a whole other element to the ecosystem.

I've connected with a professor at the University of Oregon who is knowledgeable about barley. He is interested in doing experimental barley crops with us. Barley is quite sensitive to local soil conditions. People don't really grow barley around this area anymore, but they used to. Growing barley, whether we do it or we have somebody else do it, is a goal of mine. We've only got about twenty-six acres of tillable land here. Nine have become a pasture, and another fifteen are going to be sold to a local not-for-profit that does therapy for people using animals. It's a wonderful group. My point is that we don't have a large chunk of land to grow grain on. But there are certainly people around here who could grow grain. But there are certainly people around here who could grow barley.

The goal is to be self-sufficient, although it might not get to that point. But to integrate some of these things, develop them, and get other people to do crop growing for us, we can help with the intellectual capital and time and energy. Most farmers don't have that much time to figure out new things.

We will keep Lennie's and the current brewery as they are. We considered moving that brewery, but I think it would take something away from that operation. People like to see it. I think for all the energy it would take to turn that 700-square-foot brewery that we have now into more dining space would just be more money than we should spend. As we grow, that smaller system will become the experimental brewery, and that will give us a great opportunity for creativity and fun.

Here on the farm, our restaurant brewery will start out pretty rustic, maybe not much more than a tasting room with some pizza, something real basic. From there we will just let it develop. Bloomington is not a big city, and my experience has been that it takes some time to get things going. Eventually we will want to be doing a fairly major service business out here, but that's probably ten or fifteen years out.

When we opened Lennie's in 1989, we had a huge saga getting a permit to sell alcohol, which is neither here nor there, but there was an element in the IU administration. We eventually did get a permit to sell beer and then a permit to sell wine. In the late 1980s, particularly California and Oregon were starting to make some good beers, and the whole craft beer renaissance was happening, and there was generally a lot of interest in beers. There were a lot of good imports available. Lennie's ended up having quite a few beers on our menu. We would promote an import or a microbrew a month at a time, and as I started learning about the whole craft beer industry, I just got really enamored with it. I've always been fascinated by the local, the things that become very popular at a local level but don't necessarily get big. They stay unique to their place, like "terroir." I come to see that this is part and parcel of community. It adds so much to the experience when you go somewhere and find a product that is unique and only available there. It's the antithesis of the industrialization of the world; that which the United States has so much of with Starbucks and McDonald's. It was that love and fascination of local brands that attracted me to craft beer, more than being a beer lover or brewer. I've brewed a few batches of homebrew in my life, but I'm not enough of a scientist. What I appreciate is the magic of the local brand, and that's why the Bloomington Brewing Company came into being. My marketing vision for the company is not to have our beer available all over the place, not even all over Indiana. If we make enough beer to serve our local market and have enough for visitors and we go fifty miles

The Brewers

away, I'll be satisfied. We must be big enough to have some economy of scale so we can be price competitive. That's a very big issue in brewing.

Floyd is our fourth head brewer in the history of the Bloomington Brewing Company. We had a revolving door in the brewery for a while. I never wanted that. Floyd ended up doing some work as an assistant. When he showed up, I knew he was the guy I had been looking for—someone a little bit older, more seasoned, and stable who wasn't just going to be off to the next thing.

ROSENBAUM Sometime after 1973, after leaving service in Alaska, I met Alaskans who were brewing beer with ingredients other than hops, and I developed a taste for diverse ingredients. When I got back to the lower forty-eight, I went to work as a pipefitter and got into homebrewing, paying attention to all the details. On my days off, I would come to Lennie's and the BBC. When other brewers left, I stepped in and left a seventeen-year career in the building and trades industry. I don't use fining agents. I love the traditional cask and wooden barrel to ripen.

[*We were at the pigpen at this point, meeting Matilda and her daughter, who both gave us a big, sloppy greeting.*]

MEASE They are really sweet. This is a Heritage Breed, called the English Large Black Pig, which fell out of favor with breeders, but they're very docile and personable. We're breeding her again in December 2008, and this one, too. Matilda had an unusual litter of seven boys and one girl. The boys are kept elsewhere. We already did a hog roast where we slaughtered one of the pigs out here and dressed it out. This is the first time I've done anything like that.

There's a lot of potential with pairing beer with food where different beers just taste fabulous with the right pairing and taste terrible with the wrong one. I think there are tremendously more possibilities in pairing beer with food than there are wine and food.

As far as marketing the Farmstead brewery concept, I'm just a huge believer in PR. You've got to have a story to tell, you've got to tell it, and you've got to connect with people. Live your dream and tell people about it so they can live it with you. If you do something interesting enough, people will come. You don't need to have Disneyland or have huge crowds right off the bat if you manage your overhead. Give people a good experience, and they'll tell their friends. We're going to start fairly slowly and just let it develop and not get ahead of ourselves. We want to do a bunch of different things. Our chef is interested in cured meats, so we've been learning about that—European-style cured sausage. Raise the pigs out here in a great environment, feed them brewery waste, restaurant waste, and complete that cycle with virtually no waste. I'm very interested in the whole concept of sustainability. We're already bringing all our food waste here to the farm, which is either fed to the pigs and chickens or composted. How can we make our products with more beauty and less waste? That should be the mantra of every business.

[*We were now at the water buffalo pasture.*]

Do you know where the famous Mozzarella di Bufala comes from?

Yes, water buffalo.

Interviews at Bloomington Brewing Company and the farm between 2005 and 2008 and verification in 2009

SCOTT P. KINNEY, HOMEBREWER

ROBERT SASSANO, HOMEBREWER

SCOTT I got into homebrewing in the Navy. I got into judging beer in the Navy by being in Italy and Germany. That was my start. And then when I got back to the States, I did more exploration beyond Miller Lite and Budweiser. Living in the Seattle area with this huge amount of beer out there, I got hooked on it. My buddy Cory was also in the Navy. He took me under his wing and showed me how to brew because I had no clue how to do it. The first time I brewed beer, it was a hefeweizen, and I had a huge boilover on the stove. [Laughter] Cory's pot, it caramelized the whole thing. It took me about two weekends to scrub all the junk out of the poor guy's oven. [More laughter] And I've been doing it ever since.

ROB I was in the Navy, stationed outside of Seattle. I got a real good appreciation for beer out there. It was a little town where I was stationed, Anacortes. Walking around a little town, window-shopping, I saw Northwest Homebrew Supply. I was with a friend of mine, and I told her, "Hey, let's go in and talk to this guy." She said, "You don't know anything about making beer." And I said, "I bet he does." We walked in the door, and he asked me, "What can I do for you?" I said, "I love good beer, and I know nothing about making it." So he said, "You came to the right place. I'll set you up." We walked through the store, and he put together all the equipment that I needed. I went home that night and brewed up my first batch of extract beer. It was an American pale pre-hopped extract kit. I got that in the fermenter. The next weekend, when I transferred that to the secondary, I went back to the store and I said, "Hey, Larry, my primary is empty.

I need to fill it up again. That canned extract thing was too easy. I think I need to go on to something else." So we set up a recipe, and I brewed up—it may have been a porter or a stout—and really progressed pretty fast from there. I did extracts for quite a long time. I got from bottling into kegging on my fourth batch because I got tired of bottling. I went in, and he set me up with a kegging setup. That was in 2002 when I started brewing.

Scott and I were stationed together out in the state of Washington. When I showed up to our command out there, he was on deployment. He came back shortly after that. He was one of my supervisors at work. We started hanging out together.

SCOTT It was a rash of kids that came in. By kids I don't mean like young. I mean kids that are new to the Navy. You came in with five or six people. I was one of the senior techs, but I was out the door, so I needed to pass on information. I was trying to teach the newer technicians that came in, and they were all pretty much useless except for Rob. Rob was the only one who ever paid attention, so we became friends and worked together night and day for months and hung out together outside of work, and here we are a decade later.

ROB Scott had gotten a job outside of the Navy, working with a contractor for the Navy, and had gotten a job at the base at Crane as a government employee there. When I was on my way out of the Navy, I was looking at trying to find a stopping-over point on my way back to Florida. I wanted to go back to Florida and start up a charter fishing business. I called him up. "Hey, what can you do about getting me a job so I can earn a little bit of money?" He talked to all his bosses and got me hooked up with a job.

I figured my days of good beer and home-brewing were over when I moved to the Mid-west. I got out here and I was floored by the amount of good beer coming out of Indiana, Ohio, Illinois, and Michigan. I didn't think there was good beer outside of the Pacific Northwest.

SCOTT The major difference that I see is the bottled beer that you can get here versus the Northwest. There's really good beer here, but there's a lot of beers that I miss that I wish we could get a little further out this way. [Laughter]

One of my favorites always has been Pike Place Brewery. It's a small place right down-town next to the market in Seattle. The name is Pike Place Market, so this is their brewery. They make fantabulous Scotch ale, Kilt Lifter. It's about a 9—great color, great flavor. It's one of those beers you can drink all day if you have a high alcohol tolerance.

ROB It's one of those beers like Scott said you can drink all day. It's not too heavy, but it's full of flavor. I've been asking around Bloom-ington at the liquor stores, and none of them has been able to get it yet.

SCOTT As far as I know, it's what we call a Tristate beer. You can get it in Washington, Oregon, or Idaho, and that's pretty much it. I don't know if it's gotten any bigger since we left there a decade ago. You could even get it in the grocery stores out there. There's another beer that is amazing called Mac & Jack's African Amber, and it is one of the most amazing beers I've ever had. They don't bottle anything. Everything is kegged, so the only place you can get it is in a bar. Fresh beer—always fresh—you never run into a bad keg. It's just amazing stuff. I wish they would start bottling it and distributing it or send me a couple of kegs a year. That would be nice. [Laughter]

SCOTT We brew together all the time.

ROB A year and a half ago, I got into all-grain, and I got my big setup now and make a big day out of brewing. I live in Bloomington, so it's a little harder for Scott to come over now, but it's always a big deal when we get together. I have a 2-year-old, so I don't get to brew as often as I used to. I like to make a big deal, bust out the barbeque, get some good food and good beer going. We usually try to stick to style when we do brew. If we are brewing an IPA, an IPA is on hand to drink while we are brewing. We always try to stick to homemade brew.

SCOTT If we are having a long day, we'll order a pizza. A while back we did a brew day at Bobby's house. It was kind of chilly out, not that great of a day. So I made a big batch of clam chowder, and brought it down, and we brewed out all day, trying to stay as warm as we could. [Laughter]

ROB For our first all-grain, I brewed a he-feweizen, getting ready for the summer—no, it was an American wheat. I was going to take half of it and make an apricot wheat out of it. April 14 last year, I had just gotten my setup together, the first time we were going to brew on my all-grain setup. That week I was plan-ning that brew day on Saturday. It was in the 70s all week. It was beautiful weather. Friday night the temperature just dropped down to like 28 degrees. My parents were in town to help watch my son, and we had this big brew day planned out, so it was, "We're going to brew anyway no matter if it's cold or rainy." We get out, and we set up in the driveway. Our first all-grain brew day for any of us there, and it's 28 degrees out, and it started to snow. We powered through it.

SCOTT Everyone in the house thinks we're nuts for hanging outside. We're like, we're going to get through this brew day whether we like it or not.

ROB The beer turned out excellent. Every time we brew, we let all our friends know. I send out an email to the Hop Jockeys [Homebrew Club] so everyone in the club can come over. As I have progressed, I like to get together with club members once a month. That way the guys who are just getting into homebrewing or are still brewing extracts can come and see the process done. I have a couple of the guys that were brand-new to homebrewing I met through the Hop Jockeys Club or through a couple of the online beer sites and they've come to my house, and we've sat and talked about beer and brewing, and they'll call me up a few days later and say, "Hey, I'm buying an all-grain setup. Do you want to come over on my first all-grain brew day."

SCOTT Joining Hop Jockeys for me was through Rob. How did you get hooked up with that?

ROB That was through the internet. I was new to Indiana. I'd only lived here about three and a half years. I took about a year, a year and a half, hiatus from brewing because I didn't know anybody. I didn't even know there was a homebrewers supply store in Bloomington for the first year I lived here. I just put brewing on the back burner for a little bit. I got on the internet and started searching around and came across Butler Winery, and they sell homebrew supplies, so I'd go in there and buy my supplies. At the time I was still doing extract. I was getting more advanced in the extract, getting into specialty grains and actually doing partial mashes, and I kept searching around and searching around, and finally I came across the Hop Jockeys website, and I emailed Ryan Clarke, the president, and he said, "Come on out to a meeting and see what we're all about."

I went out there and got Scott and another friend of ours, Bob, hooked up with them, and we have just been going to meetings when we can and hanging out with them.

SCOTT When I do make a meeting, I'll catch it from work. Since there's no set date we meet, I have a hard time making meetings. I try to be as supportive as I can.

ROB Scott actually designed the new T-shirt for the Hop Jockeys.

SCOTT Entering the Indiana State Fair Brewers' Cup competition for me was a mixture of emotions. You know, it would be really great to win in a local competition, but I didn't have anything on hand that I was extremely proud of. I had an APA that I really liked, but I had kegged half of the batch and I bottled half of the batch, and I used a method for bottling for the first time and every single bottle came out carbonated and shot the top off and hit the ceiling, and I was saddened by it because it would have done really well in a competition. It was a mixture of emotions because I would have liked to see a Hop Jockey or a St. Gabrinus [Benevolence Society Homebrew Club] guy winning for the first competition, making it truly local.

ROB I didn't have anything in the keg that I thought would do well in the competition. I've got an imperial stout in bottles, but it's been aging. I entered it in the Upland Brewery competition. It didn't do real well because it's pretty young, so I'm going to let it go for about another year. A friend of ours took honorable mention.

SCOTT He's a Hop Jockey. It was a Belgian wit.

ROB He didn't even like that beer at all, and everyone else told him to enter it. He said, "I don't like it." I told him, "Enter it. It's going to do well." It did.

SCOTT I don't typically brew on my own. When I was living in town, we always used to set up on his setup. There's no sense in buying another setup, since we are always brewing together. Well, now that I live here in Indianapolis, we're in the process of building one up. For my birthday this year Rob got me a keg, and we are going to cut it into a kettle and we're going to build a mash tun. I've bought some kegs, slowly picking up equipment as I go, and finally I'll have a setup, and we'll be able to brew in two cities. We'll have a good time.

ROB A brew of two cities sounds like a good name for a bar.

I've been drinking Belgians like it's going out of style lately. Anything Belgian I can get my hands on. I'm pretty excited about a lot of breweries doing Belgians for their anniversaries this year. I've been doing a couple of Belgian pales to get my feet wet in the Belgian community. I set up for a ten-gallon batch; half of it is a Flanders red that will be ready to drink 09-09-09. Long time to wait for beer, huh? The other half was fermented with 100 percent Brettanomyces and is sitting on top of some plums and cherries in the secondary fermenter and should be ready in October or November 2008.

What I'm going to play around with more now is sour beers and make a Lambic at the end of the summer, beers that are going to take awhile. So I've been getting more into more complex. I've brewed all the IPAs I can brew. I've brewed all the stouts I can brew. I need something to challenge myself, so I'm going to do sour beers that aren't going to be ready for five years.

SCOTT We keep pretty traditional. We all started out drinking IPAs, and we were big hop heads, going through the phase "We've got to have more hops, more hops."

ROB Now with the hops shortage, it's really a crunch on making beers that we love, so we've got to start working in different directions as far as going the sour route, the Belgian route, a little less hops, relying more on malt for the flavors.

SCOTT Don't get me wrong—whenever I'm at a new place, I always have to try their IPA. But I used to be nothing but IPA. Now I'll drink one and I'm ready for something to cool it off. I never really was a malty, but now I get more into the reds. I'm really enjoying some of the higher alcohol ones. I'm still not into the Belgian thing. I never liked Belgian beers.

ROB When Scott tastes it and spits it out, we know we've got it to style.

SCOTT That's how they test their beers out. [Laughter] It's just not my thing. Bobby and the others are more the experimental guys. They like to go create the off-beers. I like to take beers that I like to drink and take it to the point that "This is awesome." Back when we were brewing extract beers, we always had trouble with color. With extract it's pretty much one color. You can get a lot of flavor out of it. So we would always experiment on ways to get color. I've got one beer that I make that I call the GPA. It used berries, Irish tea, and a mix of Lipton that I brewed into the ale, and it was really good. What I want to do is to perfect that recipe as all-grain. We've never done it as an all-grain and get that to the point where it is amazing. I like to brew the same thing over and over and get it better. Those guys like to brew something different every time. He's got a few recipes of his own he's perfected and brewed multiple times, but they are few and far between. He's brewing stout one time and something I've never heard of next time that you have to age for ten years. In that way we're kind of opposite, but it works.

ROB We come up with some crazy recipes. I like to think of stuff you don't see out in the market. I've got a honey oat red ale, and I use a honey malt and oat malt, and it's pretty close to red in color. That one actually came about when somebody else posted it up on a beer forum. Looking at the ingredients I had on hand and his ingredients list, I said, "Hey, take your honey malt and oat malt and make it red, and why not add some Noble Hops for real mellow bitterness." The guy on the beer forum decided to go with barley instead. I started looking at the properties of oats and of his head retention, and if I use as much oats as I'm thinking, it's not going to have any head retention. I started looking around, and I saw that there's actually oat malt. So I looked into that and bought a bunch of that and bought some honey and some malts to make it red. I stirred together a recipe and, hey, everybody loved it. That's one of my staple beers that I brew and keep on hand. I've got ten gallons of it conditioning at home right now, getting ready for "Beer and Sweat" in Cincinnati. It's the first time I'll enter this one in a competition, so I'll see how it does.

ROB I actually just met Floyd Rosenbaum [brewer at Bloomington Brewing] a couple of weeks ago. It was great talking to him. This is actually a homebrewing story. We were sitting around talking, and he said, "Hey, do you want to come back into the brewery and see everything going on?" I said, "Sure." I started out asking him about his equipment, and in the conversation he said, "I'm just a homebrewer. I do it on a bigger scale." His equipment is a homebrew setup, just larger. His mash tun is not fired, [fire truck went by at this point] single mashes, direct fire boil kettle. It's my homebrew setup on steroids. I told him, "You are a huge inspiration for a guy like me." He's really passionate about beer, and I can see myself as a brewer. I don't know if I ever would. But it's an inspiration to see that there are guys out there making great, great beer on the same setup that I do, just a bigger batch.

About the hops shortage, I started planting hops. I made a big garden. I've got one plant that took off; the other one is not so good. That and brewing lower hops beers, Belgians and maltier beers.

SCOTT I think gone are the days of handfuls of hops. Now you have to budget for it. You have to have ten of your buddies to get the two ounces.

ROB Sitting around having too much Upland maibock at my place, Scott and I and our friend Bobby sat around, and it came down to we thought we could brew more beer in twenty-four hours than a couple of other guys. So we sat around talking. The challenge was put out there. In twenty-four hours, who could brew the most beer? So we had to follow through, and we came up with the Bloomington Hop Jockeys' twenty-four-hour brew day. Start at 8 AM, and you brew until 8 AM the next day. You are allowed a team of guys. We had two or three out there for the first time. Our team was Scott and me and Bobby. We had two mash tuns, two boil kettles, my hot liquor tank, a couple of sacks of grain, and a whole bunch of hops. We started throwing recipes together. The other guys showed up with a bunch of ingredients and equipment. Everybody showed up with giant yeast starters. That way we could share them, put together recipes on the fly. We ended up brewing nine five-gallon batches in twenty-four hours. The team that won brewed nine batches, but they had four ten-gallon batches, so they won by volume.

SCOTT Rob and I celebrated a bit long the night before, so we didn't show up at 8. We actually brewed nine batches of beer in nineteen hours. About 6 PM, we decided we couldn't do anymore. We ran out of vessels. Everyone in the club pitched in cardboard and everything, and we filled them all. We filled this guy's garage. We've got a picture of it. There were twenty-six five-gallon cardboard boxes full of beer by the end of the night.

SCOTT AND ROB (*finishing each other's sentences*) The three major highlights of the day were we had a fire. We put an extension cord on fire. The other team boiled twelve gallons of wort down to four gallons, and it clogged the wort chiller. It's still fermenting a year and half later. The other highlight was our final batch of beer. All the runnings left over from rolling back into the mash tun we dumped into a bucket, so at the end of the day we had five gallons from the drippings from everything we brewed that day. We did an EP, IPA, a stout, amber, Mexican lager; the mashes were all completely different. We dumped the bucket into the boil bucket for our ninth batch, and we started throwing in hops for the fifteen-minute boil. At one point one of the guys came up and said, "I think I've got some hops in my pocket." He reached in his pocket and pulled out some hops and threw it in the boil. There was a girl there who had never brewed before, and she thought it was fun, so she threw in some hops, and we threw in some. We don't know what the increments were, but it was pretty much a continually hopped beer. We thought this is going to be the worst beer in the world. It was

actually one of the better beers. It came out like an APA, almost amber, that was so drinkable. It took a little while for it to clear up and for the hops to mellow out and the flavors to meld together, but it was one of the smoothest APAs that has come out of any one of our brewers. We'll never be able to reproduce it again. The malt flavors were really complex, but it was in the background because the hops overpowered everything. To be continually hopped like that, you had the whole range of bitterness. It flows really well from the bitterness in the flavor into the aroma. There had to have been seven to ten varieties of hops. It was pretty low gravity, only about a 4 or 5 percent beer. It was a back-burner beer for us. If we had more vessels, we could have brewed two more batches.

ROB As a club we're trying to put together a twelve-hour brew day. I've talked to a lot of the clubs, and they're all pretty excited about a twenty-four-hour brew day, so we're going to try to set up for early summer an interclub brew day. We've talked to the guys at Upland to let us brew there in the banquet hall facility.

SCOTT The thing that's challenging is having a continuous flow of hot water.

ROB Upland is saying we can run a hose off their hot water tank and run it out for the brew day.

SCOTT It was fun having all those different beers at the same time. It was tap, tap, tap. You don't have to go buy beer, which is always nice, especially now with prices going up. It's a double slam between the shortage of hops and gas; you've got to be dedicated to drink beer anymore.

I want to mention a place called Boundary Bay Brewery and Bistro up in Bellingham, Washington, near the waterfront. I can't remember the head brewer's name. This guy brews some amazing beers. We sat down for dinner there one night. He's got a great garden out back. He throws festivals. I was sitting there. He didn't know me from Adam; he figured that I like beer because I went there after work. About the third night he sees me in there, he brought out a special cask of Reserve IPA. "Hey, man, you need to try this." If you ever get up there, I highly recommend it.

ROB I talked to Bob Ostrander before I'd gone off to Cincinnati for Oktoberfest, and I asked if anybody was going out there from Indiana Beer, and he said no. So I wrote up an article and sent it to him to put up on the website. Scott and I went to Oktoberfest together. I've been wanting to write more for them. I brought my camera today, and I'll start send-ing more things in to them. Every time I go to a new brewery they haven't reviewed, I'll send it in. I went to Flossmoor in Illinois and stopped at Three Floyds and ended up staying a little longer so I could make the drive home. I'm trying to get my feet wet in the writing world.

I don't do a lot of beer-related things other than homebrewing. I make sure I go to Micro-brew Fest every year and Cincinnati Beer and Sweat Competition. It's such an opportunity to meet other homebrewers. Everybody there is on the same page, excited about the same thing. You get a lot of good connections out of it.

Interview July 19, 2008, at Brugge Brasserie in Broad Ripple

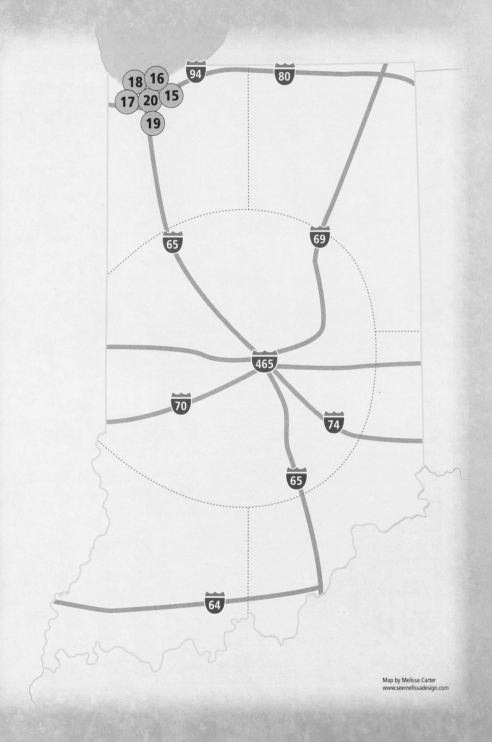

Map by Melissa Carter
www.seemelissadesign.com

Northwest Indiana

Northwest Indiana Brewpubs & Breweries

Mishawaka Brewing Company

2414 Lowell Street
Elkhart, IN 46516
514-532-2473
www.mishawakabrewingcompany.com

The Pub
408 West Cleveland Road
Mishawaka, IN 46530
574-273-5397

TOM SCHMIDT, OWNER

In the mid-1970s I was working for Miles Laboratories in Ohio when I was transferred to their headquarters in Elkhart, Indiana. It was a career change because I was a manufacturing superintendent at the Worthington Foods plant in Worthington, Ohio, but took a position in application research in Elkhart that matched with my backgrounds in science and food chemistry. My family and I moved to the area in 1978. Over the next few years I was in application research working primarily with citric acid, preservatives, and annatto food colors. During that time I was granted two U.S. patents related to annatto food colors. In 1985 I became technical services manager in the Bio-Tech Division.

In 1986 I took on the additional responsibilities with the Enzyme Division as technical services manager. At the time Miles Laboratories owned the Siebel Institute in Chicago. They were focused on the brewing industry and were selling to the larger breweries, so I had my first exposure to brewing enzymes through Siebel. I was, however, primarily working with our sales force and enzyme customers. In '86 a sales representative in the Pacific Northwest called me and wanted to know two things. One, could I make some calls with him out in the fruit growing areas around Yakima, Washington. And then he said, "While you're out here, there's a new small industry starting involving microbreweries, and they're having their annual national meeting in Portland. Is there any way you could arrange it where we could go to that?"

This guy loved visiting those small breweries. He loved drinking beer, and he loved collecting T-shirts from all these new breweries in the areas he covered in northern California, Washington, and Oregon. At the time I said, "Yeah, I can probably work that out. I'm not sure what interest we might have." And he says, "We might see if they're going to use any enzymes like the bigger breweries are using enzymes." Anyway, I arranged it for us to go to this National Microbrewers conference. At the time I wasn't much of a beer drinker. It would always give me a headache. I'd buy a six-pack once in a while and drink one and it would sit in the refrigerator until my father-in-law would visit and he'd drink it.

The first day of our trip was spent in the Yakima area visiting some of the fruit processors that were our customers. As we were driving between accounts he said, "While we're here there's a little brewpub, Bert Grant's Malting and Brewing Company. We'll stop there for lunch so you can see what I'm talking about." That was back when it was just a small place. It had a small brew kettle in the corner that heated up the room. I ordered—I think it was their Bert Grant's India Pale Ale. I tasted it and it had the most awful bitter taste I'd ever tasted in my life. He was a hop broker, so he was big into hops. Then I tried the Imperial Stout. It was too strong for my taste at the time.

When it came time for dinner, I said, "That beer I had for lunch, I kind of want to taste it again. I don't know what it is, but it left a taste that I would like to try again." It wasn't open

for dinner, so we weren't able to do that. Perhaps I had been seduced by hop flavor. The next morning we headed to the meeting in Portland at the Marriott. I think he and I were the only two at the meetings who wore suits. There were about 200 people in attendance, and they were the most relaxed, energetic group of people I'd ever been around. They seemed excited, and they had a deep passion for beer. I sat there during the talks and took notes, filling two spiral notebooks.

Nowadays when you go to these conferences they are so big they break them up. You have to pick through a menu of talks you want to hear. But in '86 it was just one talk after another. The people in attendance included Jim Koch from Boston Beer, the guys from Sierra Nevada, the guy who started Portland Brew-

ing, David Geary from Portland, Maine, Fritz Maytag, and "Buffalo Bill" Owens. Owens gave a talk and I thought, "This guy is off the wall." He was wearing a tie-dyed T-shirt, he had a butch haircut, and he's talking about owning a little brewpub: how sick you get of cleaning the toilets, how you get people in wanting Budweiser, and how he'd slide it down the bar and charge more for it. He said, "If they want to drink it, they pay more." Within about six years I knew what he was talking about and knew he wasn't "off the wall."

Many of the people attending wanted to start a brewpub or microbrewery and were there to learn as much about it as they could.

Well, it turned out there wasn't any potential for Miles products, specifically enzyme products. But I ended up with two spiral notebooks filled with notes having nothing to do with my job at Miles. I just got excited about the idea. I knew that if I ever started a business, I wanted to make something; I didn't want to go into the service industry. If I went into my own business, I wanted to be in manufacturing. I thought, "Man, this has got to be the thing." During those three days of the conference, they had many beer tastings: at ten o'clock break, at noon break, three o'clock break, and then at dinner. I'm talking responsible beer tastings—walk around and tasting just a bit. The beers I remember were Sierra Nevada, Geary's, Redhook, and beers from the bigger places like FX Matt's Saranac brand out of New York, which was very nutty and malty. I had never tasted beer like this. I began to like the taste. I ended up staying over on Saturday—they had a tour of the breweries and brewpubs that started up in Portland, Oregon. We went to Portland Brewing when it was a relatively small brewery. We also visited Columbia, Bridgeport, and one of the McMenamins brewpubs in Hillsdale that had small kettles in the corner and plastic trash bins as fermenters. They were making beers that had Mars Bars and other candy bars as ingredients. I kept thinking, this is kind of crazy, but it was the beginning of people experimenting to create new tastes.

This conference was the beginning of my interest in brewing. I had never been interested in beer per se before that.

On the last night of the conference, there was a beer tasting by Michael Jackson. After sampling all the beers at dinner and during the tasting, I was kind of buzzed. I went out and called a friend of mine who lived in Walnut Creek, California, who worked for Miles. When he came through sales training, he came to tech service for a week for technical training. We used to sit and talk about some day getting out of the corporate world. So I called him that evening and said, "I found the perfect thing to start as a business." That night he and his wife went down to Berkeley to visit Triple Rock Brewery and Alehouse. Six months later he was transferred back to Elkhart, so like big shots, we'd sit and talk about starting up a business and started putting together pro formas. We went around looking for locations. It was around '87. We actually found out you have to have some money before you start up one of these things. We had thought, oh, you can just go to a bank. It's a great idea, and they'll give us all the money we want. Well, in the end, we didn't get money from banks. In '88 we both got promotions, and I changed career direction again going into marketing. At that time we put the idea of a brewery on the back burner. In 1990 we started talking about it again, and we said, "Let's either do something or shut up." So we got together on weekends and started working on a business plan, and in a few months we ended up with a very comprehensive business plan.

We took that business plan and used it to creatively finance finish-outs that were included in our lease and, with money we had been able to save, were able to get something started. We went into it together, the two of us. We quit our jobs in August 1991 because we had signed a lease in a new development and thought everything was set to go. However, the development fell apart in November, and we were stuck without jobs and had no place to put this business. We had already purchased the brewing equipment, and it was being built by Specific Mechanical in Victoria, British Columbia. However, we now didn't have a building to put it in. The first of the equipment arrived in April, and we stored it in my garage.

After scrambling to find another location, we were shown a building that had been a fitness center and had been vacant for two years. We didn't have the money to buy the building, but there was a large car dealership in the area that had just sold property and needed to reinvest; his time was running out to avoid paying capital gains. He bought that building, and the real estate people we had been working with brought us together with him. We said, "We don't know if this is really the right place," but we were desperate, so we made a pitch, and that's really where we got most of our financing. We had purchased the brewing equipment, kitchen equipment, and tables and chairs. Getting the building and the restaurant refitted was part of the lease.

I bought out my partner, John Foster, after eight years in 2000. The original plan was that I would be the beer person and he would be the restaurant operator. Well, he found out he didn't like the restaurant business at all. It only took him a few years to realize that. But I still loved the brewery. My son Rick was working with me from the start, helping me brew. My wife was there from the start, so it became a family deal for us, but it wasn't for John.

When we were in the late planning stages, we had to take the same approach to state licensing that John Hill at Broad Ripple Brewpub went through. [In 1990 Broad Ripple Brewpub was the first; Mishawaka was the second in 1992.] Brewpubs weren't legal in Indiana, so both of us had to set up two different operations—a separate brewery and a separate restaurant. So my wife and my partner, John, split ownership of the restaurant corporation (Brew Pub Ltd), and John's wife, Sally, and I owned the brewery corporation (Mishawaka Brewing Company). Even then it was difficult with the laws because the ATF [Federal Bu-

reau of Alcohol, Tobacco, and Firearms] said that because of the Indiana law we couldn't have beer directly transferred to the restaurant. We were going to have to keg it, take it outside the brewery, and deliver it to the restaurant. At that time they had an ATF office in South Bend. The officer came out and worked with us. She found a way for us to apply for a variance where we would dedicate four tanks in the brewery cooler as being owned by the Brewpub. We had to paint a yellow line around those four tanks and have reversible signs on those four tanks. One side of the sign read "Mishawaka Brewing Company Tax Determination Tank"; the other side read "The Brewpub Ltd. Serving Tank." The way it worked was when the tank needed to be cleaned and filled, I would say, "I am extending my brewery," turn the sign over to Mishawaka Brewing, and then clean the tank, fill it, and carbonate it. Then I would say, "I am curtailing the brewery," and turn the sign over to Mishawaka Brewing Company side. The first couple of years when we gave tours, that was the story people liked the most. Most people's reactions was, "Oh, the federal government screws everything up," and I was like, "No, the feds actually helped me work around Indiana state laws."

A couple of years later, Indiana changed the laws. The state attorney general was concerned that they had set a precedent for familial relationship corporations and that bigger corporations might try to do the same. That is one of the reasons, I think, the state started to move to get the brewpub laws changed because Broad Ripple and Mishawaka had been allowed to open brewpubs with variances and they didn't want that to become widespread because it could backfire in other situations.

As far as the actual brewing, it was after I came back from the meeting in Portland that I said, "You know, I'm going to learn how to brew beer." It fit my background, being in food chemistry, so I started experimenting. I started with whole grain brewing right from the start. I spent the first year learning what different malts did as far as flavor, color, and aroma; I was experimenting with different hops. At the time there weren't that many yeast strains available. You pretty much used the dried Red Star yeast. And no matter how I changed the formula, I always ended up with the same banana ester bubblegum flavors from Red Star. Then Wyeast Labs introduced liquid strains, and I started experimenting with those, and suddenly it's "My god, this is the biggest difference of all." It just amazed me the effect the different yeast strains had as far as flavors. We selected a yeast strain we just loved, even though it had a lot of characteristics a lot of beer judges didn't like. Beer judges are trained for specific defects, and any time they detect that, they think it's a fault and the beer is unacceptable. When we won the silver medal for The Four Horsemen in the ESB category, Charlie Papazian was coming around to tasting the beers that won medals. While tasting the Four Horsemen, he said, "This is the perfect example where a little bit of diacetyl is great." The yeast strain we used gives you some diacetyl. Taking judges' comments to heart, we actually changed our yeast once to get rid of the diacetyl, and our brewpub customers didn't like it. They liked that buttery note. That's the great thing about starting with a brewpub instead of directly with a brewery. With the brewpub you can experiment a little bit more, and you get instant feedback. If you change something that is good from a judging standpoint but the customers, the regulars, don't like it, then the heck with it. You go with the customers.

In 1987 I was able to finagle my way to attend the National Microbrewers conference in Boston. At that meeting I was introduced to an ale that became my favorite beer at the time. It was Geary's Pale Ale, and I remember David Geary making the comment, "We brew our beer for our customers. We do not brew for the beer judges. We have never entered any competitions because the judges don't understand." I understood where he was coming from. But you do also want some recognition once in a while. What I found was that if you win a medal, it's not going to translate into more sales. That isn't what it really does. It basically translates into your existing customers being validated that what they think is good beer—you won an award—so, yeah, they were right.

As I was test brewing at home, I started documenting results on my computer. Using spreadsheets, I put tables in on everything I could find in the available literature—bitterness units, hops varieties, alpha acid content, taste characteristics, yeast characteristics, different colors of the different malts. After a while I was able to plug in different variables so I could model different beer formulas. I started developing recipes using the computer model that I put together. I still use it today to model specialty beers. When I started brewing beer, I thought that even if I didn't start a brewery, it was still fun. My interest in personal computers and brewing developed at the same time, and I was able to put the two together. It was fun, quite a bit of fun.

Each beer we design we approach a little bit differently. We have never really tried to brew a beer completely true to style. We use the style as a base to get started, but we are looking for different characteristics in every beer that we make. We started in 1992 with four beers on tap. Our first beers were Lake Effect Pale Ale, South Shore Amber Ale, Founders Stout, and Mishawaka Gold, which was a lager. We used different yeast for the ales and the Mishawaka Gold Lager. Four Horsemen Irish Ale was introduced as a specialty beer in 1993. It was sort of a takeoff of South Shore Amber. At the time we started the Brewpub, everybody had amber ale, but then amber ales seemed to become passé.

The Four Horsemen was very popular. What we were trying to do when we developed it was to take the South Shore and give it a little more malty richness, a little more caramel characteristic, and cut back on the initial bitterness to give it a little more mellow beginning with the residual sweetness of the malt by using a lot more of the caramel malts. It took the South Shore, which was a bit more bitter, and mellowed it out and brought out a little more of the more malt flavors. We were looking for a beer that more people would like.

There have been times over the years when we started getting carried away with hops based on what our bar customers liked: the bar regulars, the beer lovers, the guys who come in for the beer all of the time, the guys and women who talk to you the most because they are sitting at the bar. As time went by the hoppiness of the beer started increasing, and we started to really hop them up. We were getting more and more comments from bar regulars about how much they loved it. Well, I think we lost sight of the diners that are sitting at the dining tables, who don't drink beer all the time. Some of them, they'd taste it and spit it out, like the first time I tasted Bert Grant's India Pale Ale. It was too bitter for their taste. We had to pull ourselves back a couple of times because we were getting a little crazy on the hops. When we first started, Lake Effect was our mildest

ale. It was mainly Cascades and still is mainly Cascades—we've got two or three other hops in there, but it's mainly Cascade hops giving it that Northwest character that is so popular. We started out very light and gradually increased the hops as people got more accustomed to the higher hop levels. When we started, the people in our area were not used to this kind of beer. We had the Mishawaka Gold, which was a lager and which we designed so that it had characteristics like most beers that people were used to, but with more to it. We wanted a beer that people coming in for the first time could drink. They would recognize it was something different than what they drank in the past, but it still had the characteristics of a typical Pilsner that they drank. We used a lot of different malts to give it a deep gold color because we wanted to call it Mishawaka Gold, and it had a nice malty characteristic. Mishawaka Gold was our number one selling beer for the first four to six months because people found it to be most familiar to them. They were willing to experiment, but they weren't willing to go too far.

When we started, we thought more people knew what craft beers were and what brewpubs were all about. We were wrong. We had to educate people. We did beer tastings with beers from around the world and our beers. That helped educate some people to what the flavors in our beers were all about. Lake Effect was our attempt at a Northwest-style pale ale; South Shore Amber Ale was our answer for amber. With Founder's Stout—now that there is that brewery in Michigan called Founders it confuses people—we wanted to name a beer about ourselves, but we were humble, so we said, "OK, we'll call it Founders." That was the beer that we experimented the most with at the beginning because we wanted to blend six or seven flavor characteristics. We wanted to get the chocolaty flavor, the coffee flavor, the burnt toast flavor that's in there. We experimented with different dark roasted malts before we came up with the ones that seemed to give us everything we wanted. We use five kinds of roasted malts and discovered that if you eliminate one of them, it has a negative impact on the flavor.

There have been a few times when we haven't been able to get one of the malts, and we substituted with another, but it didn't taste the same. I don't know if most customers picked it up, but some of the regular stout drinkers did. They'd say, "There's something different." As a brewer, nothing makes you feel better than when you have to make a change for some reason or another and somebody notices it. The more people who notice it, the better it makes you feel. There's nothing worse than changing something and no one notices it. That means they don't really care. They don't really notice. In the last few years there has been a hop shortage that was close to critical because we had to make a few changes in our hop use. We're now getting back to where it was, but how do you explain to people why your beer tastes a little different?

Our Four Horsemen Irish-style Red Ale has become our number one selling beer. When we first started bottling Four Horsemen in 22-ounce bottles, we used printed paper labels that were pretty simple with our logo and Four Horsemen Ale printed around the logo. We did all bottling by hand using a manual three head filler that we built. Labels were hand glued on each bottle. Then we changed the name to Four Horsemen Irish-style Ale. In 1994 or '95 we changed the logo on the label to include a photo of The Four Horsemen of Notre Dame. We had a trademark for Lake Effect Pale Ale, so we decided to apply for a trademark for the Four Horsemen logo. The trademark was approved with no objections being raised. A few years back we did hear from one of the descendants of one of the Four Horsemen—Elmer Layden Jr. He was at Notre Dame for a game against Michigan State and saw our beer for sale at Notre Dame. That was the first time we had sold it to Notre Dame. We received a letter from his lawyer telling us to cease and desist using the label. I'm like, wait a minute, we've got a trademark that's been in effect for six years, and I have thirty days to respond to his letter. We reviewed all of our research, the history, and it seemed clear that no one ever owned a copyright. Notre Dame didn't, because it was only after the article was written by Grantland Rice in 1924 that a student manager, who was not an employee of the university, thought it would be a cool idea to get some horses and get these guys on them and get a picture. He arranged to have the horses and players meet so that a photographer could take the picture. He had the photographer give him the rights to the picture. He died many years ago, and no one had ever copyrighted the photo. We responded with a six-page letter back to the lawyer. After that, we think the lawyer told him to just try to work something out. The guy still hassles me once in a while. Many people are still amazed, "You have a trademark on that? How'd you do that?"

We have other regular beers including Wall Street Wheat Ale, which is primarily a beer we sold at the brewpub and the Pub and also in 22-ounce bottles. We have never really tried to push it in the wheat beer market, even though that's probably a good area for growth. The Widmer Brothers, who are well known for their Wheat Beer, were part of the brewery tour in Portland in '86 when we visited. If I remember right, they had a sign that said they were on batch 186.

We brewed a Bavarian style wheat beer when we first introduced a wheat beer called Ankenbrock Weizen using a yeast strain that gave you that clovey banana flavor. We loved it, but some customers were like, "I don't know … not sure I like the clove taste." Today I think they'd accept it. We switched to brewing American-style wheat ale. We also brew the Raspberry Wheat, which is very popular in the summer. When we take the Raspberry Wheat to beer tastings such as the big Microbrewers Festival in Broad Ripple, it goes very fast.

It's the specialty beers that have allowed us to have the most fun. Some of the specialty beers were so popular that they became regular beers, so we ended up with seven that are regular and on tap all of the time. One was the Mishawaka Kölsch, which we don't make now since we closed the original brewery and the restaurant [December 3, 2008] and now are brewing only at the brewery in Elkhart. The Mishawaka Kölsch was never a great seller outside the brewpub. With specialty beers, you find something that is really popular and you brew it maybe once or twice a year. It then became almost traditional that you brew a certain specialty at the same time of the year, like Grumpy's Oatmeal Stout. We always brewed that on my birthday. One of my customers always called me Grumpy. I told him, "Look, I'm an old man. What do you expect?" So we decided to name the Oatmeal Stout after me. So that's brewed every January.

The specialty beer that receives the most calls to find out when it will be on tap is our Jack 'O Lager Pumpkin Beer. It is totally different than any pumpkin beer on the market with a taste and sweetness that is like pumpkin pie. We have that on tap from before Halloween through Thanksgiving. In 2008 we sold over 20 barrels of it on tap and in Party Pigs, kegs, and bottles. We also brew the Russian Imperial Stout every fall, followed in December by our Resolution Ale, which is a barley wine meant to help people break their New Year's resolutions. With so many of the specialties coming out at the same time every year, we had fewer opportunities to bring out new specialty beers, which is the fun part. We go through a batch of specialty beer pretty quick at the restaurant. We haven't yet [as of January 2009] gotten back all the people who used to buy carry-out beer from the Brewpub. A lot of them don't yet know that we have carry-out beer available at the Pub. The people who buy kegs quickly learned that they could still order kegs. Party Pig sales haven't yet picked up, but we've been out of the Brewpub for only a month.

The hop shortage cut back on creativity a bit, but we're in pretty good shape now. We've got a contract for three years for most of the hops—not for all. We were set to introduce our Loopy Lupillin Double Imperial IPA in bottles last year but ran into difficulties getting the label design approved by the Federal Tax and Trade Bureau, and then the hop shortage put it on the back burner.

Our INDIAna Pale Ale is not a typical IPA in that it is not as bitter as most India pale ales, but it was the number one selling beer at the brewpub. Four Horsemen is the number one selling over all including outside sales, carry-out sales, etc. But the INDIAna Pale Ale was the most popular at the bar and in the restaurant. We take it to tastings and people say, "This isn't as bitter as I would expect an IPA." Well, it isn't if you are going strictly by the style, but we use a relatively large amount of combination of hop varieties that give the INDIAna Pale Ale different characteristics than many IPAs. We always try to formulate a hoppy beer that has lots of hop flavor and hop aroma but not necessarily a lot of hop bitterness. That's a big difference. You can get a lot of IBUs even if you're adding most of your hops later in the boil where you get more of the hop flavor. People who taste ours say, "Hmm, I don't know, this taste is . . ." They're not sure what they taste. That's kind of what we like; to have something in there so they are not sure what they taste. We try to make every beer taste different. I've gone to some breweries and brewpubs where the same characteristic is in every beer they have. That's unavoidable in some ways, but if you really mix it up, you can make every one different with a different characteristic. We don't want someone to come in and, tasting blind, pick up a Lake Effect Pale Ale, an INDIAna Pale Ale, and a Hop Head Ale and say it all came from the same brewery.

Every fall for the last ten years we have brewed Beer Garden Ale using hops grown around the beer garden at the Brewpub. In 2008, we had a good hop crop. We planted the hops ten years ago. We harvest all the hops and use all of them in the Beer Garden Ale. We were growing two varieties, Cascade and Willamette hops. Each year you get a different quantity of each with different alpha acid content, so each year the beer is different but always popular. We won't be able to do that this next year, since we closed the brewpub, unless we can transplant the hops to the Elkhart brewery.

How did I get started planting hops? My bachelor degree is in horticulture and my master's is in food chemistry, so I have always liked growing plants and using the harvest. That probably has something to do with it. It was actually a customer who started me on it. We had a little homebrew shop. He wanted

to know if we could get some hop cuttings for him to grow hops at home. That's when I started checking around to see if I could get different cuttings. I happened to call just at the right time because there's only a short period when you can order and have them sent. We ordered what they had available, and they sent the two varieties. We brought some in to sell in the homebrew shop and some to plant. The beer garden has a railing around it, and we started training them on the railing. After the first year they began to overgrow the railings, so we ran wires to the roof and trained them to grow up the wires. It made it interesting for people who wanted to know, "What are hops?"

We also have silk hop vines that we used in the brewery. We had a pipe run between the kettle and the mash tun, and we wound the silk hop vine around them to the pipe. When we gave a brewery tour, it was so nice to be able to point to them and show what hops are. Most people think beer is made out of mainly hops, and you have to point out, "That's only a little part of it—an important part but a small part."

We closed the homebrew shop when we closed the brewpub. We don't have room at the Pub or at the Elkhart brewery. We opened the homebrew shop as a convenience to the growing number of homebrewers originally. We didn't do it when we first opened because two guys had just opened a homebrew shop in Niles, Michigan, just north of us, and we didn't want to dilute their business. We referred people there if they needed something. We would sell them a bag of malt if that's all they needed. When they closed, we started one as a convenience. In 2004 the MEGA Homebrew club started [and had been meeting at the Brewpub]. They don't have a place to meet right now because the Pub is not open on Sunday. I've told them, "Give me a little time to

The Brewers

get reorganized and settled and we will work something out."

Back in '95 South Bend Brewing opened up in downtown South Bend as a brewpub. They were only there for six months. When they opened, we heard from lots of people. Our regular customers would visit and then come back to our place to give their review of what it's like, what beer was good, what beer wasn't. Yet when Granite City opened we never heard from any customer about going there. I'd even ask a few and they'd say, "No, I haven't been in there." They're more like Applebee's.

We have transferred the mug club from the brewpub; we call it the Anacreontic Society. All of the special deals we offered at the brewpub are now available at the Pub.

This is the story about Rick being a brewer. Rick is my middle son. He started working with us when we started brewing. We opened the restaurant in October of '92 but we started brewing in August of '92. So he started day one working in the brewery. We both learned to brew on the equipment at the same time. When we started he was twenty-one. At the time, he didn't know exactly what he was going to do with his life. So I said, "Let's get going in this and see where it takes us." He loves it. He just absolutely loved brewing. After I bought my partner out, I started spending a lot more time in the office handling the accounting and record keeping and operating the restaurant side of the business and Rick started doing all the brewing. He's probably brewed more batches of beer by now than I have. I spend most of my time now in Elkhart at the brewery. He helps me with the bottling, but he loves the brewing part and handling all the transfers, which is fine with me, since climbing in and out of the kettle is too hard on my shoulders, and I can't do it without pain. Rick is now 38,

and he's starting to feel the pain, too. I was 45 when I started all this, so he's getting to the age where I started. The whole idea is that in a year or two—as long as I'm healthy I won't want to quit—basically it will be his, so there is some motivation there for him to keep it up. He can do it all.

I worked in the corporate world for twenty years, and I didn't like sitting in an office and working on a computer. I've always been a little more hands-on. That's why I got into manufacturing as a production supervisor originally and then I realized that you are not really doing anything but watching other people work, giving them grief when they're not doing what somebody else thinks they should do. The research part was enjoyable because you can be creative and experiment. However, when the idea of starting a brewery presented itself, I told myself, "You can combine all the things that you like; you can work with your hands; you can be creative; you can plan; and you can experiment." The hands-on part—you're repairing equipment all of the time. I believe I can now fix anything in a restaurant or a brewery. After you've fixed these things so many times, you can almost do it in your sleep. I wouldn't want to do that for a living, but it's great to do it as part of my work. It is problem solving.

For the brewery in Elkhart, I bought all the equipment from the former Duneland Brewhouse in Michigan City, Indiana, on a whim. I wanted to buy an extra tank, and then I ended up buying the whole thing from them, put it in storage in my oldest son's building in Elkhart. That's how I ended up in Elkhart. There was a building across the street from his business. It isn't as big of a building as I would have liked, but the guy who built it decided he didn't want to lease it; he was going to sell it, so my son talked me into buying it. The idea was that I could use the lift truck and other things from my son's business across the street. It took me two years to complete the brewery. We did it ourselves. Rick helped me when he could. We did all of the plumbing, all the wiring, and the installation of the brewery equipment. We are in a light industrial area in Elkhart, sort of a mixed neighborhood.

Now, with the closing of the original brewpub and restaurant, the whole brewing operation is in Elkhart. The Pub is in Mishawaka, about two miles north of where the brewpub was located. It is relatively small and easy to manage. It seats seventy-five and specializes in hot grilled subs and gourmet pizzas.

What would I do over if I could? You learn as you go along. When we first started, we knew we wanted to be a brewing business, but when you start as a microbrewery, you don't get immediate cash flow. It takes a lot of money while you are building a market for your product, so we decided to go the brewpub route. You need time to develop your beer. What Mad Anthony's is now doing with one brewery and four or five smaller pubs—that is the route I would have taken knowing what I know now. I would probably have had five pubs. It takes fewer people to run. If you have five small pubs with one brewery, you don't have all the grief of running a big restaurant. Our brewpub was too big; we could seat 250 people. But unless you are in a large city, it is difficult to fill that size restaurant every day. At the Pub, you can have thirty people, and it looks like it is full, but at the brewpub if there were 100 people spread out, it looked dead. People do not like to go where it seems dead.

Interview January 22, 2009, at NUVO Newsweekly

Shoreline Brewery & Restaurant

208 Wabash Street
Michigan City, IN 46360
219-879-4677
www.shorelinebrewery.com

SAM STRUPECK, FOUNDER AND BREWER

Naming the beers is region related. I'm not originally from here, so I had never heard the term "Rats," but it's associated with Porter and Lake counties in general. I believe it comes from the steel mills starting the term "Mill Rats" as tying directly into this area. Nobody asks about the origin of our Region Rat Red Ale if they're from here. If they're not, we can give them the story. All the beer names have something behind them—old friends, nicknames including Sloppy Bobby and Foggy Loggy. Don't Panic! English Pale Ale was our first beer brewed here. I'm a huge fan of Douglas Adams, who wrote *The Hitchhiker's Guide to the Galaxy.* "Don't Panic" comes from the book. On the front of the book they had the guide itself. Queen Mum India Pale Ale came from Aberdeen [a now closed brewpub in Valparaiso; see also Greg Emig's story, page 42–53]. I believe one of their customers won a contest with that name, and that was kind of my baby there. I was constantly working on that beer, making it hoppier with each recipe, and now it's way different from what we started there. No Nug IPA was our answer to Sum Nug, being out of Nugget hops due to the hop shortage. I believe our last Sum Nug was made about eight months ago [June 2008]; we now use a combination of Centennial and Amarillo hops for No Nug. Leaper American Pale Ale was actually brewed February 29. A lot of the beers on the menu right now are replacements from the hops shortage.

What's happening now is so far so good with getting hops. We have contracts, so we shouldn't have any problems. I understand the hop crop was good this past year. Prices are still higher.

It may be a regional thing that people here like a hoppier beer. It may have a lot to do with Three Floyds. They've been around for twelve years now, and nobody was making IPAs like that back then, so I think Three Floyds changed people's palates and got them accustomed to it, and now we can't keep IPAs in stock. We've balanced our Queen Mum IPA a bit because we didn't want it to be too close to our Beltaine Scottish Ale [World Beer Cup silver medals for 2006 and 2008] since they're both similar in the body. We use different grains for each, but they still have that medium body. We wanted to add a little more hops content to the Amber and the Red.

We make Smokestack Porter once a year, and it's gone by the end of March. As far as dark beer goes, it's very easy drinking. We get some lighter beer drinkers who assume they don't like dark beers until they try something like Beltaine—it's smooth with chocolate notes.

As for other seasonals, the barley wine won't be around for too much longer. Last year [2008] we brought the Discombobulation Celebration Ale to the Lafayette Brewing Company Winter Warmer. It does very well in the winter. Barley wine will warm you up a little bit. A lot of the beers on the winter menu will be rotating out for spring beers. We don't make the lagers in the spring. We'll make our last lager here next week [end of February], which will be a doppelbock, and then we'll get rid of that yeast strain until next fall. We drink so much more beer in the summertime that we can't afford to lager beer. It takes us

about two and a half months to make a lager properly.

We have nine fermenters, twelve serving vessels, and a bright tank, so we added about 60 percent more capacity in the last year, and they're all full. We might not get into bottling even with that equipment. This will be our third full summer, and we'll be selling a lot more beer once again. We replace the lager with a Kölsch in the summertime. We still have that same flavor profile using that German ale yeast instead of the lager yeast.

The Dummkopf [on the winter tap menu] is a German name for an English-style beer. It makes a funny story. When Jim, our assistant brewer, makes a mistake, I'll sometimes say, "Hey, Dummkopf." Some creativity went into that brew. We made something totally different from what we were going for that day. Now we have a new recipe. We write everything down, even if it's a mistake. If you want to reproduce it, you have to know what you are doing right or wrong. We're very happy with the way it turned out. We were going to age it in bourbon barrels, but when we tried it out, we decided it was different enough from the No Nug that we could put it on tap without aging it in bourbon barrels. It's a strong beer. It started out as an IPA, and we hopped it up even more than our normal IPA. It has a little more backbone than most IPAs. If you warm it up a little more [letting the glass sit or holding it in your hands], you get more flavor. In America you're used to a cold beer, so you don't want to turn people off, and it's easier to warm up a beer than it is to make it colder. People know that, so when they're halfway done with a beer, they'll order another in advance to let it sit and warm up. That big backbone supports the hops. An IPA leaves its hops hanging out there, but this Dummkopf, even though it has the same malt as the IPA, the malt's more concentrated—it's got less water. We boiled a lot more out. We didn't gather those last runnings, which are kind of weak—weaker than the middle or first runnings. So that's how we got a German name for an English beer—because of Jim—James Knight—"Dummkopf" is what I blurted out. He's a good kid. He wants to be here, and he works his butt off. He started July 2008—a young kid, 23 years old, really enjoys craft beer, and wanted to get into the brewery. He came in and said, "I'll do anything. I'll wash dishes. I'll cook if I have to. I'll clean floors. I don't care what I have to do, but I really want to learn this." That's what we look for when we hire—team players. It's such a cliché nowadays, but I've seen my chef come out here and wait tables, I've seen people who wait tables go back and wash dishes. Everybody really helps out. It's a good atmosphere. Sure, get your work done first, have fun second—or together.

Going back to the beginning of all this for me, I was working on opening up a brewery with a couple of guys out of Chicago in the Beverly neighborhood and they're still working on it, so I backed out of that. My father was getting involved as an investor with them. I went to him and said, "I think we should do this on our own, and I prefer it to be in Indiana due to the distributing laws." Self-distribution is a major bonus for us. We can grow at our own pace instead of having to guarantee this guy [the distributor] so many cases and kegs. We really wanted to keep the quality control to make sure we weren't growing too fast. Self-distribution allows us to do that. And I think Indiana was lacking in good craft beer as far as per capita—there are only twenty-seven now, even though Granite City is expanding rapidly into the area, which doesn't bother me. They

brew all their beer on one premises, and they have some kind of patented system to ship the wort, which is a major issue in contamination, so they must know what they are doing when it comes to shipping the wort without having it fermented. Franchises haven't typically done so well in the craft brewing industry. Hops I think was the name down in Florida, and they closed all those down a few years ago. There was one in Michigan that got started.

For us here, the food is equally important with our beer. I've worked with our chef since he was 19 or 20 at Aberdeen Brewing Company. He came here and worked for a little while when we first opened. He moved on and then came back early in February 2009 and has taken over the chef's role, and we're really happy to have him. We've been down a chef since June 2008. We didn't want to hire just anybody. We were looking for someone long term. Josh stopped by one day, and we got to talking. So he's back. We like having him around—he's a good kid. He's been in the business seven years. Just like me, he started washing dishes at age 15 or 16 working in the kitchen; I got him to wait tables here for a little while. I'm happy he had that experience so he knows something about the front of the house. A lot of chefs have never stepped out, so they don't know what it's like; likewise, a lot of servers don't know what it's like back there. The mutual respect is nice to have around. I've been in a lot of restaurants where the kitchen is against the front of the house and the front of the house doesn't like the kitchen, and it doesn't make for a great experience for the customer. We'll be doing some beer dinners with Josh. It was something we wanted to do right off the bat, but we got so busy.

Our business plan was based quite loosely on Aberdeen's—as a minimum we can make this work if we are selling this amount of beer, and we have quadrupled our batches of beer compared with Aberdeen in three years, going on four. We chose Aberdeen's business plan because it wasn't the busiest brewpub in the world. When I was making a business plan, I wanted to know the least amount of money we could bring in and still make it. Banks don't prefer that. They want you to lie to them and tell them, "We're going to make a million in the first year," so we had to change that a little bit, but I knew in my own mind we could make it with a bare minimum. I wanted to know how little we needed to survive. We bought a much bigger space than what we needed, and now it seems to be growing. I knew we would be growing, but I assumed we would probably be a catering facility. But we decided against the structural changes to make that work and that we were just going to grow the brewery. We're going to make it into a more upscale area for the bar with booths, high top tables made out of the bourbon barrels, and high stools. The bar is long, but the bar will be full at eight o'clock at night, so if someone wants to sit at the bar or feel they are part of the bar, they may turn around and walk out. So we are going to make this more into a bar connected area. I think if you're a single person, for some reason it's a little more intimidating to sit down at a lower table. You're below everyone else, so we'll put high stools along the area next to the bar and tables to rest your beer on when we have music. We'll have the dining tables as well. We brought the ceiling down eight feet from what it originally was.

Originally the building was built as a lumberyard in 1857, before the Civil War, and it has been so many things in between. It's been a golf ball factory, and then it's been a camera factory. It was a NIPSCO training facility [Northern Indiana Public Service Company] for a very long time, and finally a printing company for book publisher catalogs. When I bought the building, it had been abandoned for almost ten years. I'm glad this building wasn't torn down. It was real close to being developed into condos, and they were going to try to keep the exterior as it is and develop condos, but I don't think that would have worked out. I think the building would have been torn down eventually. So we are glad to have it, and a lot of people in town are glad to have it here still. A lot of people worked here over the years. We get so many people who stop by and say, "I just came in to see what it looks like. I remember when it was a camera factory," or "I worked here in the 1970s for NIPSCO." Jim, one of Chuck's partners from Back Road Brewery in LaPorte, is retired from NIPSCO. He comes in all the time with his wife. They're great.

The town refers to this as the Big Pink Building—that's all they know it as. We've left it pink because it's going to cost a lot of money to restore it back to brick. They did a good job keeping that paint on there. It doesn't want to flake off, even though it's all cracked. I know the guy who painted it. He says, "I did a good job!" and I say, "Shame on you!" and then he says, "They asked me to paint it pink!"

I saw something posted on a beer website asking if we were still open because the outside of the building is a little deteriorated and his wife would not come in to eat, but once people get inside, they are wowed for sure, and it's definitely a clean building. We're eventually going to tear down the ratty old fence and put a natural fence around. We have some investors who own buildings and don't want to let them go because they know they are going to be worth so much more in the next ten years, but without them being bought and refurbished, it kind of keeps everything else down. It's a little bit of a catch-22. It seems to me it's the young businessmen in this town who are going to bring things around, not the city itself. We've got a lot of arts projects going on downtown. It's a great little downtown area for that. There's a company called ArtSpace that goes into certain blighted communities. They are picky about where they go, and we've got them interested in Michigan City now. It's basically a 30,000-foot gallery space with forty live-in studios in the building itself. They would build that with grants. They are doing marketing research now to see if they can get that done in Michigan City. I think they will build from the ground up because of the size. Young artists, 30 years old, are opening their own galleries downtown in these older buildings, doing a fine job, taking their time. We're going to be working with them, hopefully getting some public things going. Whatever can bring more people into this town is good for both us and the town itself. I think we've probably brought quite a few people into this town who wouldn't come here otherwise. The artists think they can make a living making art—they're all crazy. [Laughter] It is a tough living, and yet I think it has some potential being in the Chicago area just down the road from us. We have a ton of Chicago tourism here, and it's something this town needs to build on. Before they kind of shunned that. The feeling was, "Oh, we don't like those outsiders. We don't want those out-of-towners." Well, a lot of the people here now have moved from Chicago to get away from the city and realized the economy is going to have to depend on tourism; that it's a natural. This has always been industrial, and they kowtowed to industry notoriously up and down this coast.

Mount Barley is here just down the road. They harvested sand for Ball back in the 1850s and maybe even earlier. Canning has been around for over 100 years. I think this building was built out of some of that sand as well, because this is that soft sandstone brick. There are a few buildings down the railroad tracks here that have the exact same brick as this, so I'm guessing these bricks were made on-site.

Going back to how I came into brewing—well, I like beer, and I've been in the restaurant business over half my life. I was actually trying to get out of the restaurant business and go to school, finish at Lafayette for a landscape architecture degree, and I took a job at Aberdeen waiting tables in between school and basically started helping them in the brewery. Skip Bosack was the owner, and he didn't have any experience in brewing, and they had just bought the restaurant from the Emigs—Greg Emig's dad, Joe Emig [Greg Emig currently owns Lafayette Brewing Company]. Skip's son was helping him out in the brewery, and basically I learned from those two guys who didn't know too much about it. From there I just read a lot of books. I was just at the right place at the right time. I had been offered a brewer's position at the Bloomington Brewing Company. Chuck Porter was the brewer down there at the time, and Joe Jose took over for him after he left, so that would have been where I would have been, but I wasn't willing to give up school yet. You know, you get offered a brewer's position twice in your life and you've never brewed professionally and so you might take it as an omen. I was just lucky enough to be around those places. I met Chuck Porter while I was hanging out a lot at Bloomington Brewing Company and drinking their beer, so I was educating myself about the flavors of the beers before I even knew I was going to get into brewing. Once you learn those flavors, it takes off pretty quick, too. It took me a long time to figure out the different hops and the different grains, but once you do, you can really pick them out. It's fun; it's interesting.

I homebrewed a couple of times; I went out and bought a kit and did a speech for one of my college courses about homebrewing—a demonstration speech following the kit and the book. I didn't like homebrewing that much, only because I was in a very small kitchen. It was really cramped; it was hard to clean up. You make a mess. I didn't have a floor drain like I do in the brewery. I enjoyed the hobby, but it was tough to do it at the time. I didn't have a nice garage out back, so I was doing it on my stovetop. A lot of guys now have a turkey cooker out in the garage. I've brewed with quite a few people around here like that—just gone to hang out with them.

Professionally, I started at Aberdeen around 2001 and worked there for a good two years straight and then was discussing the brewery with the guys out of Chicago, and then I started this place with my father. I had to buy a liquor license from another restaurant. I didn't have to if I just wanted to do beer and wine, but since we are a full-service restaurant, I really wanted to have the alcohol as well. When we do large groups, sometimes people don't like beer or wine, they like a mixed drink, and next time they won't come back here if they can't get what they want, which is the same reason we carry a Miller Lite product, unfortunately. But we've gotten so many people who come in and have a Miller Lite and come back because we have a Miller Lite, and then one of our regulars will get on them to finally drink one of our beers—the peer pressure of becoming friends with the regulars at the bar. We've got that beautiful mug club up

there with 210 mugs, and so many of them have started out as Miller Lite drinkers.

We got the liquor license by buying a restaurant that was going out of business. It was getting run down. The tables and chairs we have here came from there. I've passed this place for years going to the beach. It's just been sitting empty. The loading dock outside was kind of the appeal to me. And the old brick building lends itself to a brewpub atmosphere. The wood is what's found in a lot of the beach houses around here from the old time. So I wanted to give it that beach house feel, warm, welcoming, natural with the brick. We bought that old restaurant in November 2004 and ran that restaurant until January 2005, which was when I bought this building. It was so cold. We didn't have any heat. We didn't get to work on it until March, and we finished it pretty quick. We did it with four people on our payroll and myself—we did it ourselves. We hired out just the plumbing and the air conditioning and the electrical. We even helped with the concrete. I had done some concrete previously, and a good friend of mine does concrete, so he was in here helping us. We picked up the brewing equipment from Puerto Rico, loaded it up on semis with a friend of mine, and we hired a crew from Puerto Rico to help us. We loaded it up and shipped it here. It took about a month and a half sitting at the port in Puerto Rico waiting to come up here until they cleared the equipment through. We weren't in a hurry to get it up here. It all got here in good shape. The equipment was used, and I got a good price on it, but after leaving Aberdeen I did some consulting work, and I went to Puerto Rico and taught people how to brew on the equipment and how to clean equipment. It was awfully dirty because they weren't cleaning their serving vessels at all. They would take a fresh batch of beer and push it right into a tank that hadn't been cleaned and sanitized. That's why I think they went out of business. The rent was extremely high, but I think they could have made it as a brewpub. It was mostly an American clientele on vacation; casinos right down the street, right off the beach. The people from whom they bought the equipment knew me so they called and asked me if I was interested, so that's how I got to Puerto Rico. I never imagined I would ever work on that equipment ever again. She offered me a job, but I was not interested. She couldn't afford to pay me to live there. The cost of living is rather high, and I wasn't willing to sacrifice my life-style to brew beer in Puerto Rico. First thing I did when I got there was try every one of their beers on tap, and they were all contaminated in one way or another, and I started cleaning the equipment, and three days later I was still cleaning, and the owner said, "I hired you to come down here and brew beer." I said, "Vicky, you don't understand. I couldn't brew beer on this equipment and feel right about giving you that product to sell." She didn't understand that. It was not her profession, and no one had told her that before. You have to have sanitary conditions so things don't start growing, and that's what happened. I tell everybody here I'm just a glorified janitor. You've got to make sure things are clean.

When we were first building here, I worked 20-hour days. Everybody else had 12 to 16, and I would continue to work the extra 4 hours or so until I had no more energy and I'd just fall asleep. The next thing I knew, it was six in the morning and my dad would be in here with the nail gun going off or the lift going beep, beep, so I'd wake up and start over. I did that for six months and another six months at a 100-plus hours a week getting this all right. And then I went back to 80 hours a week, and I didn't know what to do with myself. I spent time on the beach that first summer for a change. [Laughter] And then we started growing, and after taking some time off, I was ready to start growing the brand a little more.

Building a brand, for one, you have to know what kind of beer you are going to go for, and I particularly like English-style ale, so you might as well do something you enjoy. I'm not a huge Belgian beer drinker, even though they have become very popular. You've got to do something you love, and I love English-style beers. We do beers very true to style. We've built our reputation on Scottish ales, English ales. Even our lagers are very true to style. When we do a beer, the grains and the hops generally come from the region where that style started. So when we are making a German beer, those grains are grown in Germany, and the hops are from the Hallertau region. The same thing with our American pale ales; those grains and hops are grown in America. The English-style beers, those hops and grains are grown in England. The yeast strains I'd like to get a little more into, but yeast is very expensive and hard to keep alive, so we have a house strain that lends itself to many styles. We bring in about four strains throughout the year plus the house strain, so we go through about five strains a year, including a Belgian one in the summer for our witbier, which goes over very, very well.

You can't necessarily change the water you have. We use city water, which is pretty balanced, so we don't have to treat our water too much. I know some brewers up in Wisconsin have to add all kinds of stuff to their water to get it to come out the pH balance they want it to be, so we're blessed with Lake Michigan here. Lake Michigan water is what goes into our beer. This lake has supported many breweries over the years.

In general, not just in Indiana, brewers are very open about their profession and what they are doing, and they share information with each other. I think a lot of it has to come down to the David and Goliath of the craft brewing versus the Anheuser-Busches of the world. They really tried to keep craft brewing out of America. They didn't want competition. They'd buy out the competition. That kind of formed a special bond among the craft brewers. There's a thousand of us and only a few of them, but, boy, were they the ones making the laws! Since there are so many different craft breweries, I don't want someone to go down the road and get bad beer. I want them to have the best beer they can so that people enjoy craft beer as a whole, not just, "Oh I like that craft beer, and the rest of them are crap." I think you saw that in the early 1990s when craft breweries really took off, but unfortunately so many people didn't know what they were doing and they thought it would be fun to have a brewery, and they had the money to do it but not the experience in the restaurant business or in the brewing business, so they opened up these breweries, and the beers weren't so good, and a lot of them closed down, and we saw a little bit of a backlash on craft brewing in general. Even the good ones were struggling a bit because so many people had tried a batch of bad beer, but the good ones survived, and so it slowly came around. The good ones were surviving and staying and creating a better name for the craft brewing industry for craft brewers like myself to come along to make the name of craft brewing even better.

Steve [Mazylewski now at Crown Brewing] has been in Illinois for a long time, and he's been brewing beer a lot longer than I have. I met him at a Chicago Beer Society function when I worked at Aberdeen Brewing Company. All those guys, they give you advice. You ask them questions, they are not going to lie to you and give you bad advice and mess up your beer. I've learned more through talking to other brewers than I have from books or courses that I've gone to. The best education I've had is through sharing knowledge with other brewers.

We get many, many people from all over to come here. Lots of people from Elkhart, a lot of people from South Bend, we get a lot of people from Michigan. We are closer to a lot of towns in Michigan than we are to a lot of towns in Indiana. When you come to the parking lot on Saturday and look at the license plates, it's about 30 percent Illinois, 30 percent Michigan, 25 percent Indiana, and then some Minnesota and Wisconsin plates and New York or wherever. A lot of that has to do with proximity to the highway, of course. We'll get some travelers passing by.

Nowadays when I go on vacation, the first thing I do is look up the nearest brewpub, and I know a lot of other people do that, too. They become destination restaurants, destination brewpubs. I never really thought of AAA and how much they do for traveling and tourism. We do work directly with LaPorte County Visitors Bureau; they love us. They realize we are a destination restaurant; usually there are a couple of them sitting at the bar having lunch a few times a week. They do a fine job trying to grow LaPorte County.

I'm working with South Bend to do a festival there. We do ours here in July, and it does very well. At first it was just local—Three Floyds, Back Road, Mishawaka. We have since brought in some Michigan breweries, since we're so close to them. We had Blaine [Stuckey] up from Fort Wayne. I'm going to offer anybody in Indiana who wants to bring a keg to come. We've grown large enough to support that. It's usually the Sunday after the Fourth of July and that ties in with the city's fireworks, which is an amazing display. They are just north of us in the little harbor. They fill a barge out there and light them off. We get about 40,000 people in town for that. The first year we weren't open yet, so we threw a little party to let people know there was going to be something in this building and they were free to walk in. A friend of mine's band played. We set up the three beers we had brewed at that time, which were the American Pale Ale, Queen Mum, and Don't Panic! English Pale Ale. I think we charged two bucks a pint outside. We didn't have our license yet, so we had to get a little day permit for that. We just threw a party and had about 100 people. All the people walking by, driving by, knew there was something going on here. We are going on our fifth annual this year now [2009]. We set up a stage in our parking lot. We have three or four bands starting outside from two o'clock in the afternoon until about one in the morning. It's an all-day event. We don't do a wristband like we generally do for a beer festival; we charge by the pint. I couldn't charge twenty-five dollars and have them drink for twelve hours straight. We'd have some problems on our hands. We break even on it because we pay the bands a lot of money and we have a lot of labor. We are happy to break even; it's just a fun day for everybody.

My brother, Ben, is an agronomist. He has his degree from Lafayette [Purdue University] in agronomy. He and I have been looking into doing a hops farm, which will probably be in Michigan. I'm looking to put us right there

in the middle of the wine growing area for the tourism attraction. They've got that wine trail. I figure you could get people to the hops fields and the production facility at that point, selling six-packs to go. I wouldn't do that in Indiana because we couldn't sell six-packs to go on Sunday. What you are trying to do is to get people to come to your place to buy beer and cut off that middleman at that point—get it right from the source where it's fresh. We'd have a tasting room and merchandise, but no restaurant. People are on the move. It would be a great place to have wedding receptions. We've been fighting for Sunday sales of beer in Indiana. Wineries can sell their products on Sundays in Indiana. What makes for the unbalance between wine and beer is like that David and Goliath story I was talking about earlier where Anheuser-Busch and its large distributors have the lobbyists in place to keep those laws. The shipping laws are another factor. We need the Brewers of Indiana Guild to lobby for us. We need the Guild to help out brewers instead of brewers trying to help out the Guild.

Hops grow like weeds. Cascades thrive here, which is a highly used hops. The dwarf varieties do well generally. There's not a whole lot of information out there on what does better here. We planted some hops in Michigan on some friends' property to see which ones do better. That's our initial run at it. It might not work out. The picking equipment is very specialized and expensive, and it's all been developed for large hops farms at this point. We've been in touch with some companies out of Europe that have small family farms where wine picking equipment has been turned into hop picking equipment. They're doing smaller trellises—not fifteen, twenty feet tall but doing a ten-foot trellis. They pretty much grow to the fence. They are doing this out in Washington. They are leaving the vines up; they are not cutting them down. Instead of taking the whole plant, they are harvesting just the hops using chains to strip. The ones I have seen look pretty much like a combine. Roy Farms is working on dwarfing out several varieties, including Cascades. They are huge. They are in the Yakima Valley. They grow more hops than anyone else does. They bought out the small farms that weren't making money selling hops at three to five dollars a pound. Now the prices are fifteen dollars a pound.

I'm not the only one thinking about growing hops. It's the picking and processing the pellets, so that's a big issue. You can use the whole pellets for only a couple of batches a year at harvest time. You have to dry hops in the kiln to keep them for the rest of the year; they deteriorate easily, they lose their flavor, they oxidize. There are all kinds of issues; that's why you pelletize hops. Making hops an industry in the Midwest is a long way off, but I'm going to a conference in Wisconsin on March 14, 2009. Two guys are doing a farm, and they are all about sustainability and sharing their knowledge about what is going on up there because they are facing the same thing.

When my brother and I went out to Washington, we were hearing what seemed to me was a lot of propaganda—"You've got to have more money than God." "You don't want to do that." "You don't want to grow hops." Everything was "You don't want to do it, you can't do it." That was their answer to us instead of "This is how we do it." When you tell someone you can't do it that many times, it makes them wonder. [Laughter] Our next trip is to Europe next hops season. We are going to check out some equipment in Czechoslovakia. Those are small family-owned farms. They might co-op.

We're still learning. It's a lot of research. I'm not going to go out and plant a hop farm and think it's going to work because that's not what I do. But my brother as a professional agronomist knows about growing and the different types of diseases. The reason hop farms left the Midwest in the first place was downy mildew. The only place they don't have downy mildew is in New Zealand. They have quarantined that island so well. But it will get there eventually. Australia has got it. Growing hops where you brew is about sustainability, using less energy to get the product to the brewery. We use as many local products and people as we can. When it came to the building, everyone was local. A local farmer takes our spent grains. They feed chickens with it, and they use it for compost. They have real sandy soil, so they are working it into their soil for his wife's garden, which has unique vegetables—heirloom tomatoes, purple tomatoes, purple carrots, root vegetables. We use as many of their vegetables as we can.

My father, Dave Strupeck, is my partner. He teaches accounting at Indiana University Northwest. He's not just an accountant but a very good wood worker and a highly intelligent man. He makes my life a lot easier. He allows me to concentrate on making beer.

We sell a ton of our seasonal Bavarian Bombshell. People love that beer, even people who don't like dark beer. It's such a preconceived notion: "Oh, I don't like dark beer." At Aberdeen I used to bartend a lot, and when people would say, "Oh, I don't like dark beer," I'd say, "OK, close your eyes and try this one," and nine out of ten times they would pick the darker beer. It's hops—they don't like the bitterness of hops. They've tried Guinness, which is a very bitter beer. Some people don't like the ale strain, and it takes them a long time to figure that out. They like lagers. There is an aged-ness to a lager strain you can never get out of an ale, and some of it has to do with aging it properly. Ales are many times put out earlier than they should be because you're tying up equipment. That's why we added more tanks so we wouldn't have to put out too yeasty beer by not aging it properly or going to filtering, which I didn't want to do. We got more equipment so we could leave the beer in the tanks for five weeks to ripen. Our beers almost never go out before five weeks. Most places are putting them out in three to four weeks, and some even in two. You can tell the difference. That's not what we're going for here.

Bourbon barrel aged beers is where we are going. All the beers we are putting into bottles will have been aged in the barrels for a year. We are not growing to make pale ales for the liquor stores. We're doing large 22-ounce champagne bottles, something you can sit around and share with friends. Big, strong beers are not made for one person to drink, just as with a wine bottle. I see craft beer going into that niche. Not stuffy, but I think we can get a lot more wine drinkers drinking beer than the wine industry can get beer drinkers drinking wine. They can be gift bottles of beer. We're going to sell right out of here. This is part of growing the craft in Indiana. You can't change people's palates overnight. In Oregon they drink craft beer. Here they drink Miller Lite. We need to educate them. I've always had it in my head to go out there and talk to people, but we have to be brewing enough craft beer to satisfy the demand, so we can't get ahead of what we are producing. In Indiana we need to produce more craft beer to grow.

Interview February 17, 2009, at Shoreline Brewery & Restaurant

Crown Brewing Company

211 South East Street
Crown Point, IN 46307
219-663-4545
www.CrownBrewing.com

STEVE MAZYLEWSKI, BREWER

Welcome to Crown Brewing Company. We've only been in operation since June 2008. We're the new kids on the block.

I grew up in Berwyn, Illinois, which is a near west suburb of Chicago. My father was a schoolteacher and collected beer cans in the '70s when it was very popular. In the course of summer vacations we would tour breweries, and he collected cans from each brewery, so I've been visiting breweries since I was a young boy. It left a very big impression on me as a young man; just the sights and smells and the sounds and the workers and the tanks that went up seven stories in the buildings. It was something that intrigued me, and it was something I wanted to do from a young age, surprisingly enough. Back then there weren't microbreweries or brewpubs. These were all fairly large industrial size breweries, and we toured them all in the Great Lakes region. We would go up to Minnesota and see August Schell in New Ulm [dating to 1860]. We would do Milwaukee, so at the time you had Pabst and Blatz, Miller, of course, Chippewa Falls, Leinenkugel. We would go into Michigan and tour Strohs in Detroit, a couple of little ones, Carling, and one in Frankenmuth, Michigan. We would go to St. Louis, of course.

Wisconsin also had some midsized breweries, and one of them was called Walter Brewing Company in Eau Claire, Wisconsin. That was a 35- or 50-bbl brew house, still a good size, but not as big as the big players. I was seven years old, and we were taking a tour, and the

brewmaster was giving the tour. He was a big burly guy with overalls, a beard, and a big belly sticking out. He looked at his watch and said, "Wow, it's time to add hops." He looked at me, "Hey, kid, com'ere next to me. Climb up this ladder and put these hops in, but don't fall in." He's holding me by the seat of my pants so I don't fall in, and he hands me the bushel, and I dump the hops into the vat of boiling wort, and it was kind of like an epiphany at a young age: "This is what I want to do when I grow up." So, freshman year in high school, I sat down with my guidance counselor and he said, "So, young Mazylewski, what do you want to do with your life?" And I said, "I want to be a brewmaster." He lost it. He threw his pen right across the room and folded his arms and put his feet up on the desk and said, "After thirty-two years of doing this, I've never heard anyone say anything remotely close to this. I've heard, 'I want to own a bar' or 'I want to be a bartender,' but I've never heard anybody say, 'I want to make beer.'" He takes out his primitive Apple computer because this was in the early '80s and he says, "Lo and behold, there's actually a school in Chicago that teaches how to make beer." This being the Siebel Institute of Technology, a world-renowned school. For the longest time you either went to Munich to learn to make beer, where you better speak fluent German because they don't have English classes, or you went to Chicago to get a degree in beer making. So this is great. He recommended that I take as much chemistry, biology, and math as I could fit into my schedule, which I did, and I started working at UPS after high school to make ends meet, and I was saving my money to attend Siebel. Being the son of a schoolteacher, we lived pretty frugally. Siebel is very expensive. Even then, the diploma course was anywhere from $11,000 to $15,000, not including

transportation and housing and everything that goes along with going to school. Working at UPS helped. I started community college in Cicero, Illinois, where I was taking more chemistry and biology because I knew I would need that for a brewing career. At this time, I wasn't 21 yet, and I was looking forward to the day when I did turn 21, and I wasn't even sure if Siebel allowed underage people to attend class or not. I don't see why not, because I assume you don't have to be of age to learn how to make it.

In my hometown, a little brewery opened called the Weinkeller. I'm, "OK, this is falling into place neatly for me." Two or three days after I turned twenty-one, the owner had a free tour and tasting advertised in the local paper, so I went with my parents and my girlfriend. The owner's name was Udo Harttung, just a hard-core German guy. He was short of stature, maybe like five-two, five-four, with a really thick accent. He was very charismatic, very well spoken, well educated. He ran a liquor store with a bar attached to it, and he eventually opened a restaurant with the bar. The liquor store at one time had the largest bottle stock for sale in the United States. He made it up to over 575 different bottles of beer to buy there, and they were all available at the bar as well. He saw the writing on the wall with the microbrewery/brewpub explosion, and he put in a brewery in 1988. So I turned 21 in July 1989. During the tour, he said his son Christoff was the assistant, an apprentice, and was starting college in August, and he needed to hire someone to fill his shoes and train. So I pulled him aside after the tour and introduced myself and said I had wanted to be a brewer since I was a young kid and was saving my money to go to Siebel. He says, "That sounds good. Why don't you start tomorrow." [Laughter] So four days after I turned 21, I was working in a production brewery, which was really neat. I was there part-time. I would hand-bottle beer. I was stocking liquor store shelves. I was learning little by little in the brewery, mainly the grunt work, of course—polishing the copper, taking out the spent grains. But that worked more into cleaning tanks out. I would grow yeast in the laboratory that he had there.

After doing this part-time and still working at UPS part-time and still going to college, it really came down to after eight years at UPS there was a career decision. Was I going to drive a brown truck the rest of my life or make beer? So in July 1995, after being an apprentice for six years, I decided to give UPS notice and work full-time for Udo at the Weinkeller. During the six years I was part-time as an assistant apprentice, the owner opened a second location in Westmont, Illinois, and he had hired a full-time brewer. He had offered me the job and I said, "No, I'm working at UPS. Great benefits as a teamster. I'm still going to school. I won't be quite comfortable running a brewery on my own yet." He had offered me this head brewer job numerous times over the six years, and I always declined. He actually was quite difficult to work for. In the six years, numerous brewmasters had come and gone. Some lasted a day or two, some lasted a week or two, a month or two, a year or two. I wish I had kept a journal because I could have written a book and I would have named it "How Not to Run Your Business." He taught me a lot about how to treat people—employees, customer—with respect. Then he opened a third location in the River West neighborhood of Chicago and Halstead. I was in charge of those three breweries. That was really neat. You were never doing the same thing. One day we'd be brewing beer in Berwyn, another day we'd be

brewing beer in Westmont, another day we'd be accepting grain delivery in downtown Chicago. The change of scenery, the change of customers was great. I was living in Berwyn, so I was only fifteen miles away from any place that I had to be at.

It turns out the Berwyn location suffered a major fire. There were apartments above the brewpub, and the tenant left a candle burning that caught the drapes on fire. Berwyn closed and never reopened, so that left two breweries. River West opened in 1997. In 2000 the owner was strong-armed and robbed. We were four or five blocks away from Cabrini Green, which is the worst housing project in Chicago. He went into partnership with a black promoter, and they opened up a dance club on the second floor, and there was a $20 cover charge, and there were 800–900 people dancing every Friday and Saturday night. Someone realized the money that was being made and entered the building and waited until everybody else left and the boss locked the door and they tied him up and held machine guns to him and said, "Do what we say and we'll let you live." They took his briefcase, made him empty the safe, took his wallet, and left. He was eventually able to break free and call the police, and he voluntarily closed his doors saying, "This is not worth my life." So that left one brewery to run, and there was me and another full-time brewer. My work ethic is, when I come to work I want to work. There's always something to do in the brewing world, something always needs cleaning or changing, but it was more watching TV at the bar and every time the front door opened we'd think Udo was walking in, and we'd jump up because we didn't want to be yelled at. I was like, "I can't work like this," so I was looking for another brewing job in the area.

I ended up going to O'Grady's in Arlington Heights, Illinois. The brewer there had left, so they hired me, and after working for them for six months—it was the Monday after Easter—the owners and the manager were sitting and I walked in to start my day and I'm looking around and I say, "What's going on?" They say "Well, we're closed." I'm thinking they're going to redo the floor, shut the restaurant down. I said, "For how long?" and they say, "For good. We're bankrupt." So, no notice or anything. That threw me on unemployment after only six months of working there.

There was a brewery in Morris, Illinois, called the Firehouse, and they were looking for a brewer. Morris is off I-80 about thirty miles southwest of Joliet. It's not really considered Chicagoland. It's more central Illinois than anything. It's in Grundy County, so it's the county seat of Grundy County, so I interviewed and the boss hired me, and I really liked the job, and I liked the community. There's only about 12,000 people, and since it was the county seat, it was the largest in Grundy. It's very difficult to run a pretty large brewpub with only a base of 12,000 people with maybe 30,000 people within a fifteen- to thirty-mile area, Joliet being the closest major suburb of Chicago. I ended up working there for a year, and I sat down for my year review and I actually gave notice. My friend who I worked for as an assistant at the Weinkeller ended up winning the lottery. His family owned the Wild Onion Brewery in Lake Barrington, Illinois, and they won the country's largest Big Game. There were two tickets for the jackpot of $356 million, and they were holding one of two winning tickets. So they were multimillionaires overnight. Mike called me up and said, "We're shutting our microbrewery down, and we're building a group up brewpub. We want

you to be in charge," and I said, "I would love to—uh, let me think about that, OK?" So they hired me, and I basically built the brewery the way I wanted it and ended up working there for six years and much like O'Grady's, one day the boss sits me down and says, "Friday's your last day. We're closing the brewery down, and we're going to concentrate on the restaurant and banquet side of things." This was a complete and utter shock. My wife was doing some party planning for them. She got let go five days before me. We had an 8-month-old daughter. It was really, really bad timing because we were taking everything forward. The basement was finished, and they were supposedly putting a deposit down on a bottling line, and we were going to start distributing, and I hired a full-time assistant to do marketing. It was a complete and utter shock. That threw me on the unemployment line with an 8-month-old daughter and a wife with no job. It was a really hard pill to swallow.

I put my resume out on the web, and the owners of the Hog Haus Brewing Company in Fayetteville, Arkansas, were very interested. They had a brewer who was from Colorado and was basically homesick and wanted to go back to Colorado where his wife still was. So they brought my family down there for a full week, put us up in a hotel and made us feel very comfortable. It was a really lovely area. We were right outside of the University of Arkansas, so everything down there I saw was razorback, razorback, razorback. But what seemed very promising got worse and worse and worse. The ladies I worked for made Udo look like an angel. Some of their business practices were really ruthless and corrupt, and it became an unhealthy situation for me and for my family. So I had feelers out because I know a lot of people in the industry after doing it for so long, and Sam Strupeck called me up the beginning of December 2008 and said, "Crown Brewing lost their brewer and they're looking for someone. Would you be interested?" I said, "That's a lot closer to home." Our daughter was two, and we were ten, twelve hours away from both sides of our family. That was incredibly rough. My wife was a stay-at-home mom with no support, no family. So I said yes, and he put me in contact with the owners, and we did a couple of phone interviews, and since I was coming back for Christmas, I said I would love to visit their operation and meet them in person. On Christmas Eve they made me an offer worth pulling out of Arkansas and moving back home. So that's my story of how I ended up in Crown Point.

I think Indiana is pretty unique in that the breweries are so spread out, whereas in Illinois most of the breweries are right around the counties surrounding Chicago and in Chicago with just a few downstate. In Indiana they're all over the place. It really seems that Indiana is a beer-loving state. That was clearly evident in the last two beer fests I've done where so many people showed up we were running out of beer. What a problem to have! We went to Winterfest! 2009 and ran out. We went to Lafayette Winter Warmer with a much larger quantity of beer and they almost drank us dry, too, and that was a much smaller event with 350 paid people, and they drank almost all of our beers. We had our Winter Warlock, which is a stronger brown ale, and we went with other drinkable styles, too. So many people had big giant beers there, and that's great, but some people just wanted a beer they could drink, so we were pretty happy to have a couple of drinkable styles.

They had an outstanding homebrew club at Fayetteville. I haven't yet connected with the homebrew clubs here, though I'm aware of the Brewers of South Suburbia, BOSS. Once I get more established here we'll be working with them. Eventually we will do a mug club, a sampler plate, and that kind of thing.

Even though this is a pizzeria, they have a full menu. I appreciate that everything is made here. Nothing is mass-produced store-bought frozen stuff. We will incorporate the beer in some of the recipes the restaurant is doing. We'll start with that and down the road I will work with the owner of the pizzeria to try do a brewmaster dinner. In the next year or two, that is going to happen.

Since I am replacing a previous brewer, I will follow the house recipes, put my own spin on them, and try to perfect them and make them a little bit better. That is what I like about pub brewing as opposed to microbrewing. In microbrewing, every batch better be the same because it is going into a bottle or a keg and that is what people are buying and that is what they are used to and that's what they expect. It doesn't leave a lot of freedom. I love the creative freedom of being a pub brewer, and that is what I specialize in. The ability to substitute a hop or a grain if you run out or to tweak a recipe to try something different to see what changes it, those are the things that make my job so exciting and what makes me want to come in every day and do it again and again. Making beer is fun, of course. Even working in a microbrewery is fun. But it becomes so industrialized and processed, you know: at 1:15, you start this pump up, and at 1:30, you pull this lever and start this pump up; every beer is exactly the same, and the brewers have very little freedom of creating their own batch because they are so stuck into brewing their flagship beer. What I like is to keep my customers on their toes—what's coming out next? That's

The Brewers

probably the most commonly asked question I get: "What's coming out next? What are you making next?" That part I like a lot.

The previous brewer, Jim Cibak, had quite a following. Actually Jim and I worked together at the Weinkeller for six months, so I know Jim very well. From there he went to Goose Island, a very respectable brewery, and then to Three Floyds for a number of years. He's a great brewer and developed a huge following from his beers. After Three Floyds he ended up going to Firestone-Walker in California, which is a world-renowned brewery winning awards constantly. So when I came to Crown Point, I had some pretty big shoes to fill. He had a lot of local clientele that was very faithful to him and his beers and what he was going to do for this place. On the other hand, I come in with twenty years of experience making beers, so it was a very comfortable transition. We may have lost a tiny percentage of his friends who came in because of whatever happened—the circumstances that he left under—but that is not going to hurt us at all. The regulars that do come in have been very well receiving to the beers I have been putting out. The one main thing I think Jim was doing was making beers to appeal to his friends that were the beer lovers. That's fine, but those beer lovers are maybe only 15 or 20 percent of the clientele. The people who come in to have a pizza at a pub aren't going to want to drink a barley wine or a double IPA. They want to have something they can quench their pizza with. That is one thing, I think, he didn't really see in his vision of this place. Sure, he could make some darn fine beers, but you need to make beers that are going to appeal to the other 80 percent who are going to be walking in the front door of this place. So the first thing I had to do was make beer to appeal to them. The first one I made was a lighter style drinkable blonde ale, just to have something for the masses. We've had only two beers on tap pretty much since we've opened, and that's the other main complaint I hear. "You guys only have two beers?" So we have a serving tank cooler that's going to get hooked up with the ability to have six beers on tap. So my plan would be to have two of those lighter style drinkable beers, two in the middle of the road, and two for the beer lovers, whether they be super strong or dark or hoppy. Then you are appealing to everyone who comes into the front door.

The palate for beer differs with location. I would say Crown Point is more like Morris, Illinois.

The biggest thing in craft brewing is educating the public. Especially in the Midwest, in Chicagoland, the masses are almost brainwashed into thinking beer is light lager and nothing else. Our biggest challenge is to let people know, "Hey, there's a whole world of different beer styles out there. It doesn't all have to be pale, yellow, and tasteless." Some folks from Pennsylvania came in today, and I spent a good deal of time talking with them. They agreed that it's a notion that through mass marketing and advertising, "This is beer, this is what it is, and all it is." The community of Crown Point is more a light beer type of crowd with about 20 percent seeking us out because they know we are a brewpub and they know there is going to be special beer on tap. You have to cater to the mainly 80 percent coming in that just wants a beer because we don't have anything but our own beer in this building they are not able to have a Miller Lite with their pizza. So we need something like that. As far as other breweries I've worked in Chicago the ratio is more fifty-fifty. We always had a bottle selection of beers for people who wanted their Budweiser. You charged more for it than a glass of your own beer but if they want it that bad they'll pay and you're still making money.

Thinking about our growth, we have to get our serving tank cooler running and get beer in the tanks. Once we have the capacity to have six beers on tap, we want to start getting some draught accounts. We already have a number of restaurants that said, "As soon as you have beer ready, we'll put it on tap." We'll start small, but since we are such a small startup company, that gives me the freedom to create a flagship brand. I think an ideal flagship brand for this immediate area would be a lighter lager, not something bland and tasteless like a light beer, but maybe a pilsner or a helles. A nice drinkable German helles is one of my favorite styles of beer. Craft beer is great, but a lot of times you have a pint or two and that's it. You want to have a glass of water or iced tea after that. I like Session Beer. I like a beer you can have four or five pints of it and still function and not be completely bloated because it's really sugary sweet or too hoppy where it's all stuck on your tongue for a few days. A thirst-quenching drinkable lager might work to be our flagship beer to keep on tap at a country club and a restaurant or two in the area. The more medium to long-range goals ties to there definitely being a demand in this area and once we establish a name for ourselves, a brand for ourselves, we can then get into bottling. It might not happen this year or next year, but possibly the year after.

The building we are in is the old boiler house for the county jail that is closed next door. The big chimney that's right outside was for the boiler house. The jail is where Dillinger escaped out of. He carved a gun out of soap, and he got out of one of the windows in the back alley over here. There's a lot of history here. The owners, Tim Walsh and Dave Bryan, are on really good terms with the Historical Society that owns the jail that has been closed since the mid-1950s and they already said, "As little or as much as you need, we can work with you." Once we max out our little 7-bbl system, when all our tanks are full and we are brewing multiple times per week and it's time to expand, we have an opportunity to build a bigger brew house and possibly a bottling line in the old county jail. With the right investors you could do a huge revitalization of the old jail building that would be something else. You could put tables in the cells. Dining in the old jail cells would be a pretty unique concept. Who knows what the future brings on that!

Interview February 17, 2009, at Crown Brewing

Back Road Brewery

Brewery address:
308 Perry Street
LaPorte, IN 46350

Mailing address:
1315 Michigan Ave.
LaPorte, IN 46350
219-362-7623
www.backroadbrewery.com

CHUCK KRCILEK, PRESIDENT

I started brewing as a hobby back in 1990. I had recently graduated from Purdue University, so I had lots of time on my hands. [Laughter] I bought beer kits through the mail and followed the directions that came with them. After a few years of brewing like that, I branched out and started designing my own recipes. By blending my own malt and hops together, total control of color and flavor was achieved.

Homebrewed beer tasted so much better than the thin pale stuff consumed in college. I got to thinking about how I could make more beer. Maybe bigger batches or more fermenters would increase my home production. I drank my share, but I also gave a lot of beer away, probably too much. Sometime in 1995 an idea was starting to form in my mind. Start a small brewery and SELL the beer. The idea was compelling and would not go away. I knew nothing about starting a brewery. Immediately, I started researching on how this could be done. All this sounds pretty corny. It was the start of my brewery endeavors and eventual entry into craft brewing. I started my brewery because it felt like the right thing to do.

Brick Road Brewery was incorporated in August 1996. The name has a very solid and traditional feel to it. It is metaphorically rich and sounds good, too. Bricks are solid and last

a long time. Roads are a way to take you into the future. Think of it as a long lasting path. That is how we got our name. Next, I found a great location in LaPorte, Indiana to house the brewery. It was an old brick warehouse that oozed character and had everything I was looking for. You know, stuff like docks, cement floors, big doors, three phase electric, and a big parking lot. While permits and paperwork were completed and sent in, work inside the building progressed, too. Floor drains had to be cut-in and installed. Lots of plumbing was needed for water and gas. Drywall, painting and all the small detail stuff was completed. The majority of the work was done by family and friends. I contracted some of the work out as well. Most of that was electrical and re-frigeration related. Having never designed a brewery before, I figured on keeping things as simple and straightforward as possible. Common sense can take a person a long way, too. The actual brewing equipment was the last to be installed. All in all, the brewery turned out to be efficient and easy flowing. Our first batch of beer was sold on April 22, 1997. Things were starting to look up, or so I thought.

Misadventures can make you stronger. In August 1997, only one year after organizing, I had to make a big decision. Pay someone else a licensing fee for the use of our company name or change it altogether. I really liked the "Brick" Road Brewery name, and so did James Brickman. James Brickman owned Brick Brewing Company in Ontario, Canada. Jim's lawyers said that the name "Brick," as applied to the brewing industry, is owned by him. Any use of the word in a brewery company name or beer brand would require a licensed agreement and subsequent user fee. Well, needless to say, that was not a good day for me. What was I going to do with all the newly made labels? So I called Jim Brickman and we spoke for nearly thirty minutes. It is amazing what can be accomplished when two people actually communicate. In the end, all got what they wanted. I was able to use the remainder of my label stock and keep our original corporate structure intact. Brickman succeeded in protecting his proprietary "Brick" brand-name. On January 1, 1998, Brick Road Brewery Corporation d.b.a. Back Road Brewery was born. "Back Road" Brewery is now a registered trademark and is exclusively marketed and sold as such. The new name has been beloved ever since.

Back Road Brewery is unique in several ways. First, we are still in business. What I mean is, I've seen a lot of breweries come and go over the years. It can be a tough industry if you're in it just for a quick buck. Making beer is one thing. Anybody can do that. But to make money making beer is another story. What has kept us going is a lot of great customers drinking great beer. Second, we are small enough to turn on a dime. People's palates for beer do change. We are able to offer new beers on a regular basis. Our house beers are consistent, but it is fun to introduce new beers, too. We make over forty-four styles of beer. Our customers know that. That is what they want. Third, there are only three people who work at the brewery (me, myself, and I). We do everything from brewing to bottling to kegging to delivering all our beer with just three people. It makes it easy on payroll, too. Just kidding. There really are three of us.

Our specialties would probably be brewing lagers. Lagers are more time-consuming and require careful attention during fermentation. It can be difficult for a brewery to devote this time and energy to lagers when you are already struggling to get ale production out. Our lagers include Millennium Lager, Maple City Gold, Aviator Doppelbock, and Koza Brada Bock. We have had good luck with a schwarzbier as well.

I think the biggest change in craft brewing has been in the quality of the beer. Quality is way up. Seriously! Indiana breweries are consistently putting out some of the best beer in the country. Indiana can hold its own when it comes to brewing beer. Who says the Midwest is ten years behind the east and west coasts? Other than that, prices are out of control. Everything a brewery needs like energy, water, grain, glass, packaging, kegs, and HOPS have skyrocketed in the last year. In my eighteen years of brewing, I have never seen anything like this. I think just about everyone in the industry has had to raise prices at least 10 to 15 percent since November 2007. The good news is that our customers are smart. They see what is going on, and they know why the prices have gone up. They are still buying the beer. As long as the beer is high quality, they will pay the price. As far as the brewery is concerned, we try to operate as smoothly and efficiently as possible.

As for the BIG [Brewers of Indiana Guild] Microbrewers Festival, the biggest change is increased attendance. More people want good beer. They are attracted to festivals that are well organized and have great Indiana beer! BIG Microbrewers Festival has really come a long way. It is a great festival.

Email interview August 21, 2008

Three Floyds Brewing Company

9750 Indiana Parkway
Munster, IN 46321
219-922-4425
www.3floyds.com

TRAVIS FASANO, STAFF

I have never worked in a brewery prior to working at Three Floyds Brewing in Munster, Indiana. I got into the craft beer industry through a close friend, the typical "tired of drinking tasteless beers and wanting a higher standard." My friend worked for a small liquor store, and he would bring home barley wines, pale ales, and IPAs. After this discovery of beer, we began homebrewing. Homebrewing consumed my whole mind. I obsessed over reading, researching, and wanting to create crazy beers of extreme calibers. After college I found Three Floyds, and on Fridays after work

a few friends and I would head up there for a few beers and pick up a six-pack or growler. The place captivated me for some odd reason. I asked the brewers lots of questions and simply loved walking around and analyzing all the tanks and pallets of grain. I always said to my friends, "I would love to someday work in a brewery."

Five or so years went by, until my first Darklord Day in Munster. Thousands of people lined up to buy the Russian Imperial Stout, including me. We stood in line for hours, drinking beers and meeting new people as we discussed craft beer. I still thought it would be fun to work in a brewery. On our way out the door, I saw the owner of the brewery, Nick Floyd. I said hello and thanked him for making awesome beer and inspiring a homebrewing beer geek like myself. I also mentioned to him I wasn't happy in my current career choice and that I would do anything in the brewery if there was a position open. He chuckled and said, "Seriously, bring your resume in on Monday."

I figured I had nothing to lose and mailed my resume in. A few days later I got a call. Three Floyds needed someone to make boxes, help on the bottling line, and load trucks. The rest is history, and now almost two years later I am still there and still in love with my job. After years of college and graduate school, I've found my passion, and it resides in a brewery. One could witness a day in the life of Travis at Three Floyds and call it busy, maybe chaotic. But each day is enjoyable and composed. My fellow employees took me, a psychology graduate student with zero brewery experience, and taught me the operations of a brewery. I learn things every day and am thankful to be in such a well respected brewery. For once in

my life, I can honestly say I love my job, and I take pleasure in going to work each day.

Despite our current economy and the rising costs of packaging and raw materials, my job continues to flourish, and I am thankful for that. The brewing industry is a large family. Competition exists; however, there is a strong connection between brewers sharing in a skilled craft and having a high regard of respect for other breweries and brewers.

Phone and email interview February 18, 2009

Brickworks Brewing Company

327 Main Street
Hobart, IN 46342
219-942-BEER [2337]
www.brickworksbrewing.com

THOMAS D. COSTER JR., OWNER
AND BREWMASTER

My passion for beer began, or came to an abrupt halt I should say, when I was a child. One summer day when I was about 10, I opened the fridge to get something to drink, and there it was . . . a full pitcher of crisp, cold, sparkling apple juice. Being a slob, as most little boys are, I grabbed that pitcher and began to chug its contents.

Whoops. It wasn't apple juice.

My stomach hurt, and I was going to die. "Who would do that to the apple juice?" My father had a good laugh at my expense, for it was the last of a keg from the night before that was being saved in that pitcher. "You people DRINK this stuff . . . and LIKE it?"

Anybody who knew me well when I was young knew how I scolded the adults of the family at cookouts and gatherings. "You're killing your brain cells! You're killing your brain cells!" I remember how they would laugh when I told them that I would never, ever drink a single drop of alcohol. When I turned 21, my sister Cathy convinced me to drink beer at the taverns; otherwise, she said, I would go broke drinking all of those fruity little drinks with the straws. But they tasted so sweet, like JUICE, one might say.

I hated beer. I absolutely HATED it. But at $1.50 a bottle versus $4.00 for a fruit cocktail foo-foo drink, I chose economics over quality or taste. I drank beer for almost a year and a half and tried all of the big brands, but they all tasted the same. I could not understand it, a multibillion dollar per year industry, and this is what they were selling. I simply could not wrap my head around it. I thought that maybe it was just me; that my taste buds just didn't care for beer. Then when I was about 21 ½, I was driving to meet a few buddies of mine at a little bar called Pass Times in Valparaiso to have a few drinks when I heard a radio ad for Samuel Adams Boston Lager. Just hearing Jim Koch talk about the Hallertau Mittelfruh and Tettnang Tettnanger hops, the selected malts, and the rich flavor and color made me very, very curious. But my expectations were low; after all, it was still beer. So upon meeting my friends and placing our drink orders, I decided to opt for a Samuel Adams to quell the curiosity and to reaffirm that beer was not good. The beer came, and my friends were joking that I was going to drink this stuff that none of us had ever tried or heard of before. I could immediately smell the difference coming from the bottle, and I was a little nervous about trying it. "It can't be any worse than any other beer I've tried," I thought. I cannot tell you how wrong I was. This was most definitely different! It had flavor, aroma, mouthfeel . . . but did I like it? I don't know. This was new to me! I tried another.

So this is what beer was supposed to taste like. Before Prohibition drove all but the most tenacious of breweries out of business, this is what beer, real beer, was supposed to taste like. Forget the writings of the philosophers Plato, Aristotle and Socrates, forget Sir Isaac Newton and his discovery of gravity . . . and that Einstein fellow, who needs that Theory of Relativity nonsense . . . I discovered BEER! Not for mankind, of course, but for ME!

With new eyes and new palate, I began trying all of these so-called "microbrews," discovering new tastes, aromas, and gastronomical consequences. I found out that there was a brewery in Chicago by the name of Goose Island, and I went there and enjoyed beers directly from the source. I could not believe it, but I liked beer. I LOVED BEER! The passion for good beer grew in a matter of months, and I started visiting more breweries and trying more beers, exotic beers with flavor. They actually sell beer with flavor. Did you know that?

Then I thought, "I want to try to make my own." By then my wife, Nancy, was in the picture, and I tried to instill into her my passion for beer, that I want to brew my own and someday I want to open my own brewery! How nice for Nancy. It was so cute that she had a man who had himself a little dream or fantasy that he wanted to chase . . . it was so sweet . . . now shut up and get ready, you're going to be late for work.

Like most brewers, I began in my home. There is nothing like opening up one of those pre-made beer kits with their bags of malt extract and packets of dry yeast! My wife and I brewed several batches in rapid succession, and we quickly moved from all-extract to all-grain recipes. Not long after that, we were milling our own malt and developing our own recipes. Nancy is a chemist, so I like to refer to her as the "science" behind our beer, with me being the "art" behind it. We make a pretty good team.

Soon our homebrewing equipment became more elaborate. New vessels were purchased along with new instrumentation, and we began to refine our process. I still have fond memories of that copper wort-chilling coil that I simply could not wait to get home and try out. Our brewing reference library grew along with our recipe database. Many brewers from the local brewpubs around Chicago were more than happy to discuss the brewing process, to demonstrate how things worked with their commercial equipment. They freely gave me terrific advice. I was very surprised to find that the process of how I brewed at home was not much different on larger-scale equipment.

Eventually I entered a homebrewing competition. The category: India Pale Ale. Being a hop-head, I went about developing an India Pale that was over 100 IBUs . . . a real toe-curler! It ended up placing fourth in the competition, and I could not be happier. Then there was the time I brewed a batch of my dunkelweizen. Up to this point I had never had any major "problems" with my beers. I would normally keep back a portion of the unfermented wort for this recipe and use it as my priming agent before bottling. I must have measured the amount wrong for this particular fateful brew. Everything went smoothly. The beer aged well, and into the beer fridge it went. About two days later, the beer fridge shorted out and I had to unplug it. As I was upstairs on the telephone talking to someone about repairing it, I heard a "pop." What the heck was that? Then I heard it again. Then another . . . and another. Within a few seconds it sounded as if an M60 machine gun was being fired in my basement. I frantically rushed downstairs to a most dreadful sight. There stood my beer fridge, door wide open with glass and beer everywhere. It seems there was a little carbonation problem with the beer as it warmed up in a fridge that was not maintaining a cold temperature. The first few exploding bottles caused a chain reaction that blew the fridge door open, spraying my office with shattered glass and beer. It was a sad, sad day . . . even more so that my wife told me that it was my mess and I would be cleaning it up alone.

A disappointment to be sure, but it was enough to make me stop and think about my dream of a brewery. Of course, other homebrewers assured me that it has happened to the best of them. But the dream lived on; sometimes it was in a coma, but it was still alive. At every job I held after that, I would keep daydreaming of the day I would walk away, start my brewery, and be successful. But dreams have no calories, and you can't live off of them unless you do something about it. The road was a long one and a hard one with many ups and downs, roadblocks, frustrations, and detours. It took me several years to finally compile all of my research into a business plan complete with a three-year financial pro forma. Now I find it hard to believe that after almost fourteen years of chasing a fantasy . . . a dream, it is all coming true. Even more so, that this dream started out as nothing more than a few ideas and hopes on some scratch paper, coming from a man who absolutely hated beer when he turned 21.

I decided that my hometown of Hobart was the perfect place to start my brewery. It had a quaint downtown area with a lakefront, and the city was investing substantially in the development and beautification of the area. It was also nestled firmly in an area between the only other local breweries in Michigan City, Crown Point, and Munster; we will just fill in the gap. Anybody that has grown up in Hobart and still lives here could attest that there is an extremely high level of hometown pride. So after I talked with Mike Adams, the executive director of the Hobart Chamber of Commerce, letting him know that I was finally going to make my move and open a brewery, he was ecstatic. Word soon spread, and public enthusiasm for the project was completely off the charts.

We mulled over several locations. The first one was perfect: it had the correct square footage and the right amount of traffic and storefront visibility. I am still unsure how that deal fell apart. Our next location was around the corner, but after money was spent and after months of planning, that location fell through as well. It just seemed like we were not meant to open in Hobart. Thankfully we had the city and the chamber of commerce behind us. Talks were resurrected with the first location, and we signed our lease. The building is at 327 Main Street, the location of the old Hobart Furniture store. We could not be happier with our location. The building was built in 1940 and was a Kroger's grocery store. After Kroger left, it became a pharmacy, then the furniture store. Now it is home to the region's newest brewery. It still has the original tin ceiling tiles, which we are in the process of restoring and painting. The building owner, John Sakes, has been wonderful to work with. He views this as a passing of the torch, as he was my age when he first started his business, and now that he is retired, he wants to see his building thrive in the hands of someone who can bring a unique business to downtown Hobart. We secured our financing through our local MainSource bank and began the final leg of our journey.

We named ourselves Brickworks after the town's past. Hobart was a major brick manufacturer from the 1850s to around 1964, with the brick mills employing a majority of the town's residents. We recently went on an excursion to recover bricks from the site of the old brick mills while cleaning up the lakeshore where they were located. Divers from Aquatics, Inc., aided us by retrieving bricks and artifacts from the lake's murky bottom. Our plan is to clean them up and give them a good home in our brewery, to touch on a bit of that hometown pride. Our brewing system is a 7-bbl stainless direct-fire from Premier Stainless Systems, and it will be arriving in the second week of June 2009. I am a seasonal brewer, so the styles will be changing through the months. My best beer is my dunkelweizen; it is the most popular among my friends, with banana, walnut, and clove overtones. A few of our flagship beers will include Cornerstone— an American-style pale ale; Foundation—an American-style lager; Earle's Extra Special Bitter—named after the town's founder, George Earle, who named Hobart after his brother, Frederick Hobart Earle.

It has been a dream almost fourteen years in the making, and it is surreal that we are almost there. We are looking at an opening date sometime in July 2009.

Special thanks go to my wife, Nancy, and children, Brianna and Tommy, my inner circle of beer geek friends, my investors and lenders, the city of Hobart, my contractors, and everyone that played a part, however minor, in helping to make this dream come true. Also, a warm thank-you to Clay Robinson of Sun King Brewing Company in Indianapolis for his input.

Phone and email interview May 28, 2009

Notes

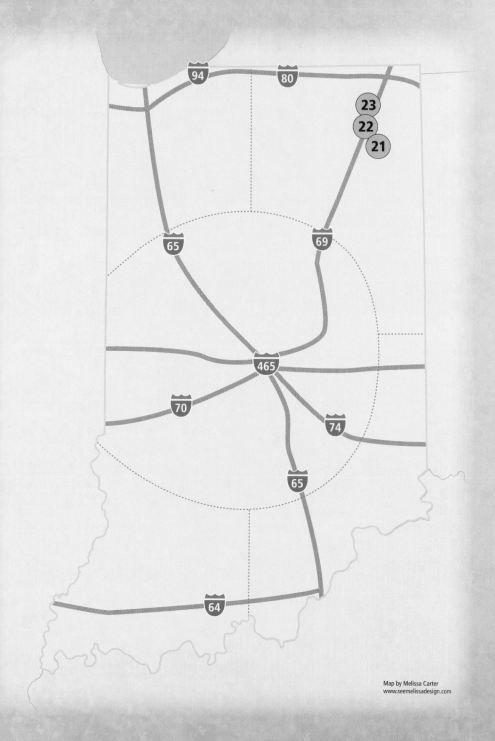

Northeast Indiana

Northeast Indiana Brewpubs & Breweries

Mad Anthony Brewing Company

2002 Broadway
Fort Wayne, IN 46802
260-426-2537
www.madbrew.com

Mad Anthony Taproom
114 North Main Street
Auburn, IN 46706
260-927-0500

Mad Anthony's Lake City Taphouse
113 East Center Street
Warsaw, IN 46580
574-269-2537

Elkhart Beer Garden
526 South Main Street
Elkhart, IN 46514
574-293-5100

BLAINE STUCKEY, PRESIDENT

Mad Anthony opened in 1998. It was the first brewpub in Fort Wayne. Opening extensions at other locations is a great way to share our beer styles that aren't targeted by some of the other craft brewers. We've found a way to send our beer up and have our alehouses out there. There's a long way for Indiana craft beer to go. We hope to see quite a few more breweries open up these next couple of years. We're into promoting this. Our own drive is to open one or two more brewpubs and keep building our distribution inside our state.

As to educating ourselves and our customers, thank goodness my partner, Todd Grantham, and I are able to travel around and sample beers all over the nation and have a passion for great craft beers and seek them out to build that all-time ideal six-pack for you and your buddies to sample all evening. This built the whole idea of opening a brewpub. This happens every day, not just when we opened. We've been in Fort Wayne for ten years and

in Auburn for seven, in Warsaw for three, and we're opening Elkhart in December 2008. We choose historic buildings and renovate them.

Mad Anthony Taproom in Auburn is in the former Blackwell's department store. Mad Anthony's Lake City Tap House in Warsaw is in the former Eagles building and Senger's department store.

When we go into a new community, we fill up samplers for sharing. For people who order lighter beers, it's an opportunity to share what we brew with them. It's not just at the pubs but at all the philanthropic tastings that we are able to see folks and promote not just Mad Anthony but also Lafayette or Brugge craft beers. It's all of us.

We were very fortunate in Fort Wayne to have an existing restaurant that already carried a lot of bottled beers, so the brewpub was a gradual step to craft brews on draught. We slid right into it. It was fantastic. Customers still had their favorites, and we don't want to pull their hands away from their Guinness or Bass or Harp, but we want to introduce them to a lot of great beers produced in Indiana. I love the "Drink Indiana, great beer made here." It's getting that through. It's always an opportunity. Sometimes you're going to find people who are not going to change their minds, and so you don't get upset about that. You just move on to the next person. We don't want to force anything on them; we want to share. If they like it, that's great.

When we first started, we had to wait to see if we were going to make it. The last brewery in town was Falstaff. At Mad Anthony it was going to be very different from what they brewed. They closed in 1990. Falstaff is said to be the first to legally brew beer after Prohibition. So we had to win the customers over. To be honest, we had a lot of supporters immediately. It

did well, and at the end of that first year [1999] we won the silver medal at the Great American Beer Festival for the Auburn Lager, and that really put some merit to our brewing company and opened people's eyes—"Hey, these guys know what they're doing."

I've been on the craft brew bandwagon, going to all of the events, having a good time, and even if I didn't enter beer in the competition, we'd still go and support our fellow brewers. Indiana is so young in this business. So many brewers in other states are so much larger than we are. We see this when we go out of state to events. It inspires us to know that things are going to go in the right direction. We are going to have little setbacks, but it will be all right.

Good beer and good food in the brewpub has grown over the years. It is something we

have learned as owners, and we still need to maintain that goal to make sure our customers are satisfied with the style of beer we are pairing with food here and with our friends who carry our beer in their restaurants. I had a great time in Bloomington talking with the folks at Max's, who serve my pale ale there, and the Farm, who are putting my lager on draught. We just set ourselves up for another event next year for Slow Food all raised on the Farm. I can't wait to do more of those.

With the internet and all the promotion you get from the fantastic *Midwest Brewing News*, along with the Brewers Association, everybody shares getting the word out. That's what I love. Everybody can share ideas, what works and what doesn't. At a Brewers of Indiana Guild annual meeting, we had a discussion about distribution. We were making decisions based on what's going on now. But you can't say, "Yeah, that's OK," because you have to make decisions on what's going to grow the business. You have to allow individual brewers to make their own decisions on what's best for them, not be forced into a specific pattern by legislation.

I myself don't want to go so far out of my state to go to California with my beer. But if someone from out of town comes over, say, from Oregon or Colorado or Washington, and they buy my beer to take home, that's the kick. We feel proud when someone from all these places with a fantastic history of brewing craft beer says, "You guys are doing the right thing." That's really neat. For them to order a shirt or a growler, and all of a sudden one of their friends who does business in the area is supposed to pick something up for them, it's a kick. We get a lot of that.

The best way to bring people to any of our sites is word-of-mouth and tastings, and those are normally charitable. Every month is something different. We do Cystic Fibrosis, Paws and Claws for the ASPCA Animal Shelters, Toys for Tots, Phoenix Theatre in Indianapolis—I can't even remember them all, they are all over Indiana. That's how we reach all those areas. Kendallville is fifteen miles from my closest brewpub, so we sell our beer in the local package and grocery stores. I find philanthropy much more effective, not that there's anything wrong with putting an ad in papers. But we can offer a sample of beer to someone and see the expression on their face and say, "OK, did you like that? Now try this," and they say, "Oh, that's more my style" or "I liked the first one better." I take them all the way to Imperial IPAs and dry stouts, oatmeal stouts,

very different beers, so this gives them a broad understanding of all the beers we make. "We don't just make this one beer you first tasted. There are perhaps fifty different beers we make annually, so come out and try them."

I'm looking forward to pubs and restaurants all over Indiana recognizing that they can carry Indiana craft beer and introduce it to their customers. That is going to do a lot for our whole state. I've been working with folks in demographics to learn where we can target markets. For places we [Mad Anthony] open, we find spots with a little bit of history and do the renovation. We like being in an eclectic area like this that has great seafood down the street, a great Italian restaurant, a classic steak house, and then our brewpub joining them. There is a push here in Fort Wayne to mirror Broadway, to be something like Broad Ripple in Indianapolis. People who used to live here come into our places and share their memories and their stories.

Jeff Neels joined us a year after we opened, so Todd and I were the partners prior to opening. We were always drinking different beers. We were doing the same thing that all enthusiasts do, grabbing an Anchor Steam or a Nevada. Anything we could get our hands on to try different beers. Right now we want to be diverse like that, to offer a full-flavored lager, to an amber lager, to a hopped-up ale, to a dark ale, to a bourbon barrel aged Imperial porter that's in the barrel right now. That's the anniversary ale that will come out in April 2009. Just to be able to grow and do the things everyone else is brewing and learn from our brewers all over the United States to keep people engaged, keep them happy that there's always something new coming out. But we have people who like what's been here from the opening. A gentleman just ordered a T-shirt and a mug club shirt that has his favorite beer on the back, customized. They want their mug club number on the front, and the back says, "I like to fill my mug with (their choice beer). He said to list Plumb Stout. I said, "We haven't made Plumb Stout in two and a half years." He said, "Yeah, I know." We're always busy doing fun stuff. We have to bring back old classics like Big Daddy Brown, which is on tap right now, and Oatmeal Stout, which we started our brewing on. Jeff is still running the restaurant operations. It's been a great partnership for ten years. We all have our positions and things we need to focus on, but we all work together on many different things and lean on each other to get those things done. There's not just one deciding voice. When it comes to an opportunity for opening an alehouse, I lean on the guys if they like the idea and what they think of it. It makes financial sense. We are all on the same page for what we are looking for. Todd basically has fantastic recipes, and he brews great styles, and if there's something unique I might say, "Can we brew this or that?" It's fun to do that. We bottle only our five flagship styles: Gabby Blonde Lager, Auburn Lager, Ol' Woody Pale Ale, IPA, and Old Fort Porter.

We increased our staff, getting ready for Elkhart to open. We do all our brewing here in Fort Wayne. It might be cool to have a small brewery in each of our locations sometime, just like McMullen [in England]. They have all the little ale houses all over, and they brew in each one of them. I think that's neat. Todd does an awesome job and knows the personalities he is looking for in an assistant brewer. We've got a handful of brewers who work well together. Some of our Indiana brewers go to work elsewhere and take our reputation with them, and that's not bad, and then maybe they'll come back and open their own brewpub or brewery like Ted Miller did. He traveled abroad, and then he came back with his experience, and look what he brought back to Indiana. It's fantastic. Same thing with our friend in northwest Indiana, Sam Strupeck, who opened his brewery, Shoreline Brewery and Restaurant. They are all great folks. We try to make as much time as possible to get together, but we get caught up in our own business so much, it's hard to get together. That's why the Brewers of Indiana Guild having two events annually will help keep that chain of communication going.

We started out with just Todd and me in the brewery attached to this restaurant, and we'd come out and watch people drink our beer. A group of three gentlemen owned the restaurant and then sold it to us a year later, and that's when Jeff got involved. So it was three guys working in one pub, and so we said, "Hey, we've got some energy. Let's do this again but keep the brewery here." That makes sense. And then we said, "Hey, opening in Auburn was great. Let's do it again in Warsaw. It's exciting, and there's a need for it. Maybe down the way there will be a brewery opening in Warsaw or Elkhart or Auburn. I'd love to see another brewery down the street here on Broadway. It's better for everyone the more excitement we can get.

Interview November 1, 2008, at Mad Anthony Brewing Company in Fort Wayne

Warbird Brewing Company

DAVID HOLMES, OWNER/
FOUNDER/BREWER

Warbird ceased operation October 2009.

The Warbird Beer Show started out as a joke. The fellows who were here in this building for four or five years had a business where they basically used radio technology for special venues like air shows. They live in Fort Wayne and know a lot about technology. Their idea was to develop a content-specific radio station like in the old days when radio served a community. If it were Marion, Indiana, the DJ would talk about everything going on in the community. Modern radio has gotten away from that. They don't have anyone teaching them, so these guys are creating their own path for content-specific radio for aviation. Instead of your community being Marion, Indiana, your community is in airplanes. So this station is called Flight Line Internet Radio Network, and you're listening to a radio broadcast right now. They play music; they have shows.

I jokingly said to them, "I'd make a great talk show radio host because I'm a psychiatrist and a pilot and I own a brewery, so if they got depressed I could talk about Prozac, flying a plane, or drinking good beer." And they said, "That sounds pretty good." [Laughter] So we did a dummy show, and they liked it, so we started doing them. We record them live, and they get a little bit of editing, since we're not exactly pros yet. But it will go on at five o'clock this afternoon and will broadcast worldwide. We added almost 18,000 listeners in the last six weeks worldwide, and 50 percent of them are regulars. Ten percent are what we call addicts: they listen constantly. So it's gone from a joke to a real program. We talk about beer sometimes, but mostly it's the fact that I make beer that gives it some kitsch. We talk pilot stuff, aviation stuff. If you've ever heard "Click and Clack" on NPR, we have that kind of banter. It's just fun. The great thing is I invited my friend Greg Muir to do it with me because he was my backseater when I flew in the T-6, and he is just a fun guy to be with, and we can talk with each other and have a great time, and I think that really comes through on the show because we have a lot of people emailing us now. They love the show, they love the banter, and they listen to us in the office now. We started this whole thing in September 2008, and we were their first produced show. They're helping us do stuff we don't know how to do. Of course, we know how to do stuff they don't know how to do, like joke around. [Laughter] You can get all broadcast information on our website, www.WarbirdBeerShow.com. I go by the name "Sidney" because that was my call sign in the military. Greg goes by his call sign, "Scratch."

Warbird started in 2004. We won a gold at the Indiana State Fair Brewers' Cup for our T-6 Red Ale in 2005. The medal for the Shanty Irish-Style Ale was this year [2008], so we actually have two gold medals. We forgot about the contest for 2006, so the Warbird guys just pulled bottles off the shelves and the beer wasn't exactly new. You can't put your best foot forward if it's been out there in the trade for a while. We had a lot of comments that it was a good beer, but it had a little bit of trade damage, which is just code for it's been sitting in the sunlight or it's been warm for a length of time.

People ask about our name. "What's a Warbird?" A Warbird is a retired military aircraft. Some people mistakenly believe we somehow

promote war. Actually we honor the people who have served so we can live in a free country and have that kind of discussion.

Our company actually started in my home. I was a homebrewer. After many years of making beer at home, I finally made a batch of beer for my wife, who wasn't a big beer drinker. I made the T-6 Red Ale for her. It was a light-bodied, easy to drink red ale, and she said, "We can sell this." So nine years later we have a company. We named it the T-6 after the first Warbird I ever owned and flew. I owned one for twelve years. We name all of our beers after airplanes. It's not a marketing idea. It's something we do and love. We think of an airplane, and then we make a beer for it.

The only label we've done for a person's individual aircraft is the Shanty Irish. That happened when the owner of J. K. Donald's Irish Pub here in Fort Wayne came to me at the end of a tour of the brewery and said, "What will it take to get you to make me a house ale?" I said, "You probably will have to buy a batch." He said, "What will it taste like?" I said, "It will taste good." I described it and said, "I always wanted to make a beer called Shanty Irish."

He said, "What's a Shanty Irish?" I said, "Well, Shanty Irish is actually the name of a guy's airplane. He was the son of an Irish immigrant. His name is Gilbert O'Brien, and he grew up in a shanty town in Manhattan. When WWII kicked off, he joined the Army and the Army Air Corps, where when you reached a certain level they gave you an airplane. So instead of naming the airplane after his girl-friend or his mom or his wife, he named his airplane Shanty Irish to remind people that's where he came from. He painted a shamrock on it."

The Shanty Irish is our best-selling beer partly because the Rathskeller in Indianapo-lis is selling it on tap. It's their house amber, so they sell many, many kegs of that. Our two leading sellers are the Shanty and the Mustang Gold Ale. Those are big draught sellers for us. In actual volume they are relatively close, but the Shanty is in the lead. For the recipe for Shanty, we said, "Let's add a couple more crystal malts, some extra malts for substance, and use English hops instead of American hops because we want it to be UK-style Irish ale." The recipe formulation is part of the process.

For our packaging, the idea is a unitary theme of all the different beers. Two sides of each six-pack box are identical about Warbird beer and Warbirds and the others are specific to the plane, why it was important, the type of beer named for the plane, and why the beer is made that way.

I started homebrewing when I came back from the Gulf War in fall of 1991. I was a doctor in the Gulf War. I've always been a beer guy; my dad was a beer guy. I grew up in Albuquer-que, New Mexico. Back then, when people heard we could get Coors, that was pretty neat out there in the West. If there is an alcoholic beverage choice, I'll always take beer. My dad and I never drank in bars. When I'd go over to Dad's house, I'd sit and have a beer with him, and now when he comes to visit us, we sit and drink my beer. Isn't that cool?

The T-6, I made at home. The second beer we made was a light red ale with a little crystal malt, to give it some flavor, and German hops. My wife doesn't like beers that have a big after-taste, so our whole beer philosophy is keeping my wife happy. Having an easy finishing beer was important when we started. Then I made a traditional German hefeweizen for the best man at our wedding when I was at home in Las Vegas, and we ended up making that com-mercially for the brewery as the wheat. He was a Thunderbolt pilot, so we ended naming it for Thunderbolt P-47.

The story about our golden ale is that my brewer wanted to make a fancy golden beer, and I wanted to make a simple golden beer. He was more of a whiskey guy, and I was more of a Scotch guy, so I was familiar with whole single malt Scotch story. So I said, "I want to make a single malt beer." He said, "What are you talking about?" I said, "I want to make a beer where we use one malt, one hop, yeast, and water—that's it—and that became the Mustang for people who just appreciate the purity of the process and the flavor of the malt. Some people think it's just a single malt beer and it's not very special, but it's actually quite rare to find single malt beers made with a 100 percent varietal malt. It has taken me a while to get that message out. The Mustang Gold Ale is a single malt beer. We are grandiose enough to call it "America's single malt beer." How's that? [Laughter] We'll see what happens.

On the six-pack we add: "For a special treat, gently pour one part Shanty Irish on top of two parts of Mustang Gold to make one of our in-house brewery favorites, the Fightin' Irish, a lighter version of the un-cut Shanty."

And then we made the pale ale. The pale ale is actually between the Red Ale and the Gold Ale. My brewer and I agreed that we needed to make the credibility beer for the microbrewery. Once again I wanted to have something that is drinkable. We went through several six-packs of pale ale that had credibility, and I ended up saying, "I want this to be as good as Bell's Two Hearted, but I want it to be maltier." Traditionally, American pale ales are overbalanced for the hop. It's like a Ping-Pong ball with a coating of hops, a sort of hollow. I wanted a solid golf ball of malt with

hops around it so it has that substance behind the hop. That's what we did with the Warhawk Pale Ale. We get criticized by professionals; it doesn't meet the style guide because it is too malty, which I accept as a compliment. The finishing hop is Amarillo; a lot of people appreciate that.

As I talk with people about our brewers and who makes the decisions, I'm ultimately going to be the guy who decides what the beer is, no matter who is making it. I'm the guy who decides whether a beer is going to leave the building. Structurally in our company that's our brand. We keep recipes consistent in our individual products. I can show you the book. The idea behind the book is that any competent brewer ought to be able to walk in tomorrow, use our book, and make that beer identical to the last batch. That is something to aspire to. It may not be 100 percent true, even though we keep track of all the important elements— the temperature, the mash, the consistency, the amount of water, the times and temperatures of fermentation. We can taste individual variations between batches because we have extreme sensitivity to them, but in general we have never had anybody come back and say, "That beer was really different," which is good news.

I've been here today thinking about my latest problem, so I'm not sure if I should be talking about this brew. I don't want to make a promise I can't fulfill. I'll give you an expectation. Something dramatically different is coming out of our brewery, but I promise it will still be drinkable. How's that? It's a chemical challenge. We are trying to achieve some chemical things that average small breweries don't try to get. It will be a very popular, easily recognizable beer. Making a beer is not that difficult. It's the rest of it that's difficult. Getting it packaged is the hard part. I can't wait to tell you the story.

The Warbird niche goes beyond Indiana. There's one other aviation beer—in Montana—and they have different types of airplanes, but no one really focuses on the types of airplanes you see at air shows. When I was getting the marketing ideas together, my wife took out a piece of paper, two stamps, and an ink pad, and said, "How does this look?" I said, "Wow, Warbirds and beer, my two favorite things." So I bought the web domain, Warbirdbrewing.com, and I had to build a brewery. Certainly, the appeal is there for people who go to air shows, but we can't compete with Budweiser and Coors. Those guys are sponsoring air shows, and they won't let us serve our beer there. We end up in air shows in different ways. About a month ago [October 2008] some guys came into the Huntington airport in a Torpedo bomber and then came here and asked if they could buy ten cases of beer. So I called Cavalier, our distributor, and I said, "Mat, I don't normally sell beer outside of you, but these guys want ten cases of beer," and Mat said, "For the PR value I'm happy to have you do it." So we loaded up ten cases of beer, and they flew to Terre Haute and sent us pictures of them unloading our beer at the air show. We are appealing to people who really, really appreciate what the airplanes are.

We always want to provide beer to people who don't have to be extreme beer aficionados. If you look at the air show crowd, there's not a big percentage asking for a strong American pale ale or a double IPA. You take an air show with 10,000 people, you might have 100 people who do. I personally want to have a broader appeal with our beers. At air shows, when we show them our Gold Ale, people are just thrilled that it tastes great, clean, and refresh-ing; it's thirst quenching, and it's got an airplane on the bottle. Well, they think that's awesome. The only palate consideration we have is that we want them to be able to enjoy it and not feel like they've hit their mouth with a big slug. For stretching the palate on the credibility side, there's not that many American breweries making traditional hefeweizen. There's a lot of American wheat beers. Many use things to try to Americanize them. We make a pure Bavarian wheat beer. A lot of people in America have never had one. So we are broadening what people perceive to be enjoyable in a pure wheat beer. What I think expands people's palates is appreciation of balance.

From what I have seen since I've been in the craft beer business in the last five years, most people are not looking for more hops. Most are looking for a beer that is more balanced. What we are doing is trying to put balance and quality at the forefront. We're in the minority in the craft beer industry. When you look at what is selling, what beer geeks are looking for are 120 IBUs and higher alcohol and different combinations of hops and hop preparations. Warbird is in the minority of educating people about the value of balanced beers in the craft segment. I don't see a big weedout from hops. We still have ample ground to cover.

If you automatically think craft brewers are supposed to make over-hoppy beers, you are immediately disappointed with our Gold. If you are opening a bottle of Gold and thinking you are getting a whole bunch of hops, you're not. You're getting an exquisitely noble German Hauertau to make that varietal malt, nicely balanced so you can taste the whole thing and just enjoy it. We get a few comments, but not enough to dissuade me. Our growth is still exponential. We're adding a state every two or three months, and that's a lot of volume.

The craft beer distributors that already have beers that are heavily influenced for hops are actually relieved to have a drinkable craft beer. I think there is a need within the market.

Our tastings typically start with a bunch of people showing up at the tap, and guys are very aggressive about, "What can we get, what's different, what's new?" Typically, if they have a girlfriend, the girl looks right at us and says, "What do you have that's light. I'm not really a beer drinker." So we say, "We are happy about that. You are our customer. Come over here." We pour the Red. The Red started our company for a woman who didn't like beer. So the girlfriend tastes it and says, "That's really good." By the end of the show [beer tasting], the guys are bringing their girlfriends to our tap, saying, "Taste this." And then they leave, saying, "This is the best beer of the whole show." Now we've got these women who always showed up because they were on a date but now are excited about craft beer because they don't have to be handcuffed to something that is really hoppy. So I absolutely believe we are serving an important part of the market.

When we get criticism from the really intense craft people that we're not doing complex enough beers, I say we are still serving the market, and we are providing beers that we want to provide. It's not that we can't make more complicated beers, and someday we might, but right now we want to build a reputation that you need never get burned if you buy a six-pack of Warbird.

The Warhawk, wonderfully balanced 45 IBUs, 7.2 percent alcohol, just a nice American pale ale, gets bad reviews if you go according to style because it is a little malty. Our T-6 Red Ale, because it is generally perceived as an American amber, doesn't have enough hops. We know, and we typically don't care if we get

awards. The award comes when the customer lays down $8.50 or $9 on the counter. That's what my focus is. I didn't get into this to get awards. I got into it because my wife said, "We can sell this."

This is a way to share our beer in areas that were not targeted by some of the other craft brewers.

Interview November 1, 2008, at Warbird Brewing Company

Granite City Food & Brewery

3909 Coldwater Road
Fort Wayne, IN 46805
260-471-3030
www.gcfb.com

JOSH GALLOF, MANAGING PARTNER

There is no full-time brewer on site.

We have five fermentation vessels here at the restaurant. We do the fermentation, but we do not begin the brewing process here. The essential brewing is at Ellsworth, Iowa, for all twenty-five of our restaurants across the Midwest. What we are doing is having the ingredients go through the mash tun at the brewery. No fermentation has happened yet. Once we get it here, we begin the fermentation process in these vessels. We add the yeast and take the readings every day to the point where we want to stop the fermentation process and are at the point where we are able to finish the beer inside the cooler here, and then send the beer directly to the bar. We patented this process. It is called "Fermentus Interruptus." We have nine years left on that patent. We can't believe that nobody had ever thought of doing that before us, but it is so much less expensive to do it this way, and the product is absolutely amazing. With the India Pale Ale we do a dry hopping process.

We don't adjust our beers to local tastes, but we have seasonal beers. Every couple of months we have a different seasonal brew. We just finished our Oktoberfest and finished it in under two weeks—a 350-gallon batch. It is our most popular seasonal beer. Right now we are expecting a delivery of Scottish ale, which we will serve in December for however long that lasts. We'll receive it in ten days, and then it takes eighteen days or so to finish the fermentation, so it should be ready to serve by the end of the month. There is no tweaking by the brewer here. Everything is set to recipe. The process has been refined, perfected. As long as we follow this, we are going to end up with a great product. Locally, we can certainly follow our standard operating procedures.

We started in 1999 in St. Cloud, Minnesota. St. Cloud was known as "the Granite City," so that is how we got our name. I don't know the specifics for picking Fort Wayne as our first city in Indiana. We choose secondary markets over major metropolitan cities. We are already a public company, so our goal was to show Wall Street that we were able to secure secondary markets so in the future we can go for primary markets. In Indiana we are open in South Bend and Mishawaka and moving into Fishers and Carmel.

I was moved here from California to take over this Fort Wayne operation. Here in Fort Wayne we've enrolled more members in our mug club than in any other Granite City location. We coordinate our mug club parties with tappings, and we have a day-by-day mug club calendar every week.

We support different charity events. We don't do any advertising, so we rely on community events to be able to get our word out and have people try our product. Many people don't know who we are, where we are, or what we do, so that's a great opportunity to spread our word.

We are members of the Brewers of Indiana Guild. We're not officially connected with the local homebrew club, but individual members are interested in our process, so we are able to tour them through our brewery from start to finish. Fort Wayne definitely is a city that loves its beer.

We don't advertise because we feel that execution on a daily basis is so important to us that the service, the food, and the ambiance are going to stand on their own. While advertising can be beneficial for certain markets and certain businesses, we feel we do such a good job of taking care of people when they come in here that we feel they will want to go out and share with others the experience they had here.

We narrow our focus on four brands of beer plus the seasonals we do every couple of months. By doing that we concentrate on our success story. We don't bottle, but we do fill growlers. Our Northern Light Lager is our best-selling beer. It appeals the most to our people because it is a very broad kind of thing. Not many people are familiar with what a bock is. Some people may know stout for Guinness. Our other three beers have a very distinct flavor, whereas they'll say, "Oh, the Northern Light Lager is very similar to something I've already had."

The Duke of Wellington, which is our India pale ale, happens to do very well here compared with some of our other markets. An IPA is a very distinct flavor. It's more hoppy; we dry hop. We also have a two-pull by request by our guests, so it's half Northern Light and half Mai Bock. There are quite a few different combinations that would be admirable, such as "The Admiral," which is two-thirds Northern Light Lager and one-third IPA. There are several combinations that our guests seem to like. We do a sample platter with all our different beers that people can try to find out which beers suit them the best.

Anyone in the restaurant business will tell you that people are our finest asset. It's difficult to find them and difficult to retain them once you find them. We go through a very intense hiring and training process; several interviews, assessment checks, and questionnaires to be sure the people we are hiring are guest driven and understand they are really responsible for people coming back. Once people are hired, they go through a week of classroom training that covers everything from computer usage to our menu, our services, and our beer. They have to know our brewing process so they can talk to our guests about it and really know how to sell it.

We want to have information on every table to help describe what we do here. We are very proud of our beer process and how each complements our food menu. We want to give everybody the opportunity to see for themselves. People are very hands-on. If you are able to look at the process in your own time and try to understand it, it makes a difference. With each of our beers we go through what kind of style, the different malts and hops that are used, gravity, the color, the body, the flavor, and of course the alcohol by volume, ABV. The brew guide goes through all four brews and the two-pulls, our seasonal beers and the intended

tapping dates for them, and the mug club parties in conjunction with tappings.

On our menu we do have suggestions for each one of our beers. What we recommend goes very well with each beer in the same way that you can do it with wine. Because our beer is a unique flavor, each can go with certain dishes. We definitely recommend to a guest the full Granite City experience.

For the restaurant, we get all of our produce from local vendors in each one of our restaurants across the country, and we have a relationship within each particular city. Some of our other items are through a national company that we have contract prices for because we spend so much money on food we have to have a company that meets our standards but also can supply us companywide. So it's a little bit of both, local and national purchasing.

The founders of Granite City have a beer background and are beer fans. Several worked for a company called Champps. They don't have a brewery, but they have an extensive beer menu.

Every week we update our volume of sales and coordinate that with deliveries to ensure we are never out of a beer, based on the length of time needed to ferment. Our beer is kept fresh and rotated. It's a complicated process, but it works. The brewery at Ellsworth, Iowa, has been around for as long as we have been around. I know that they have to expand beyond the brewery in Toledo, so we may have to open one in Ohio or Pennsylvania. We are looking at Pennsylvania and Ohio for additional markets. We are looking at Texas, Oklahoma, Kentucky, and Tennessee.

Interview November 1, 2008, at Granite City Food and Brewery, Fort Wayne

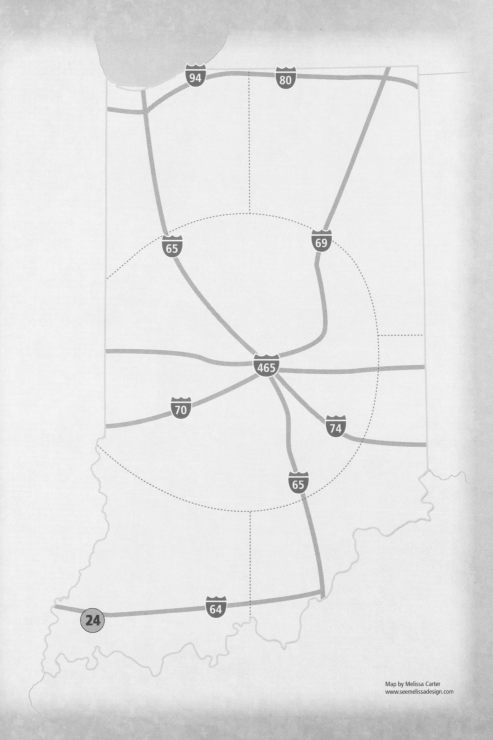

Southwest Indiana

Southwest Indiana Brewpubs & Breweries

Turoni's Pizzeria & Brewery

412 North Main Street
Evansville, IN 47711
812-424-9871
www.turonis.com

Turoni's FOR-GET-ME-NOT-INN
4 North Weinbach Avenue
Evansville, IN 47711

Under construction: a new site in
Newburgh, Indiana

JACK FREY, HEAD BREWER

COREY FISHER, ASSISTANT BREWER

JACK The brewery opened in 1996. The whole inspiration for opening this brewpub was from McGuire's in Florida. The owner has a small fortune in Evansville beer advertising stuff as décor on the walls. They sponsor a lot of sports. Judy and Jerry Turner are the owners. Judy is Don Mattingly's sister; you know he used to play for the Yankees.

We have a 7-bbl net system. Jerry Turner is the founder. His son, Tom Turner, was the first brewer. Eric Watson was the first brewer with a brewing degree. I think we're the only brewery in Indiana with open fermenters. You climb in and scrub 'em out.

I started here in the fall of 2003, when Eric was here; he left in 2004.

Most little breweries like this, this is what you see. It's all manual. We have a mash paddle and a shovel. We do have a mill right above us, in the granary upstairs. When they opened, they didn't have the mill, and they just got pre-ground grain, but they had the mill when I got here. Eric was responsible for helping get the mill. It's a much bigger mill than we need. We can grind grain as fast as we can throw it in there. I brew twice a week.

We inherited all the beer names other than our seasonals. We have changed some recipes a little; it can change from batch to batch just by what hops we get in, what grains we get in. We make some minor changes, but basically they stay. The Moose [Blue Eyed Moose IPA] I changed. It's not a real super IPA. Our customers like malty beers. What's nice about our IPA is you can drink 'em all night long whereas some you have one and you're all puckered up and you don't want to drink anymore. You can drink several of ours, but they don't do well in competition. Judges say they are not hoppy enough. I've changed that recipe probably more than any, but I've gone back to the original recipe because I haven't been able to get the hops that I've had before, so we are back to making it with all Cascade hops. I was using some English Fuggles.

The seasonals are all ours, whatever we come up with. The pumpkin beer was Corey's first recipe. We made it last year, and it sold out real quick, so we made two batches this year, and we made it to the final round of the GABF 2008.

We've got six serving tanks, six conditioning tanks, and four fermenters. We are looking for at least one more fermenter, maybe two. Everything we make is served on tap. We've got six on tap, five regulars and the seasonal. We don't have a bottling line. When we bottle for the competition, we do like the homebrewer does, one bottle at a time, and we hate it. [Laughter] Everything we send to the east side [the second site] is by keg. Keeping inventory is pretty easy. When we've got the serving tanks full for here, we've got fourteen kegs. Always on tap we've got the Honey Blonde Ale, an English-style ale, Vinny's Light Lager, an all-malt German-style pilsner, Thunderbolt

The Brewers

Red Ale, which was developed as a German-style altbier, but it's not hoppy enough to be a true altbier. We also have Blue Eyed Moose IPA and Black Light Lager with Indiana wildflower honey.

This calendar has all of our records of what we've done for a year. I couldn't live without this calendar. It's easy with color-coding for every beer. I also list all the festivals and all that kind of stuff we are going to. I just got an email that on December 11 a local jewelry store is having a men's night and they want us to come and serve beer. I'm planning to go, but I don't know all the details. I don't know if they want us to donate the beer or they're going to buy it, if they want us to serve it, or if they're

getting a license. I don't know how it's all going to work out yet.

The last annual festival we have is "Spirit of New Harmony" on the Saturday after Thanksgiving. It's very small; sort of a local party that the public is invited to, but not too many people go to. It's progressive. They start in the Athenaeum with wine for an hour or so, and then they come to the double log cabin with no heat or electricity—I got chilled until we built a fire last year, and until they lit the candles in the chandeliers, the only light I had was from the fireplace. Last year one side of the cabin was beer and the other side had a classical guitarist. From there they went to some other property in historic New Harmony and had cider and mead, and then I think they ended up in the Granary.

The local homebrewers were all up there. Historic New Harmony is part of the University of Southern Indiana now. They don't advertise much. They've done it for five, ten years, and I'd never heard of it. The only reason I heard about it last year was because Chris Norrick, who is in the homebrew club [Ohio Valley Homebrewers Association], works for USI, and somebody with Historic New Harmony knew he was a homebrewer and asked if they would like to get involved, and that got us involved. I don't think they had beer before. I think it was just wine. At the Granary, they have a cash bar with all sorts of alcoholic beverages.

They lost their cider guy, so they want the homebrewers to supply cider. The homebrewers this year used an 1815 cider press to make cider, and it was real good fresh. But once we fermented it, the iron from the cider press came out. It's got a real iron kind of taste. So I don't think any of us has any cider fit to drink. I haven't tasted mine for a while. I'm hoping I can either spice it or add some fruit extract. I don't know if we can ever get the press cleaned out enough to be able to get rid of that iron.

When I got here, we filtered 75 percent or more of our beer, and our filter pump went out. By the time we got that fixed, it was several weeks, and we realized we didn't really have to filter. Every one of those tanks has a sampler valve. We'll pour some every day, and when we're ready to put it on, we'll pour a sample and we'll decide if it's clear enough. If it is, we don't filter it. The only one currently up there that's filtered is the Vinny's. There's a little plate filter that we use. It's not a sterile filtration; it just gets rid of most of the yeast. Yesterday we

emptied one conditioning vessel, and today we emptied four.

Rudolph's Revenge is our Christmas beer. What we had left over is aging in the barrel. We put it in about a week ago. It's a Belgian strong ale. It's about 9 percent alcohol. We had a smoked porter that we put in the barrel, and we got to the final round of the GABF with that one, too. We entered it last year, and we got to the final round with it one year old, and this year it was one year older, and we got to the final round, and it's all gone now, so we cleaned the barrel to age the Christmas ale.

COREY We've got some bottles left of the barrel-aged smoked porter.

JACK I forgot about those. We can bottle-age them another year, but we don't have enough to send to GABF again. What's funny, at the Indiana State Fair, they hated it. One judge didn't even sign; he just put down numbers. But I knew it was a better beer than that, so I sent it out to Denver. It's subjective. We've never gone up to Chicago [for the barrel-aged competition].

From a business perspective, it doesn't make sense for us to go to Denver, but it's for education. Hanging out with Corey, when I think it's time to go to bed, he's ready to go out drinking! [Laughter] He comes back from Denver charged up, and I come back tired.

I've got some hops planted out here by the light pole. The guys that come around to cut grass take weed whackers and whack them down so they get only two feet high. It's only the second year that I've had them, and I haven't gotten any pellets at all. Then in the summer, somebody took the middle of the plant out over the weekend. There weren't any cones on them, so what were they after? I need to cut them to the ground before it freezes hard. I've planted them at home, but I don't water them enough at home. My aunt out by Huntingburg died a year ago, and we're about to settle that estate, so I'll have one-seventh of four-fifths of the family farm. But my question about hops is how much specialty equipment you need unless you're going to do it all by hand. If you get it too big, you probably can't get it all by hand. There's been some discussion about growing hops. There's a couple from Illinois by Vincennes and another guy that wants to try several acres of hops. Corey took one Cascade hops home this year, and usually they don't produce any cones at all, but for the first year he got a lot of pellets off it, but if you open them up, they don't have much of the yellowish powder that you're actually after. There wasn't much in there, but he had cones.

The "Brewski Tray" is actually a little ski—unusual for a tasting tray. We give five plus the seasonal off the tray. They serve it by color, but actually the Honey Blonde Ale should come first in the taste order. The Light Lager is a little bit lighter in color, but it's got a substantial hop. It's supposed to be a German pilsner, but I'm using Argentine Cascade. I happen to like the flavor of it with the Argentine Cascade, but it knocks it out of the German pilsner category.

Since we're the little guy that never had any contracts, the only thing I could get at the beginning of the year was Argentine Cascades. It didn't work in the Honey Blonde Ale. It had enough of a hop bite for the Honey that it changed it, but the Honey drinkers drank it and didn't complain too much.

We applied for the Samuel Adams gift, but we didn't get any. When they announced it would be a drawing, I knew there would be more requests than what they were giving away. I get some Cascade hops from brewer-ies in Alaska and Modesta, California. I had a decent supply, and when I talked to our supplier about getting a contract before the shortage, they said, "We're only renewing existing contracts." So all they had was Argentine Cascades when I called. It works for us. But since then I've been able to get some German Select, some German Traditional, and some of the other hops we normally use anyway. I needed around 300 to 350 pounds of hops. I bought over 500 last year. From talking to people this year, it doesn't look quite as bad, but I'm not real sure how it is this year.

For us, more malty beers work out. Blue Eyed Moose is by far our hoppiest beer. The last time I entered it in the Indiana State Fair it was a batch that I had dry-hopped in Fuggles. It was an all-Fuggles batch. A couple of years ago at GABF, I won 44 pounds of Fuggles [an excellent aroma hop that's a traditional ale hop]. Fuggles is what I used with Cascade, but since I had so much Fuggles I made a couple of batches all-Fuggles. I dry-hopped with Fuggles. I actually got a 41 average score at the State Fair, but I didn't win.

The Honey is our biggest seller. We'll go through a seven-barrel batch of Honey in a week to ten days, the Red in about three weeks for a batch, and the rest are more like a month to six weeks. Eric thought that a dry stout drinker would drink a sweet stout if that was all that was offered but that sweet stout drinkers wouldn't drink a dry stout. He sweetened up the stout when he got here. I've gone back and dried it out. I happen to like a dry stout better. I'd go to something else rather than a real sweet stout. One of our big stout drinkers likes it dryer, too, so it's dryer now than when I first started. The year that I was the assistant to Eric, we entered it in the Indiana State Fair as a porter and a stout, and we got a silver medal in both—the same beer. But I've never entered it in the Fair since I've been here because we don't have it on at that time [midsummer].

As a homebrewer, my highest score in competition was for my black lagers, so I brought that on as my first seasonal beer. Stout's really a pretty light beer, but in the summertime people just stop drinking it, so Black Light Lager is our dark beer for the summertime. That's what we got the gold medal for at the State Fair this year. It's the first time I've entered it.

I got into brewing at the right place at the right time. My ex-wife and I, with our neighbors, always had a Fourth of July party with probably 100 or so people. I lived downtown. We had a fireworks show at the river, so it was a pre-fireworks party. We always had a keg of beer. One year my neighbor said, "I've got a video about brewing beer. Next year we'll make our own beer." But we never did. My wife moved out in January 1996, so it was the first year we had a party without her, and we talked about making beer. I had the week off after the Fourth, so I went up to Indianapolis to the Wine Art. I didn't know about Great Fermentations, but got my first ingredient kit from Wine Art there on Keystone and came home and told Tom, "Well, let's make it." We never got together, so I made it myself. He was my taster, but he never did brew with me. After that I brewed all the beer for the Fourth of July party.

I worked for Old National Bank for almost thirty years as a computer programmer, and the last several years I was the technical supporter on the HR payroll system. In 2003 the director of HR finally got the PeopleSoft system, and I saw I was working my way out of a job, because everyone else was working on the new system, and come May they said, "Oh, by the way, the 13th is your last day." I had a trip to Europe planned with my girlfriend for the fall, so I took the summer off, since I had benefits coming in from the bank for being laid off. During that summer I came into Turoni's Main Street Brewery when Eric was brewing. I don't remember helping him; I may have helped him shovel out the mash tun.

I took my trip and got home and thought, now what am I going to do? So I started looking for a job. After thirty years as a programmer, I really didn't want to do that. There was only one brewery that was running here in town, and they had a brewer who had been here awhile, so I didn't think that was an option, but Eric called shortly after I got back in town and said, "I need an assistant." So I came in and helped him part-time. Had Eric not left a year after I got here, I probably would have had to find a real job. Two thousand four was my first time at the GABF, and on the way there Eric told me he was leaving, and then he told the owner's son on the floor of the GABF on Saturday afternoon that he was leaving, so I found out that I would be taking his place.

Corey, my assistant, was a server. Corey is the most experienced employee they have for doing anything. He's worked in the kitchen, he's worked behind the bar, he's worked as a server, he can handle the brewery. If someone doesn't show up out here, they'll call him. "Can you come out and serve? Can you come back and help us make pizzas?" Once they get the third location opened up, we have to make beer for three. We probably aren't going to let him come out as much to help them as he does now.

Once I came here, I took the Siebel Institute Class in Chicago, and I've taken the craft brewers class out in Philadelphia at Vinestadtner.

I'm one of the founding members of the Ohio Valley Homebrewers Association. There was a nice little local beer and wine homebrew shop owned by a couple from Newburgh that might have been open at the time I got into homebrewing, but I didn't know it at the time. It was open for about six years, and they closed it when they split up. When I first met him, he was working here in Evansville at one of the Internet providers, and then he was in Columbus. They were instrumental in trying to start a club in 1997. There were some old-timers who were making stuff with a whole lot of sugar and a little bit of malt in an old crock kind of thing, but most of us were fairly new homebrewers when we got started. We probably started with about ten or so of us. We've probably got about thirty members now. The website has helped a whole lot, but I'll still get people in here who say, "Oh, I homebrew." "Have you heard of the local homebrew club?" "No, I never heard of them." We're not super big.

We've been part of the Southern Indiana Council on Aging Homebrew Festival here in town; two or three years ago they added wine to it, so it's a wine and beer festival now. Without the local homebrewers doing all the manual labor and grunt work, they wouldn't be able to have it. At the art museum there's a social group that raises money for the museum. I think this is their tenth or eleventh year that they've had their beer festival. The local homebrewers serve beer at that. Until about four or five years ago, one of the local distributors that handles Anheuser-Busch products was supplying beer, so they didn't have much in the way of craft beer. It was a beer festival that had no beer except for local homebrewers. Even Turoni's never participated—they never asked Turoni's to participate, so we just started since I've been here. World Class has participated in

the last few years. The homebrewers had some thirty beers on tap.

I usually try to get to the Brewers Guild of Indiana annual meeting, and there's a festival in St. Louis that I've been going for years. It's a nice little festival at Forest Park at Muni Theatre. In St. Louis you can take a drink from a bar and go out on the street with it. We go to the Brew-at-the-Zoo in Louisville. I've gone up to Fort Wayne in the past, but that is so far away to go for us. Mad Anthony's has come down here, but it's far for him to come, too. Warbird has come to our summer Freedom Festival. We have a boat race with an air show. It's been a hydroplane race in the past five years.

We used to make the T-47 here [in Evansville during World War II]. They also had a big shipyard here during the war. My dad was an inspector. We now have an LST. It's one of the few remaining that was built in Pittsburgh, but we made about 160 of them here.

I had no connections with the beer tradition in Evansville until I started brewing. I'm a late bloomer with craft beer.

COREY All this started for me five years ago. I'm twenty-eight now.

JACK It was about four and half years ago, November 2004, when I took over as a brewer

COREY I've been with Turoni's for seven years. I started off as a buser. I started waiting tables after that, working in the kitchen and over in the brewery with Jack. I actually have to be back in an hour and a half to wait on tables tonight. Just working here at Turoni's got me interested in brewing.

JACK When I heard you were interested in coming to work at the brewery, I was happy and I wanted to see how much of a pain you could be! If you ask me how we work together, I'd say I do it all. But if you ask him, he'll say he does it all while I stand around and tell him what to do.

COREY Yeah, he makes appointments like this [oral history interview] so he can sit down at the table or give a brewery tour, and I do it all. [Laughter]

JACK Actually, when I started here with Eric, we had much more defined duties. I was more the cellar man. He did everything up at the brew house to the fermenter, and I took it from the fermenter. But Corey and I do things together. I'm still primary brewer, but he can do everything in the brew house, start to finish, so we do commingle our responsibilities a lot more than Eric and I did. It worked out pretty good. He knows everything. It makes my job easy because he knows what needs to be done. I don't have much supervising to do.

COREY Basically making recipes is my downfall because I didn't do much homebrewing beforehand. The formulation of recipes isn't something I'm real big on.

JACK He's not real experienced at it, and we're working on that. He came up with the pumpkin recipe. I helped him a little, but basically it was all his recipe. He made the recipe, and I helped him get it to our grains. It turned out very well. He's supposed to be thinking about another one. He hasn't come up with something yet. As a homebrewer you get into recipes, and if you decide you want to make a brown recipe, you go online. You don't have to bring it up all by yourself. You can get different examples, and then once you get the examples, you can play around and come up with what you want. You can use Promash, which is what I used as a homebrewer, and for no more than what you pay for it you can come up with a pretty good recipe. It's what Eric used, and when I took over I brought my computer in. You can take it up from five- or ten-gallon batches to seven-barrel batches. He has done some homebrewing since he's been here. Back in the cooler there's a watermelon wine that he's working on.

COREY When I wait on tables at night, a lot of people don't know I'm assistant brewer here, and they'll sit at the table and talk about the beer. So I'll say, "I'm the assistant brewer here," and they're happy to talk to me. "Wow, he's the guy who's actually making the beer." So I learn what they're thinking.

Interview November 18, 2008, at Turoni's Main Street Brewery

Notes

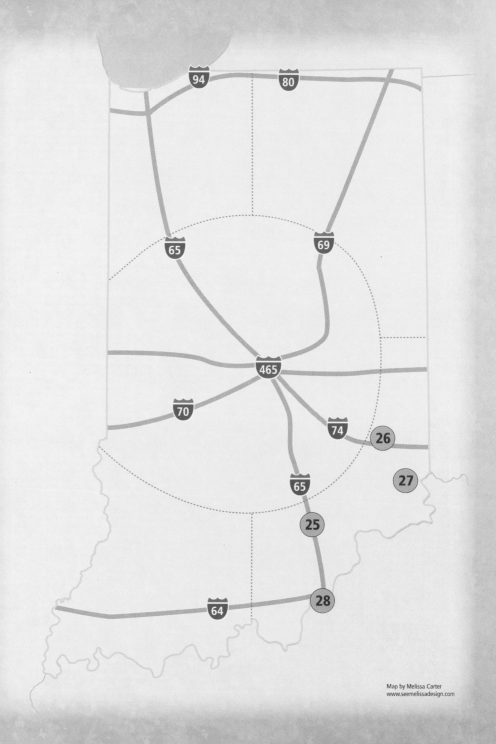

Southeast Indiana

Southeast Indiana Brewpubs & Breweries

Power House
Brewing Company

322 4th Street
Columbus, IN 47201
812-375-8800
www.powerhousebrewingco.com

JON A. MYERS, OWNER/HEAD BREWER

DAVID BAUGHER, ASSISTANT BREWER

JON I think I loved beer from the very beginning. My dad likes to tell the story when I was a baby he'd give me little sips of his Strohs and I seemed to enjoy it. When I turned 21, this was the first bar I came to—the Columbus Bar. They had imported beers that at the time had the reputation of being the better quality, so I've always had an affinity for better quality beer. That would have been around 1994. I'll be 35 in December 2008.

DAVID When I started getting into beer is a story about my dad. My dad grew up in the same house I did. He'd talk about sitting on the porch with his dad and drinking beer and how much better it tasted and how tastes have changed and that started my interest in beer and fermentation and I started homebrewing at an early age and really got into it. I'd say that was about 2001. The first beer I made was really good. The second one didn't turn out too well, but I kept at it. I had a lot of support from my parents and input about the history of beers, how much things have changed, and how much we owe to beer for civilization. I'm a huge history addict in every aspect. I didn't finish college. I realized I wanted to be a brewer. I should have gone to the Siebel Institute, but I was working. When I was 21, my mom gave me a real brewing kit. I'm 25 now. I'm fifth-generation Columbus. My grandma's cousin was one of the first owners of the Columbus Bar.

JON Starting Power House Brewing is a little bit of a long story. I was born in Columbus, and I moved away to go to college, where I started working for Mike DeWeese. He had the BW3 in Muncie. I started working with him there in the kitchen and worked my way up to general manager. At the time he would take his managers from the Muncie store to other stores he was opening. I got to learn a tremendous amount about beers and how to run a restaurant. I went to school in Muncie and was working for Mike and actually lived just two blocks from the Heorot, another wonderful place for beer. So I got a very good education in beer.

Mike was opening other stores, and he opened one in downtown Indianapolis, and I worked at that store after I graduated from Ball State. Then I decided I had enough of the restaurant business. My father had some rental properties when I was growing up. I didn't want to get into the rental properties game, but at this point in my life I started looking into maybe dad had the right idea. He was wanting to get out of it, so he sold about half his properties to another gentleman. I inquired about the other half and moved back to take over those properties. When I moved back to Columbus, I was terribly disappointed in the beer. I had been in places that had an excellent beer selection, and I took it for granted that it was the way things were going, that it was a trend and basically thought that everybody would be on board. It was drastically not true. So when I moved to Columbus, there was no beer, and I ran across a liquor license that was for sale, and with financial backing from my dad, we started a bar called It's All the Buzz

on the west side of Columbus. The idea was to have a great beer selection with twenty tap lines. I think we had eighty beers all together that we offered. It was a small place. But while I was running the Buzz and bar tending there, I became friends with Doug Memering. He's my business partner here, and we had a similar idea that there's a building here downtown, a senior center that used to be the city power house, and we both had a notion that that would make a good brewpub. So we started meeting to discuss how we might want our brewpub to look and what we might want to do. In the meantime the Buzz wasn't doing very well financially, and my dad found a buyer to purchase the business. It's still open. So I got out of the Buzz. I think about nine months later, Doug and I took over this facility. Since 1939 this building housed the Columbus Bar. Every time I came back from college this is where I would come. Back then it was falling apart. We heard a rumor this place was for sale, and we thought it would be a shame for it to go under, so we decided that we could start brewing small batches here, which is what we are currently doing, and then expand the brewing side at a later date once we got this place operating and sell our beer through this restaurant like brewpubs do only we just have to bring it in from across town [when we expand to brew offsite]. We got possession of the place in March 2005, closed the doors, and started remodeling. We reopened May 31, 2006.

DAVID People still call it the CB.

JON It's Power House Brewing's Columbus Bar. This whole thing was spawned by the idea that the old senior center would make a nice brewpub. The seniors are building a new facility. We're still hoping we can put a brewery in that location. We have the little brewery in the front of this building. It's twenty gallons. It's small and it's easy to overlook it.

Andrew Lewis [Brass Monkey] in Kokomo is smaller, but he actually has out produced us. One thing that's nice about his operation is he gets to focus on beer; somebody else is handling the restaurant. Andrew and I had a conversation at the Microbrewers Brewers Festival in Broad Ripple, and really I'm a restaurant manager who brews part-time. [Sycamore Marketplace closed in fall 2008, and Brass Monkey lost its base of operation.]

That's why we have David here. He helps facilitate that. He'll be a bigger part of that as we expand the business. We'll have to get a separate license for that brewing facility. We'll probably see about transferring this license there, but I'm not sure if we can do that or have to apply for a new one. But even with a new brewery we'll have two, and this will become like a test batch.

I actually tried to get the homebrewers together when we had the Buzz, to get some kind of club going, but to no avail. It didn't seem there were a lot of homebrewers. I don't know if because we're now here it attracted a different quality of patrons because we're a brewery interested in brewing and maybe homebrewing spiked more in Indiana in the last five years and more people are taking up the hobby, but it's worked here getting people together.

DAVID When I worked at Big Red Liquors, I got all kinds of homebrewers who came there who didn't realize they could get decent beers. They didn't know the Buzz existed, and it just kept growing. The Big Red is actually where I met Jon.

JON I miss Big Red.

DAVID It seems a lot of people from Scotland work for Cummins. It's not people who have always actually lived here, have had roots here, but it's a combination of people from somewhere else who were coming into Big Red and looking for good beers.

JON We have a really diverse population here because of Cummins, and because of Camp Atterbury we get a lot of military people who have been stationed overseas.

DAVID There just wasn't a focal point before.

JON Here we've made an effort to market ourselves more broadly as far as our Internet and our email. We've got IndianaBeer.com and all those great websites. We have a lot of people coming here that are passing through Columbus, or they are going to be in Columbus for a short time and have sought us out from our website and other beer-related websites. We get a lot of compliments on our web sites. Actually, it's a pre-packaged deal through Discover, the credit card, that is template-based. With no prior knowledge of web design, we just follow it. We have a pretty creative staff here, and we all meet frequently and discuss what we are going to do. Some of the promos are stuff we've seen other people do. We always have a pint day on a weekday when we feature everything on tap at a discounted price.

The homebrew club is called the Columbus Area Classic Alers [CACA]. There's some dispute about the name, so that might get changed. We wanted to promote homebrewing. As was mentioned at the NUVO Indiana Brewers Roundtable, there's a connection between homebrewers and professional brewers that you really don't have in other areas. So we want to promote beer, we want to educate people, and have homebrewers around you excited about what you are doing and help spread the word.

We just picked a date and hung up flyers saying we're having a meeting.

DAVID We posted them here in the bar.

JON People who just came in from here and there told other people they knew.

DAVID Word of mouth.

JON I'm not sure when the first meeting was.

DAVID It's been almost two years, right? It's when I started second shift, so I wasn't coming for about a year.

JON We don't have officers. We're completely unorganized. That's the biggest complaint about our club. Everybody complains about it, but nobody wants to step up to be an officer of the club. Hopefully we'll get over that hump. We wanted to start it to spread the word and help get people interested in brewing, but I didn't really want the homebrew club to be a division of Power House Brewing Company. We wanted people to make their own club.

Right now we have the single malt challenge. The only rule is you have to make a beer with only one type of malt. The last competition we had [2007] the only rule was it had to have pumpkin in the beer. All the brews have to be here on December 2 at 8:00 PM. That's actually the December homebrew meeting. The judging will be the following Saturday, December 6. To judge, we have Bob Ostrander from IndianaBeer.com. He is our only certified judge. And also judging are Chris Nulting, who is a member of the homebrew club who is not making an entry for this competition, and Brian Snider from Great Fermentations. For the last competition, we had Bob Ostrander as our only certified judge. We used the judging sheets. Bob was instrumental in helping us get that organized. It's a friendly competition. Everybody wanted to make their beers, and everybody wanted to talk about them after they were done. When we're done, we brew the winning beer on our system and sell it here. We're still small batches, we're still homebrew system, so it's not too bad. We ran into a problem with the last recipe [2007] because he used a canned pumpkin in it, and it clogged up the pulls bar. It was still a good beer, but it wasn't the beer that won the competition. We renamed it "Disaster Ale."

Our facility here wasn't affected by the flood [summer 2008]. Unfortunately, David's personal house was affected.

DAVID Our house was flooded, but it didn't affect the hops I planted. This year I planted Nugget and Cascade. My parents just purchased some land in Brown County, and he's offering a small portion of land, so I'm figuring I can plant ten more vines. I'm really looking at doing that next year. My backyard is limited space, so I had to have some of the starter vines growing toward each other. It seemed to work out all right. I think the vines to the north didn't get as much sunlight. I think I can change that around to make it work better. I pretty much did everything by the book. First time out it says it usually takes a year before you actually get a yield, and I got quite a bit off each vine.

JON This last batch, we brewed about half an ounce from David's hops. It's our Diesel Oil Stout. That has emerged as our flagship beer.

DAVID I wish my trellis could have been a little bit taller. It started growing a good 15–16 feet. I really enjoyed doing it. It's definitely something I would pursue gladly. For two vines, harvesting worked pretty well. When it dried, I did the traditional, pulled 'em down by the string, picked 'em off the ground, and peeled 'em off. I just now got back to my house

[October 2008], so I didn't dry the hops as much as I wanted to. It's sort of a cross between having a kilned hop and a fresh hop, so it's the best of both worlds.

JON We don't know how it'll affect the taste of the beer. It's still in the fermenter [October 11, 2008].

DAVID I don't know how much it has been done before; I don't know much about the kilning of hops. I just thought it was nice to have somewhat of a vegetable, green smell to it.

I got downy mildew at the beginning of the planting. The book I had told me how to get rid of it with seaweed and baking soda. It worked. I had to dig up one of the roots and kill it all the way down. I think it came with it. I noticed some stuff on it before I planted. I'm planning on spraying the plants down next year before I plant them.

In general in Indiana for agriculture it would be nice to have crops of hops growing. I'm planning on dividing the roots and donating them to the homebrew club so people can grow them if they want. The frost is actually beneficial to the rootstock somehow. When I got the book, I read that that creates a more hardy hop for next year. I don't know how that works or that it's necessarily correct, but that's what I read.

JON When Big Red closed their store down, it was probably the catalyst for this. David came to work for us. With his extensive beer knowledge and his interest in brewing, we put him to work right away. We had him waiting tables and helping me brew. We've been brewing a little over a year, and we've been learning to brew on this system and how to perfect our operation. We have it down to a science now. We both come in and go right to work and know what to do. The first few months we didn't really know how the equipment worked and, if it didn't work right, how to fix it. David has certainly been instrumental in fixing some of those things and having ideas on how we can make it easier. We can't keep up at all. We run out of beer frequently. David is going to start doing a batch each week to help us keep up. We anticipate opening another facility with a larger brewery, so that will alleviate the problem. We change beers every so often as well as seasonally. On our website there's a section that has our beers we've brewed.

We brewed a common ale and a Scotch ale; a dark wheat beer that David brewed; we brewed an amber and our Working Man Wheat. The Diesel Oil Stout has been the most popular. They've all been popular. There's not any one that people haven't been into. Everybody's been excited about them. One week we'll do a single batch, and one week we'll do a double batch. So we usually do at least three batches. The Working Man Wheat we do more over the summer. There's more of a demand in the summer.

[Power House Brewing Co.'s White River Brown Ale won the bronze medal at the 2007 Indiana State Fair Brewer's Cup.]

We carry other beers on tap, especially other Indiana-brewed beer. It was very intimidating to put our beer up against some of my favorite beers, but the idea of us taking over the Columbus Bar and brewing the small batches here meant we had to have a good beer selection to define ourselves as a beer place.

There are two things we try to do with our beer list. One of them is to support Indiana beers. We have six of them on tap right now. I try to have at least four tap lines dedicated to Indiana beers. I try to get everybody in our Guild on our tap at some point. The other thing we try to do is educate people about beer, so our draft list is designed to have entry-level beers and then get people to stair-step up into different styles. We have a good cross-section of styles, and we teach people about these. There's no domestic or light beers on tap. The closest thing we have is Stella Artois. We try to put a nice pilsner on every once in a while. The idea is that pilsner is a first step for somebody who comes in. If they are used to Budweiser, we get them on the Stella. They've made a step, they've opened their minds, and then maybe we can move them to something else, our common ales, our wheat beers. Luckily, our staff is excited about beer, and part of wanting to work here may be wanting to learn about beer and maybe experience beer, and maybe our enthusiasm about it motivates them to do well. We do meetings where we go over this stair-step strategy. They ask a lot of questions when we put something on. If your staff is excited about a beer that you put on, you have no problem selling it. They'll sell it. They'll tell people about it. If they're not excited, it won't sell.

We have daily luncheon food specials. Unfortunately, for a lot of people, their jobs frown on them having a beer with lunch. We usually have a few beer sales at lunch, like on Saturdays people come in and have a beer with lunch. Our beer sales are definitely evening meals, the after work crowd. We have ten-ounce beers all of the time, and Doug and I have talked about brewing light-level alcohol beers; we were going to call them lunch-box beers, 2–3 percent beers to serve at lunch. I homebrewed a wheat beer once; it was OK. I didn't quite get the flavor. That was the hard part. It didn't have much body. But it was something maybe we could do. We would have to do it a couple of times to get it right.

Well, for our Diesel Oil Stout, which we've been trying to keep consistent it's been hard because we can't get the hops we need. Last year almost every batch of Diesel Oil we made had a different hop line-up. We changed the name to Junk Yard Diesel. We wanted people to understand that it may change from batch to batch, but surprisingly it's been very subtle. Each beer I've had is amazingly distinctive. That beer had so many roasted grains in it that profile dominated. My wife, Robin, was pouring one last week, and it came out of the tap black—black—and she said, "That's a beer with character. It looks like a beer that's been smoking for twenty years." [Laughter]

As you know, there's some redevelopment happening here in downtown Columbus. We have a new hotel a block away from us. There's 500 new jobs coming in across the street; another new office building has opened up around the corner, so we're getting new people downtown all the time. People are coming in and asking what we're making that day, what we're brewing, what's going to be coming up. I hear a lot less of, "Oh, you're making that dark beer again." It's like Paul Edwards said at the NUVO Brewers Roundtable about the Broad Ripple Brew Pub, when after a while people started picking up the nuances of each batch. Their palates had changed. I think we're seeing some of that with our regular customers. They know a lot of the styles, and they can differentiate different brands.

We have a great cook, Nana Wiley, who does a lot of the menu planning. I wrote the first menu we had, and since then she and I and Doug and all the managers have collaborated to improve upon the menu, to improve upon the quality of food, have specials we can offer. This is a small town. We get a lot of

repeat business. The 80-20 rule is a good one in that 80 percent of our business is from 20 percent of the population, so instead of having the one menu with the same stuff all the time, we change the back page each quarter to have seasonal things, and every day we try to have different specials for everybody to get excited about. So we keep a standard menu that has all the old favorites on it, but we spice it up every couple of months. The physical side of our menu has prohibited us from putting too many suggestions for pairing beer with food, but a lot of time with the specials we'll suggest a beer to go with it or the servers will recommend a beer.

DAVID I think for the most part Jon and I have a pretty similar idea of what we would like to make. At home I used to brew creative things, but here there's still a lot of styles I enjoy brewing.

JON We haven't done a lot of David's recipes. David's been working part-time, so we haven't been able to develop them, but I'd like to get more of his. He definitely has a twist on things, like we should use this instead of that, change ingredients a little bit. One of the nice things about our small brewery is that we've been able to tweak our recipes and play with them a little bit. I know once we have a bigger brewery and we're starting to bottle, we're going to be a lot more limited with what we can make, but at the same time I think we'll be able to make a batch of something interesting. Starting out small, I've learned a lot about the brewing business. I've learned a lot about brewing beer. I've learned a lot from David, too. Honestly, if we had started out with the big brewery I think we would have had a lot of trouble. We would have been trying to learn something that was too big for us, and I think

The Brewers

the hop crisis would have got us. We would have been one of the newest breweries without hops, and $100,000 worth of equipment to pay for, and no way to make any beer. In a lot of ways it's been great.

As we grow, we are going to want to brew different styles of beer. I put that on our website, and that's been our guide. When you see the beers we brew they're all unique. The Scotch ale has a smoky, peaty flavor to it that is very present; the Diesel Oil Stout is very black, but it's still a session beer that you can have two of at a sitting. When we went to Evansville for their Wine and Beer Festival we were an extreme beer. We brought Diesel Oil Stout and we were the extreme beer to people in Evansville. It was like, "Whoa, look how black that is."

It was strange having a session beer wind up as the extreme beer. People who tried it seemed to like it. It always does well when we take it to festivals. People who attended the NUVO Brewers Roundtable put us on Beer-Advocate.com. It was the first time any of our beer made it on BeerAdvocate.

We have a lot of community events, especially this summer, that we're involved with. There's some we don't do because we don't have the manpower to do everything. The city wants Fourth Street to become the cultural epicenter; they want more restaurants, so we're a perfect fit downtown. We've had a lot of support—not financial but emotional support. The Columbus Bar is an icon. It's historic, and people come in and look for the seat their grandpa sat in. Guys come in and tell me stories about the beers in the '50s and '60s when they came in here. The hard part is that a lot of people are resistant to the changes we've made in here. It's amazing to me be-cause the place was in such bad shape when we took over, and they don't recognize we took something that was floundering and turned it around. It is frustrating to put so much effort into it and the perception to be so wrong. A customer summed it up perfectly: "People remember the place the way it never was."

DAVID When a place is important to people and you make any changes, they're not going to like it.

JON We have other customers who think it's great.

DAVID What I think is so amazing is that you have your homebrewers and professional brewers and other people who come in who are interested, so anyone you talk with, anyone you brew with, I feel like I'm a teacher and I'm learning. All the brewers are willing to help each other. It's like a brotherhood.

JON I'd like to reiterate something David said. Beer is about people coming together and enjoying life. I think that's really important, and I think that's what fundamentally motivates us. We have what I call the end of the day philosophy, and that is, at the end of the day, to look back and realize that you've made an impact and done good work and you've made a living doing something you enjoy.

We did an exchange with Brass Monkey. We traded them Working Man Wheat for one of their pale ales, which was very exciting. I hope to do more of that. The Brewers Guild is trying to get the brewpubs to carry each other's beers. That's when we dedicate four lines to get as many as we can. My wife, Robin, used to live in Ashville, North Carolina. We go there often. A lot of their local places carry a lot of local brews, and here we're getting up to that; we're starting to get quite a few brewpubs and breweries, so I think it would be nice to give each other that kind of support. There's no place for us to go but up. It would be nice if we could get a logo for Indiana beer.

DAVID When you travel, you're looking for places like that. I think some of the best breweries in the United States are in the Midwest. Indiana has Three Floyds, and Brugge is amazing.

JON In North Carolina, a lot of the breweries are making similar beers, and here all the breweries definitely have their own distinct craft on all their brews.

DAVID For a while, Indiana was a dark spot for beer.

JON That's what motivated us. You couldn't get a decent beer. There was no excuse for it. People were afraid to try it as a business, but we've proved it could work. In a similar vein, we have a smoking ordinance in Columbus, and the argument was that people should be able to make their own decisions. People wanted places to be smoke-free, but all the business owners were afraid to be smoke-free because they looked around their bar and people were smoking. So it either took an ordinance or an entrepreneur to try it. We get a lot of smokers here, and they just step outside. We did a catering one time, and a lady came up to me and said she likes to come to our place for lunch but that she won't come at night because there's always a gang hanging out outside, and she was afraid of that. So I explained that they were just smokers who step outside. So she said "Oh" in a way that I hope gets her unafraid and she'll come. [Laughter]

Interview October 11, 2008, at Power House

JON FISCHER, HOMEBREWER

Jon Fischer of Columbus, Indiana, won the second annual Power House Brewing Company/ Columbus Area Classic Alers Brew Club competition in 2008 with his 6 Row Pale Ale.

Since the challenge was to make a single malt beer, pale malted barley seemed to me to be the obvious choice. But which one? I chose Rahr six-row barley, hoping that it would provide a little more malt character than the usual two-row. True to the pale ale style, I used an English ale yeast and a moderate share of hops. In this case, it was a blend of Willamette and Columbus, giving the beer a great balance of aroma and bitterness. It has a slight cloudiness to it (I don't use any Irish moss or other means to clarify my beer), so it almost looks like a wheat beer. It has an original gravity of about 1.056 and has about 5 percent alcohol.

I'm a 47-year-old average guy. I started homebrewing in 1991, and I got more serious about it in 1999. The love of great beer and a kit that I received as a gift got me into homebrewing. I lived in California, when microbrewing took off in the late 1980s. I was inspired by the great variety of new beers available in stores, bars, and pubs. But the high cost and low availability of my favorite styles drove me to make it myself. My wife and my brother have both been great supporters of my hobby, always willing to pay for my barley and hops and always willing to participate in quality control.

Email interview, fall 2008

The Brewers

LiL' Charlie's Restaurant & Brewery

504 East Pearl Street
Batesville, IN 47006
812-934-6392
www.lilcharlies.com

ADAM ISRAEL, CHEF AND BREWER

Why a brewery in Batesville? Well, Batesville is dominantly a Roman Catholic and German town, so the interest in craft beer is high. Plus we wanted to be the first. The tentative opening date is September 14, 2009. But we will be selling some of our New Beer Varieties at the Oldenburg Firemen's Festival on June 27 and 28 and the Oldenburg Freudenfest on July 17 and 18.

To start out, we are only going to do draughts. We have four staples: Batesville Blonde Pilsner, BullRam Bock, Father Franz's Hefeweizzen, and our Red Ale (which still needs a name). For our grand opening we will also have our Oktoberfest beer. The nondrinkers can still appreciate Unkle Buck's Rootbeer. We will have eight other craft beers on tap, with domestics only in bottles.

It all just started out making small five-gallon homebrew batches, then with the interest of expanding our restaurant, a microbrewery just sounded right.

Well, without any professional schooling in brewing, my sister and brother-in-law [the owners] and I have just had to use trial-and-error, so there have been some letdowns. But as with anything, it is coming along with time. Also being a chef, figuring out the process came a little easier.

I went to school at the Culinary Institute of America in Hyde Park, New York.

As a beginning microbrewer, I don't have too many tales, but the knowledge I have gained (very quickly, I might add) is unbelievable. The brewery is coming along nicely, the bar and new restaurant are looking great, and the new menu is going to complement our beers very well and vice versa. With the warm and cozy atmosphere we are wanting to provide, we are hoping LiL' Charlie's will be the spot to come to enjoy great food and great beer.

LiL' Charlie's is not a chain restaurant. In fact, LiL' Charlie is actually co-owner Tricia Miller, who acquired the nickname from her father's friends (who said she looked just her father, Charlie). As part of the décor, you can find antique farm equipment, including an ox yoke that belonged to Tricia's great-great-great-grandfather, Bernhard Wilhelm Schmidt.

LiL' Charlie's opened in June 1999 and has expanded three times in five years.

Email interview June 5 and 6, 2009

Great Crescent Brewery

327 Second Street
Aurora, IN 47001
812-655-2435
www.gcbeer.com

DAN VALAS, BREWMASTER

brewmaster@gcbeercom

I have been a homebrewer since my wife, Lani, purchased some basic equipment and supplies from a local delicatessen/homebrew store I immediately took to the hobby and began studying the craft.

I had the great good fortune of being able to work in Brussels, Belgium, at the time. This made me even more aware of all the beer styles that were not in the mainstream lager and ales. I decided that entering my beers in amateur competitions would be a way to get feedback from experienced judges. I entered local, regional, and national competitions. I won several awards and got the feedback I was seeking.

I took the feedback and applied it to improving the beers I was creating. I selected a small group of beers as a focus for starting a commercial brewery on a microbrewery scale.

After nearly eighteen years of amateur brewing, Lani and I decided that we would like to start a microbrewery in our community. We have always enjoyed travel and learning about local history. Shortly after moving to Aurora in 1994, we took a tour of one of the Hillforest Mansion. During this tour they explained the history of the Crescent Brewing Company, which was known as the Great Crescent Brewery. This nickname and local connection appealed to us very much, and the idea to build a brewery in the local area was born. It took another fourteen years before we would take

The Brewers

the leap and create our own Great Crescent Brewery.

The first challenge was to find a facility that was available, inexpensive, and suitable. We found a storefront in downtown Aurora and applied for a federal brewers notice and a state brewers permit. We selected recipes that would introduce a broad range of beer styles to the local market.

I attended two courses at Siebel Institute of Technology in Chicago in 2006 and 2007 to gain further knowledge of the brewing process, the chemistry involved, and brewery operations. I also joined professional organizations like the Brewers Association and Master Brewers Association of the Americas. It was during this time that we began to purchase the equipment that would be suitable for an operation of our size—three-barrel capacity. In May 2008 we signed a lease and began to purchase and outfit the facility for brewery operations. We received our federal brewers notice within forty-five days and applied to the state for our

brewers permit, which we received in August 2008.

The Great Crescent Brewery opened for sales on November 15, 2008—just in time for Thanksgiving. We offered three beers at our opening—a blonde ale, British-style mild ale, and an American-style stout. We have expanded our beer offerings to include a Belgian-style witbier, cherry ale, coconut porter, and an India pale ale. We plan to continue expanding the number of beer styles we create.

The greatest part of running a brewery is the opportunity to meet the customers face-to-face and be part of their beer drinking experience. We understand that only a small segment of the beer-drinking population appreciates our craft, and we intend to make sure they have only the best experience with our beers.

Phone and email interview May 7, 2009

New Albanian Brewing Company

812-944-2517

Sportstime Pizzeria
812-944-2577

Rich O's Public House
812-949-2804

3312 Plaza Drive/Grant Line Road
New Albany, IN 47150

NABC Bank Street Brewhouse &
Brasserie
415 Bank Street
New Albany, IN 47150
812-725-9585
www.newalbanian.com

ROGER A. BAYLOR, OWNER

The building that houses the new NABC Bank Street Brewhouse dates to about 1950. It was originally a garage for delivery vehicles from a bakery that was across the alley to the west. The bakery got bought out and for almost thirty years it was known as Rainbow and Day Old Bread Store. In my efforts to familiarize people with this location, I'll say it's on Bank Street, and no one knows; it's across from the Carnegie Center Museum, and no one knows; it's around the corner from this . . . , and no one knows; it's the Day Old Bread Store, and everyone knows what I'm talking about.

It's just a concrete block building, but it was built very, very solid. There's a lot we can potentially do with the building. The fellow we are buying it from is also the contractor who is doing the work. His name is Steve Resch. He's done a lot of renovations downtown. Where we are standing now, there used to be a big garage door at the rear. Originally there was another garage door at the front. That got ripped out years ago. When they had the vehicles, they used to drive them in and out through the building. This was then being used as just a storefront for years and years. What we have it divided into is roughly 40 percent devoted for the front of the house. We completely changed the plans in the last month for a lot of reasons. We now seem to be on track, so we should have this finished by March 2009. Brewing will be in back.

We have a pretty big parking lot for downtown New Albany standards. We'll take up space adjacent to building for walk-in coolers and an outdoor patio. We had to move walk-in coolers outdoors to make room for a bigger kitchen to serve more food than we imagined we were going to. We had a chance to get a chef who is worth having, so we revised everything. We figure we can seat between fifty and sixty. There will be a bar on the south side of the building. We're not going to do serving tanks here. We're going to build the bar around keg boxes. We're going to get a three-way license simply because we have the potential ability to tap into the mechanism of the riverfront development, which is a very handy thing. We can get a three-way for marginally more than beer and wine, so we will have the capability for liquor, if we wish, even though we are not planning on doing it.

There is not much foot traffic going by here, but it is a reviving urban center that does not yet have a critical mass of residency. It's developing; it's coming in. Part of it is based on faith, but I think we have enough things going on here now we might be able to get the walk-in, walk-by. They are going to have to park someplace, then walk between sites. The residential sites they're opening downtown demographically are not the target audience for us. The Carnegie Center we know real well; they're old friends. I think we'll be able to do a lot of things with them. A couple of other es-

tablishments have opened in downtown New Albany, so we want to position ourselves as an entertainment option. I'm a bicyclist, so I have a lot of interest in bicyclists to put us on their path in better weather.

We're adding to our brewing capacity. We are going to continue to run the one we have. One of the reasons is to make more beer and sell it in other places. We want to do outside distribution. The current brewery will continue, and Jared Williamson will stay there. That's where the seasonals and the specialties will come out of, so we should be able to make more different beers because we'll have a small

4 bbl, 8 bbl that is meant for that. This downtown site will be larger, a 15-bbl system, 30-bbl fermenters. It's going to be the distribution system, and Jesse Williams will be down here. We hope to create a whole new product line with the small brewery—small batch specials. There will be no bottling now, but when this downtown site gets up and running, we will look into the canning line. We would like to do big cans, the 750 ml cans that everybody refers to as "holding cans."

The buzz we hear now, especially if you go west, is that cans are preferred. You shouldn't use the word *suddenly* to describe this preference; it's been there all along. I think what changed is that (a) the technology caught up with it, and there is better quality equipment to do it now, and (b) the environment thing, the green thing, has come into thinking. It's not mass thinking yet, but it is more widespread than before. Aluminum cans can always be recycled. You can't say that about a bottle. Bottles can be recycled, but just as easily dropped or thrown away; aluminum gets kept, and that's a good thing. There's no issue about light harming beer in aluminum cans. So there's a lot of good reasons for cans if the equipment is good. We won't have enough room here to store cans, and one thing we didn't calculate is that if we want to get any economy on buying cans, we're looking at a delivery of 30,000, so we'll store them in a warehouse a mile from here. The canning operation itself is not that large, 12 feet by 4–5 feet. The printing is done on the can.

Outside we'll have a storage area for the kegs, the walk-in cooler, and the outdoor seating area. We still have a tentative notion that someday we'll have a rooftop garden, which is going to require a little bit of money to make that happen, so we're not ready for that quite yet. This building is just rock-solid. My contractor thinks you could add two stories on this building. It's an excellent building. It took me a long time to figure that out. I was prowling around downtown New Albany for three years looking for buildings and kept doing the square peg in the round hole by looking for historic buildings. I saw this a couple of times and never thought about it. Then finally, one day, it clicked: "Yeah, this is built for what we want."

We wanted to have something we could open up, to have something on the street at some juncture—by my reckoning in about three more years. The city is amenable to extending the sidewalk out into the street and making more area for serving outdoors. The weather comes at us from the southwest, so we have a little protection on the building side so we can open the front doors and have protection if it rains. That's consciously playing to the new urbanism downtown. We don't have much of that right now. We're on the fringe of comprehension, so we're trying to visibly demonstrate—you see that in Louisville to some extent in a couple of corridors, but it hasn't yet caught on here. We want to be able to open up the front and interact with the environment.

In Indiana we have a few more challenges with ATF laws to make sure we comply with that. But, yeah, we can rope that off and get away with it.

If we do what the business plan says we should do, in about three years we'll be out of space again, but we'll see what happens then.

We decided early on we were going to buy new brewing equipment. Everybody has a different opinion about that. You save money buying old, but it takes a lot of time going out to look at equipment. Buying new, you start out fresh with tech support. Main Source is our regional bank, which fits into the whole notion of shopping locally, which is what we are trying to get across. We think the equipment will be delivered May 1, 2009, and then we'll put it together and be brewing by June. We'll do some initial gatherings for VIPs— government officials, contractors—for a soft opening for a while. This is a totally new experience for us. We originally slowly evolved, and now we're moving real fast. This place adds to Rich O's. Nothing will change there except that I won't be there as often. I have a beer manager now, Mike Bauman. He's one of our longtime employees, and I've trained him to do what I do, maybe not in the exact same way, but that doesn't matter. We have a separate entity form to run this for liability purposes. The new entity is going to run all the brewing operations. We need to do some spiffing up at Rich O's. The overall strategic aim here is to get the new revenue source pumped up and be able to take what we are saving and reinvest it into the business.

In the beginning, there was me in the 1980s traveling around a lot in Europe and learning about beer and reading Michael Jackson's books and deciding that there were a lot of other angles and aspects to it than I had realized.

In 1987, I got back from one of my trips to Europe, and a friend of mine said, "Go check out this new place on Grant Line Road called Sportstime Pizza. You'll like the guy running it." This turned out to be Rich, who had two daughters, Amy and Kate. Amy married me in 1993.

In 1987, what was originally called Rich O's was an aborted plan of Rich's. He wanted to have a barbecue place in the same building. It was kind of strange. It lasted a couple of months. Amy took it over. At this point we were dating, and we began experimenting with the idea of having different beers there; that's where Rich O's came from. We didn't have any microbrews then because there weren't any microbrews, at least not here. So we had mostly imports to begin with. We kept on traveling together. Rich O's Public House took off in 1992 because I started doing it full-time, and we built that into what it is today. I wrote my own job description.

In 2000 or thereabouts, we had a chance to get the brewing system that had been used at Tucker in Salem, Indiana. It had been bought by the Silver Creek Brewing Corporation, which later purchased what was left of Oldenburg. This turned out to be a mistake because trying to absorb what was left of Oldenburg dragged these guys down. So what we ended up with in 2000 was this Elliot Bay Brewing System, formerly of Salem, which then moved to Sellersburg and then shut down when the Silver Creek organization went belly up. We also had the acquaintance of their brewer, Michael Borchers, whose idea all along was to do the brewing at Silver Creek Brewing Operation, but it got out of his hands. In early 1999, they had this building in Sellersburg. The owner was Michael's boss. They had an internet company, a service provider. They outfitted part of the building for the brewery. It was Michael's idea, but these guys were part of the dot com bubble. Michael was helping his friend Jeff run the company, and Michael was bored. Michael wanted to be a brewer. Todd Tucker in Salem, who was in the process of going out after thirty years, called me and asked, "Do you guys want to buy my system? I'm going to quit." I said, "No, but I know someone who might," and I hooked Todd up with Michael. Michael talked his bosses into investing in the brewery. We didn't have any money, or we would have bought it. So they got the equipment, they moved it to Sellersburg, and the guy who had been brewing in Salem abruptly quit. Michael had to do it himself, and it got away from him. His bosses were under the impression that because they knew something about the internet, they knew something about brewing, too. And as we all know, several people thought that, and most of them failed. So Michael got caught in a situation where he couldn't do what he really wanted to do. They said, "We don't want to take any chances. We don't want to do anything different. Do those beers like they were doing them in Salem."

Now you're trading on the equity of the beers in Salem, and that was a mixed bag. Then they decided the only way to go was to get bigger, so they bought Oldenburg, which dragged them down because they couldn't digest it. By 2000 the whole thing was in disarray, and at the end of 2001 everything was coming apart at the seams. They didn't even use the Tucker System once they bought the Oldenburg. So we negotiated that we would get it. We invested money in Silver Creek. We lost the money. They let us have the brewing system for a few bucks, so we put it into storage, and we started making plans to brew with it. The reason for that all along was that no matter how good you are at doing other people's things with their beers and their ideas and their art, if you want to create your own art, you have to do it yourself.

We had been successful with the food. Originally the pizza was Noble Roman's. By this time, Rich was my ex-father-in-law. He divorced himself out of the family in 1994, and I divorced myself out of the family in 2003, right after the brewery got up and running, but we're still partners. In any case, Rich had taken the Noble Roman's template and adapted it. Even that wasn't entirely original. So I had to find my own idea. I did want to create my own stuff. Besides, we had Michael out there, who wanted to be a brewer, and I was of the opinion that if Michael could do what he wanted, he could create good things for as long as he wanted to stay. I knew he wouldn't stay forever. I wanted to show that Michael could have done great things for Silver Creek. One thing led to another.

For the first time, I borrowed money, and we added on to the building and set the equipment up, and Michael started brewing, and here we are now. It was a creative thing with me all along. At some point you want to do

that. The implications of what we had done before and for what we started to do in 2002 with the brewery was something that requires a little bit of explanation. Most brewpubs start as brewpubs. Some start as a restaurant and add a brewing system to it. But I don't think you often see somebody like us that started as a good beer bar in the Belgian sense with the best of everybody's good beer that we could find. We didn't have Budweiser or Miller or anything like that. We were doing only imports and then micros and then decided to start brewing. You don't have to understand too much about this to know this poses a challenge. Seven years after we started, we are still trying to work out what the answers are to those challenges of comparison between what we were already selling and what we were brewing. Not that I didn't think Michael could make good beer. He could. But you avoid the comparison by not brewing the styles you are already selling.

Two things we did first were Community Dark and Beak's Best. We've done the Community Dark for seven years. The rationale for those two beers: with Community Dark we wanted to make a lighter beer, but we didn't want to make a golden beer, because I wanted to have a teaching tool to show that just because a beer is dark doesn't mean it has to be heavy and solid, so the model there was English Mild. Beak's was going to be English influenced (we've changed that a little now). It was to be an ESB that was more affordable because people at that point wanted to drink Fuller's, but if we could make something that was an English bitter that cost less money, it was a good price point difference. So those were two things we did. We also decided we were not going to treat the water. We have super hard water here, so we were going to use the minerals we already have, so we decided in 2001 when Michael and I were plotting all this out to determine which style category is underrepresented that we can buy or that if it's represented meets favorable price points. So we decided to go the English and British route because we can use English ale yeast that's calibrated for harder water; that way we can have that match.

The third we did was the Elector. That was serendipity. It was supposed to be a winter warmer with English yeast. Michael decided to put a lot of American hops in it, and it turned out to be an overhopped red ale, so we decided we liked that. For the most part we tried to do things we otherwise couldn't get.

Jesse Williams came on board in 2005, working with us as a server, and he was interested in the beer. He went to Sullivan University in Louisville in the culinary program. He wanted to do beer. Michael taught him. He wanted to do different things, so we started playing with Anchorstine, a hybrid yeast from California.

For seven years we've been trying to find something different from what we're already selling [imports and microbrews]. And that speaks directly to why we have a certain clientele base, and there's no sense taking that away. With our own brewery, we've done close to about 500 bbl, which is where we've been for the last couple of years. At the same time we sell four kegs of Spatten Lager every week. Our import sales didn't change. It's always been strong, kegs and bottles both. We still have some 200 bottles, 30 Lambics; the Belgian core is what we're renowned for. Because our own beers are going to get overshadowed by the reputation we already have for imports, we've had to aggressively sell our own beers in our own brewpubs to make sure everyone knows it is there. We found that out because

some brewpubs are selling buckets of Miller Lite and forgetting about their own brewery. Customers see the brewing equipment, but they may not know what it means.

About two years ago, we had to do a remarketing of our own beers. What that has done in turn in the Louisville Metro area is to get people there to associate what we are doing with the brewing in addition to what we are doing with the pizza and the outside beers.

We knew what we had to do when we got into this, but we didn't understand all the nooks and crannies and nuances of it. We never intended our beers to take over. I can't really do that. What I have been very good at in my career is to have all the great beers in the world where nobody expects it. The question now is how to grow our brand, and the answer is having a place to do it. In the community here we have a brand already known as Sportstime Pizza, where people have come for twenty years, so a certain segment of the community knows us for the pizza. That's one brand. The second brand we have is for beers from all over the world. Our own beer brand was diminished by those two brands, so we've worked very hard the last two or three years to elevate our beer brand. If we want to elevate that further, we can't do it in that building [Rich O's Public House], and I wouldn't want to do it in that building, because that building does what that building does. That's what we're already renowned for, so why change that brand? If we take these beers and attach them to a different interface downtown, a far more contemporary setting, that's working on that brand and giving that brand someplace to grow. We've gotten positive feedback from consumers when we've gone to festivals in Indianapolis, many of whom know we have a pub and a pizzeria. But lately the younger people just know us for the brewery. Since the self-made beer side grew the most over the past two years, isn't that the one you would want to maximize?

There's already 5,000 places around here making pizza. There's only five breweries in metro Louisville. There's only one brewery in southern Indiana in metro Louisville. You have to travel an hour and a half to get to Aurora. I don't know how long it takes to get to Columbus. And it's about an hour and a half to Evansville. I don't want to conquer the world, but we have the backing to go from 500 bbls every year to 2,000. We're obviously trying to parlay this new urbanism that's creeping into the downtown area here. So is it possible to have two destinations for the same sort of brand? Sharing the beer brand is definitely possible because what we have in downtown New Albany but don't have on Grant Line Road is the urban ambience. My instincts become contrarianism, so this is why the Pub, which people think on the inside looks traditional, is going to end up being by the Beltway in the suburbs, and the Pub that's going to be the brand-new architecture is going to be downtown in the middle of all the historic buildings because that's the way to do it. After all the time I spent looking at historic buildings, I realized that's not what I want to do. I want to have something modern. That's one of the attributes of the NABC brand. What we may end up with from Louisville will be a younger crowd, and the older crowd will be at the Pub. That's my hunch. What John Campbell has been doing a lot of is what he did at the Fringe Festival at the parking lot downtown was very much geared to trying to hit some sort of twenty-something to thirty demographics with the music, the entertainment, the whole ambiance of it that never happens in downtown Louisville, it never happens in downtown New Albany so someone should do it. Now we're taking the classic brand and keeping it out toward the suburbs and doing the new one downtown because contrarianism and serendipity is what works. There's also going to be a winery downtown. How good it will be I don't know, but the people are certainly well intentioned. They'll be in a historic building on Pearl Street. We'll have a winery downtown, a brewery downtown, a couple of nice restaurants, a wedding hall/convention center, and a brand-new YMCA on the waterfront up near the floodwall.

The FOSSILS started in 1990. We call ourselves the homebrewing and beer appreciation club. I didn't know anything about homebrewing, but my cousin, Dennis Barry, had started babbling about homebrewing. A friend of mine, Barrie Ottersbach, had been getting into homebrewing somewhat. I had been traveling and was coming home from Europe, ogling the beers I could get in Europe. Even before I got actively involved in the business, he was willing to indulge me and get some imports in there at what became Rich O's. I had a little experience from the retail end because I worked at a liquor store, package store, in New Albany. It's no longer there; the building's gone. But from 1983, on and off during all the time I traveled, I was working with those guys, called Schoolboys Liquors. I was the expert. I didn't know very much at all, but one door of the cooler was the imports, and it was one of the better selections around. It pales in comparison with what's available today. The reason for FOSSILS [Fermenters of Special Southern Indiana Libations] was this embryonic thing to pool our money together once a month and buy a case or two of beer you couldn't ordinarily afford and start learning

The Brewers

what all this meant. It was before books were coming out, before the internet, but we wanted to start learning. Plus, if everybody liked the beer that week, it would be added to the list at Sportstime and Rich O's, so we would have a base to start building on. We had seven people at the first meeting in September 1990. I don't know what the actual numbers are now, but at one point we had gotten up to 200. It's lower than that now. In 1990, the LAGERS Club [Louisville Area Grain Extract Research Society] had been formed in Louisville, eight or nine months before FOSSILS, because people in Louisville were a little bit further into it.

David Pierce has been at Bluegrass Brewing Company one way or another since 1993. He was the first person we called for homebrewing help because he was famous already for that. I had known Dave when I was in high school; I went to school with his brother, but I lost track of Dave, so we got reacquainted. We got the homebrewing part started. I wasn't really qualified to do the homebrewing, but I could do the appreciation part. We have always functioned both ways, and we have an advantage with FOSSILS because Rich O's has been the headquarters for FOSSILS since it was started. We still meet once a month. My cousin Dennis came up with FOSSILS because in 1990 when he was 40, he thought he was becoming a fossil. Actually it also was a connection to Clarksville with the fossil beds along the Ohio. That's at the Falls of the Ohio. The neighborhood is called Portland, which provided portage in and out of the Falls. There were a whole lot of Native American settlements that turned out to be archaeologically interesting. That's where they would have followed the river for the buffalo trail up to the Knobs. State Street goes up to where the buffalo went—actually, bison. Louisville was the

crossroads for all that. When the locks and dams got built, they were exposing the fossil beds and the trails at different times. Springtime it's overrun, but in the summer and fall they're seen. So it was that and our increasing age.

Michael decided to leave in early 2005 to go to graduate school. He's now an environmental engineer. We started plotting how we were going to replace him. Unbeknownst to me, Jesse Williams had approached Michael because he wanted to try to learn. So Michael surreptitiously trained Jesse for about three weeks before I knew what was going on. I'm running errands and trying to figure out what's happening. I think it's interesting because Michael approached brewing more in the "traditional" way, yet he was a homebrewer. He got into it that way. Jesse had never homebrewed. He had a culinary background, and I think you see that more now in the younger generation. That wasn't something anybody thought about in the '90s. We weren't talking much about food and beer. It wasn't really a coherent ideology the way it is now. Beer and food is a second-generation phenomenon. And Jared Williamson is much the same. Jared knows almost everything there is to do at Grant Line Road: make dough, run the kitchen, wait on tables, serve. We had an assistant brewer when Michael was here and Joey had already gone, so Jared nominated himself to brew. It all worked out pretty well. Jared will now be at the old operation on Grant Line Road, and Jesse will be downtown, and we will hire another person to be downtown. So we'll have three, and we'll have some part-timers going back and forth doing grunt work. Jesse and Jared have complementary skills.

Interesting names for the beers has been part of it, and we have interesting artwork.

Tony Beard is the graphic artist. He has been living in New Zealand. He'll be back at some point in 2009, but through the wonders of the wired planet, he can do the work for us from afar, and we trust him enough. No one has ever looked over Tony's shoulder. It's like what I recall from Elton John and Bernie Taupin saying they never collaborated in the same room; Elton John wrote the music, Taupin wrote the lyrics. We give Tony the basic things—here's the name, and here's what it's supposed to represent.

The names all have a story. Community Dark is named after the biggest park in New Albany, just down the street from us on Grant Line Road. Beak's Best—Beak is the nickname for Don, Denny's older brother, and he's the guy who introduced me to world traveling. His nickname is Beak because of a prominent proboscis. The third beer we made was Elector back in 2000; we brewed on Election Day 2000, and being all good Leftists we were miffed at the 2000 presidential election, so it seemed electors make democracy pointless because the popular vote was overruled. Tony had just developed the whole devil woman theme to go with that. Thunderfoot is in reference to the size of my feet. Hoptimus was Jesse and Jared together on the Transformer thing. If it were my choice, I would have called it Hoptimismus because *optimismus* is German for "optimism," thus *h-optimism*. If you can have a pun that goes more than one way, you're better off. Mt. Lee is supposed to be the California Common Anchor Steam [style] Light Beer. Tony named it after the mountain in Los Angeles where the Hollywood sign is. Of course, Tony didn't know that California Common is San Francisco, but we said, "What the hell," and left it. Hoosier Daddy was Jared's idea. It's a hoppy cream red ale, creamy crimson. Elsa

and Malcolm and Jasmine were the brewers' best friend series for the names of their dogs. Elsa Von Horizon is imperial pilsner, Jasmine the Mastiff is sweet stout, and Malcolm's Old Setters Ale is an old ale—all determined by the disposition of the dogs.

We had a lot of fun with Bob's Old 15–B. The FOSSILS had had a porter competition each November for years and years. In 2002 we said we would brew the winner of the porter competition, which we did in 2003. (We need to bring that back someday. It's my favorite name—the Black Hand.) Bob Capshew won the following year, and everybody liked it so much we decided to keep doing it. We asked Bob what he wanted to call it. About that time Bob went to Ireland with his wife, and when he came back, he was talking about how much fun he had had in Ireland, and I said let's call it Bob's Craic House Porter, which means atmosphere and conviviality and gemütlichkeit. My idea got overruled, and he wouldn't come up with his own, and we had to release the beer, so I said, "OK, I'll go look to see what the robust porter designation is in the beer judge certification guidelines, and we'll call it that." It was 15–B, so we called it Bob's 15–B, and Tony came up with the airplane fuselage like in World War II with the girl on it. But, at the very same time, unbeknownst to us, they changed the numerical rendering of the styles: now 15–B is Bavarian-style hefeweizen or German hefeweizen. That's where the "old" comes in. It's not an old ale. It's an old number. No one gets it; we have to explain it. It's a shame we couldn't call it Craic House Porter. No one would have gotten that.

I get overruled a lot because what I propose is way too esoteric. Kaiser 2nd Reising is because the building that was torn down to make way for the Holiday Inn Express in the mid-1960s was the site of New Albany's most famous brewery before World War I, called Paul Reising. So the official name of this beer is Kaiser 2nd Reising, which is a return. One of the Brewiana people brought me a label for a pre–World War I Paul Reising Brewery beer, not a pilsner, so we changed that part of it. I think it was a dark lager that was called Kaiser. The fascinating thing to me is that in New Albany, Indiana, in the year 1899, somebody was making a beer called Kaiser with the image of Kaiser Wilhelm II on the label. They went out of business before World War I. We decided to make it a pre–Prohibition pilsner because I didn't want to try to do a German or a Bohemian or a Bavarian or anything like that. I surely don't want to do an American-style in the modern sense. There were built-in problems, because we can't really lager it the way it should be; we can't get the same yeast. If we are making a pre-Prohibition pilsner that has corn in it, that has six-row barley in it, then we are free to create something new. We're going to pretend that what we are doing is the Kaiser pilsner made by Paul Reising in 1899. It's not entirely true that he did make a beer like that, so we were taking some liberties. I saw the film *Frost-Nixon* last night, and

I know liberties were taken with the chronology. I'm taking some artistic license with this. No one remembers. I wanted to be able to tell that story, too, which our customers can get on the website. Most of the servers should know the basics.

You can usually tell which of the labels are mine. Bonfire of the Valkyries is because one of my favorite places to get beer in Germany is Bamberg, which is only an hour away from Bayreuth. Bayreuth is Wagner, Wagner is Valkyries, and *Bonfire of the Vanities* is something different, but it makes sense. So it's a black lager, swartz rauch bier, a smoky beer. Cone Smoker is the first we did.

The building we have downtown is surrounded by two parking lots. Two buildings standing on each of those parking lots were torn down. One was the headquarters of the Women's Christian Temperance Union in New Albany. So we have people in the outdoor seating area consuming beer on the spot that the Carrie Nation sect occupied for fifty years.

Interview January 25, 2009, at the site of the soon-to-be-opened New Albanian extension on the corner of Market and Bank in downtown New Albany

3

The Business

Brewers of Indiana Guild Penn Jensen

Brewers of Indiana Guild

www.brewersofindianaguild.com

PENN JENSEN, EXECUTIVE
DIRECTOR (2008–2009)

While still a graduate student at San Francisco State University, I was invited by the publisher of *Rolling Stone* to edit a start-up environmental magazine. The *Stone* offices were on Third Street across from the Southern Pacific Railroad station. There was a young photographer in town driving a cab, and almost every time he got a fare to the station, he'd come up to the offices looking for work. Since I was the most junior person there, I'd be told, "Talk to this guy." His name was Bill Owens, and we became pals. Later Bill opened a brewpub across the Bay in Hayward called Buffalo Bill's. It was arguably the first brewpub of the modern era in America. That was in '74. He once grew a pumpkin in his backyard and called me up to say, "I'm going to make punk'n ale out of this big punk'n I grew!" Although Bill sold the brand and the brewpub long ago, you can go out today and buy a six-pack of Buffalo Bill's Pumpkin Ale in any major

liquor store. World Class Beverages distributes it.

The beer of choice at that time was Anchor Steam, when we could afford it, and Rainier Ale, fondly known as "green death" for its green bottle and devastating effects. Fritz Maytag of Anchor Brewing was very influential in my college years. He would open up the brewery for us on occasion when we were planning peaceful anti–Vietnam War activities. He'd provide us with beer and bread and cheese. For many of us, it was our only meal. Between Fritz and Bill, I developed an enduring love and respect for craft beer.

Bill Owens and I still work together. We are partners in the American Distilling Institute, itself an offshoot of the craft brewing phenomenon. Craft distilling is a growing movement around the world and nowhere more so than here in the United States. In distilling whiskey, beer is the critical ingredient. In brewing, sugar water obtained from malted barley is called wort; after fermentation it's called beer. In distilling, the beer is called wash, and it's basically a beer without any hops or anything else in it other than grain. A single-malt whiskey is exactly that—fermented barley malt distilled into spirit. Bill also brought *American Brewer* out of its retirement and published it for several years, and off and on I worked with him on the business side of that publication. I believe Blaine Stuckey from Mad Anthony used Bill's business plan for starting a brewpub to formulate his own.

I moved to Bloomington because my wife was finishing her doctoral dissertation and wanted to be near her aging parents. I was reluctant to move at first, but it made sense to be here and to be with them. Besides, one of her selling points was, "You'll love Bloomington; it has a great brewpub!" Indeed, Upland was an oasis, and it was there that I met and befriended the owner, Marc Sattinger. Upland had reached a plateau, a classic "stage one" situation where the choice is either to stop growing or find new financing. So Marc hired me to build a business plan and to help manage the operation. This fit my background as someone who had owned his own companies and had developed several businesses for other people. I also understood the basics of the brewing business, although not at that scale. I was there for three years and was instrumental in making a smooth transition of ownership from Marc Sattinger to Doug Dayhoff. Doug and his team, with head brewer Caleb Staton, now run Upland and are making great beer.

It was essential for me to reach out to Upland's distributors and key accounts to deal with the core issues of distribution, sales, advertising, and promotion. The relationships I made during that time are precious to me. As Upland's representative with the Brewers of Indiana Guild and then as a member of its board of directors, I could see how craft brewing in Indiana was evolving and how the dramatic growth over the previous five years was demanding a more focused approach than what had been working in the past. Given that craft beer growth has been 20–30 percent per year in Indiana, and we're still less than 3 percent of the market, it behooved the Guild to step up and be more of a representative organization for all the brewers in Indiana. Our goals are to expand the Indiana Brewers' Cup, which the Guild now runs, to reach out to all the breweries in the Midwest, and to make Indiana a powerhouse for craft brewing. We've got a lot of support from Pat Berger and the other State Fair people who see in the Brewers of Indiana Guild a potential equal to that of the Indiana Wine Council.

In fact, a key goal of the Brewers of Indiana Guild as I represent it is to achieve parity with Indiana's wineries. For example, the Wine Council is funded by the state, and wineries can sell their products at their wineries on Sundays—which brewers cannot. If wineries can have those benefits and rights, why can't we? Along with that ambition is our resolve to be as professional as we can and to be as good as we can. The Guild represents every commercial brewer in our state. I don't think any other brewing organization can claim that distinction.

The signature public event for the Guild is its annual Microbrew Festival, which benefits the Lymphoma and Leukemia Society. In 2007, we had over 4,200 attendees and completely filled Opti Park in Broad Ripple. We are now planning several new projects that we believe will greatly enhance the profile of Indiana's brewers. The first new project is Winterfest! slated for January 24, 2009. Over time, we believe Winterfest! can be a really big deal, like the Cowboy Poets Festival in Elko, Nevada, held on the last weekend in January, which draws thousands. We're holding Winterfest! in the Champions Pavilion on the Indiana State Fairgrounds—inside with good facilities and food and plenty of parking.

There's a range of things in our decision to launch Winterfest! First off, you want to do something at a time of the year when not much is going on to promote communication and education about craft beer. We're talking about winter beers, so it's not just your lagers and ales but also your darker beers, porters, stouts, and barley wines. It's not all high-gravity beers, although they're obviously an element. It's beers brewed for the wintertime, so we can talk abut that side of the style sheet that isn't always promoted. Second, we want to create something for the weekend before Super Bowl. In 2012 the Super Bowl is going to be here in Indiana. We're going to have an established major event by that weekend. You can be sure there'll be a lot of hoopla all over town! What we are doing is positioning ourselves to capture the high end of the winter sports fever with high-quality Indiana brewed beers and other Hoosier products. The goal is to make it a cultural winter event for the Indiana craft world.

The second major Guild project is the Indiana Brewers' Cup. Anita Johnson of Great Fermentations has been the driving force behind it, but she's now handing it over to the Guild. The Cup is funded by the Indiana State Fair, and the goal is to bring it to the same level of recognition as the Indiana Wine Fair. It makes sense for the Brewers of Indiana Guild as a representative of all the commercial brewers in Indiana to take a major role in this. The ambition of the Brewers' Cup is to reach out to other brewers in the region and make

the awards much more valuable by increasing the level and quality of competition. We want brewers who win a medal to say, "This is really worth something."

The third Guild project is the "Drink Indiana, Great Beer · Made Here" program. On an individual basis, Indiana's brewers are significant contributors to the arts and culture of their local communities. The Drink Indiana program attempts to augment this on two levels. The first level is an ongoing effort to promote Indiana beers in retail outlets and restaurants. The second level is to focus on smaller Indiana communities by sponsoring and supporting specific events in cooperation with local efforts. Local communities are largely ignored by the industrial brewers, but it is in those communities where the brewers live, where they work, and where they provide support to the visual artists, musicians, and other arts people who also work and live there. There is a mini-renaissance of interest in localized arts and cultural, locally grown produce, and so on. There is a concerted effort by many organizations to support the rebirth of small towns by reversing the flow from the mall back into the downtown. That's part of what the Guild wants to build, as well as increasing tourism and creating jobs.

There are many obstacles ahead, and nothing is going to happen overnight. The downturn in the economy is no doubt going to impact craft brewing to a degree, but, as I like to say, lifestyle has a very bad reverse gear. People don't like to go backwards unless they're forced to. They don't want to go back to Budweiser or Bud Light if their preference is for IPA or porter. Price point is going to be significant for people, but I think it's going to be something they are willing to pay because it makes them feel good. It's kind of a growing confidence in their own sense of values and in their own sense of identity. I think the situation we're now entering into the craft world is very much heartened by the election issues we just faced, that there's a sense of intelligence rather than corporate power running things, we hope. [Laughter] I won't go very far with that, but the point is there is a sense of renewed challenge that things are such we can work through it.

I believe strongly that the core Indiana beers, the core midwestern beers are going to stand with the beers of the world. For example, Three Floyds Dark Lord has won some pretty amazing accolades, but it's a very specialized beer. It's not a beer you are going to drink every day, and you're not likely to drink very much of it. A regional competition such as we're planning with the Brewers' Cup brings the Rogues and Dogfish Heads onto the playing field to match against our own high-gravity beers. All of a sudden we've generated a great interest in that category, and we've provided a process for professionally calibrating the true merits of those beers.

I also think it is of real importance that more and more people are beginning to understand and appreciate the wide variety of craft beer styles available to them. Other parts of the country are way ahead of us in this regard. But the curiosity about craft beers is contagious. People have begun to be familiar with what a pale ale is; they recognize what a Weißbier is; they can discern among various IPAs. But then again there's pressure coming from the industrial beer world that seeks to capture the growth in the craft beer market. Time will tell, but I think that the strength of Indiana's brewers will be their ability to hold their price while they maintain their quality and their consistency. But we have no control over barley prices, no control over hops. There are market forces that militate against craft brewers, and we may see a few fall away, but overall we are going to see growth.

I used to resent deeply the clout of the Big Three [Bud, Miller, and Coors] in their attempts to invade the craft category. I don't feel that way as much anymore. For example, until Blue Moon [wheat beer] came along, the premier wheat beer in Indiana was Upland Wheat. But Blue Moon had the advertising and promotional guns. Their pricing was better, and there was nothing we could do about it. I saw that Blue Moon was actually supporting the category, and by supporting the category I mean that most people didn't see Blue Moon as a Coors product and still don't. They see it as craft beer. The point is that if Blue Moon wasn't on tap, they weren't reflexively going to ask for a Coors Light; they were going to ask for another craft beer. I then realized that these guys are really helping us in the long term. They are converting conventional beer drinkers to the craft category. Once you open up people's minds, open the door to a new and wonderful world, guess what? People are going to walk through it and find all these exciting styles of beer.

In that sense, craft brewing possesses a rebellious spirit. It is a step away from factory beer, away from the industrial mega-brews. People regard craft beer as a handmade product, and it is. And that's why we love to do festivals because it's the interaction of the brewer with the person who is actually drinking the beer, and it's the opportunity for the person drinking the beer to interact and share with the brewer. That is an irreplaceable element of the craft culture that cannot be overemphasized. If someone can sample Indiana beer at a festival, they can earn some bragging rights, go back home and say, "I met 'Ale-Leen' [Eileen] Martin, or Jeff Eaton, or Ted Miller, and here, try this and tell me what you think." And everyone sits around and enjoys that beer. It's a matter of the community propagating itself. It's more than just making widget beer to turn a profit.

Nevertheless, branding and distribution are universally serious concerns for our commercial brewers. It's a very delicate process—not going too fast, at the same time not going too slow—you build your capacity in sync with your market. So creating pull is important because you can't push it. Without the marketing bucks to push the brand, you depend on people to ask for it. So how do you get people to ask for it? You get them to taste it, and they say, "I really like that," and then they go to the store and they say, "I really want Barley Island's Majic Porter or Three Floyds' Alpha King," and so on. Taking that further, the customer goes into a tavern or pub and sees Mad Anthony's Auburn Ale on tap and says, "Yeah, I tasted that last summer. I'll have that!" Brand building is cumulative, achieved through innumerable small experiences that ultimately create a pleasurable recognition.

I think the core mission of the Brewers of Indiana Guild is to build Indiana craft beer as a brand and to educate people about what that means. We can achieve that through the media by communicating the quality of the beers and of the brewing process. Our goal is to communicate and educate the public about the excellence of Indiana beer and to build the sense that these are serious professionals committed to serious commercial endeavors. Breweries will be sustained by being focused on what

they do best for what they sell for the best quality, the best amount for the best profit. Maybe they can't be all things for all people. Maybe they won't be the brand that goes all throughout the Midwest or out to the West Coast or even into Europe or on to anywhere else.

Fritz Maytag speaks well to the point of so many authorities complaining about kids drinking and of the tragedies of alcohol abuse. His point is that drinking is not the problem; the problem is that most of us have never been taught how to drink. I come from a family that loved to drink. It was viewed as a pleasure, a gift. The trips into the wine country with my father to visit wineries, meet vintners, and purchase wine are some of my fondest memories. If, on the other hand, drinking consists of knocking back vodka shooters or playing "Beer Pong" or "Sink the Bismarck" until you sink yourself, then, indeed, drinking is a problem. In contradiction to that, a large part of what we are trying to do, a large part of the culture of craft beer, is to communicate the enjoyment of it. Key to that is knowing what you are drinking and why you are drinking it. Cultural separation occurs here because there is a large contingent that doesn't care what they drink and who think beer is a monoculture consisting of four or five brands of essentially the same thing. This has been a deliberate and carefully architected deceit. The cultural segment knocking back ten beers while watching a Colts game tends to be deaf to craft, but you can sit down and drink one or two really good beers and watch a Colts game. That's all you need.

During the early stages of planning Winterfest! I had a conversation with Jim Schembre [owner, World Class Beverages], who rightly cautioned, "You can't say for twenty bucks you get to drink all the beer you want."

Consumption control is our professional obligation. What we are trying to communicate is the enjoyment and the knowledge of what is in your glass. We want people to understand there are these great styles and within those styles there are numerous versions, some of which you will enjoy more than others. You will begin to build a palate. It's building a sense of identity. As they say, if three people taste the same beer, you'll get four opinions about it. Personal identity is part of the culture of craft beer.

Being a guide, being a resource, supporting the great adventure that is brewing and enjoying craft beer, that's what the Brewers of Indiana Guild is all about.

Interview November 16, 2008, at Broad Ripple Brewpub

Indiana State Fair
Andy Klotz

Indiana State Fair

1202 East 38th Street
Indianapolis, IN 46205
www.brewerscup.org
brewerscup@indianastatefair.com

ANDREW L. KLOTZ, PUBLIC
RELATIONS MANAGER

The Brewers' Cup is a successful competition at the Indiana State Fair that began in 1999. Julie Grelle approached the Fair about having a competition, and at the time it saw the success of the wine competition that was going on and it really wanted to do for the brewing industry what that was doing for wineries and wine in Indiana. That was the impetus of the competition. It also involved the Brewers of Indiana Guild. They got the interest, they got the people, they got it off the ground. If I'm not mistaken, Julie may have been involved a year, maybe two, but it was enough to get it off the ground. Then Anita Johnson came in, took it over, and really, really developed it and improved the competition to the point—just to throw out a few numbers—56 brewers entered the first competition with 123 total entries. In 2008 we were up well over 100 brewers and over 800 entries. That's quite a leap in ten years.

As Anita kept growing the competition, Brian Snider, Tom Stilabower, and Matt Maurer became involved. The whole purpose is to emulate the wine competition, which has grown to be the third largest in the country. This beer competition has become a very well respected event that draws a lot of people from the region, and it is focused on the amateur, on the homebrewer. That is really the connection to the State Fair in terms of having an agricultural tie to it. We don't produce a lot of materials, but we do honor the fact that this is an agricultural product, and it is a craft much like quilting or cake decorating or something else that you find at the State Fair. So that is really what we try to do.

The reward, as you know, is having that amateur [best of show] beer brewed and served at the Broad Ripple Brewpub. It's quite an honor, and I know that all the competitors take a lot of pride in this. It has been a great way for brewers to gather, display, and educate the public about Indiana craft beer. The only ironic part about this is that we have a dry fair. That subject has come up a couple of times in recent years, but to my knowledge there are no plans to change our fair. You can't come to the State Fair and taste these beers except on the day of the competition.

One of the reasons the competition hasn't grown even more is because there are a limited number of qualified judges. We are trying to work with the Brewers of Indiana Guild to help get them more people qualified and provide more access and more building space for judging that day. That is the bulk of our tie to the Brewers' Cup competition.

The wine and beer exhibits are located in the Agriculture/Horticulture Building.

The competition is held prior to the State Fair because of the dry rule. Many fairs have beer gardens, and that's fine. But we have tried to emphasize our family atmosphere.

[Regarding an exclusive beer serving contract at Indiana State Fair:] In the 1940s, after Prohibition, as I understand it, they had beers at the Fair, and then it was voted to take beer out of the Fair, but I believe a specific brewer had what we call now "exclusive pouring rights."

Now that Oktoberfest has moved out to the State Fairgrounds, which obviously celebrates and promotes beer as well, I'm hopeful that Winterfest! will be one of those annual events people look forward to and associate a good, enjoyable, entertaining time at the State Fairgrounds with their many other experiences—just like at the Fair that obviously doesn't just revolve around beer, but with the Brewers' Cup competition in particular some people find the Fairgrounds as a destination point—as someplace to go and know that there are a myriad of events that they can enjoy. With Winterfest! and Oktoberfest, which celebrate beer and different types of beer, we are hopeful what will happen is a nice se-

quence of events: the Brewers' Cup in the summertime and then when we move into the fall you've got Oktoberfest and then in the dead of winter you have one more event. So hopefully people put all three on their calendars.

For the agricultural emphasis of the State Fair, it would be ideal if some brewers were self-sustaining with growing the ingredients of beer and could add that element to the competition, which would further underscore how it fits into our mission at the Fair to educate people about agriculture just as we do with so many other exhibits to show people where their food comes from, where their clothing comes from. We want to show them where their beer comes from, and if you can actually grow all of the necessary ingredients in Indiana, that would be perfectly in line with what we are trying to do with the competition.

Since water is the major ingredient of beer, an exhibit about Indiana's water and beer might be an interesting way to show how local water conditions affect brewing decisions.

The wine competition brings more and more wineries from all over, and so it just blossomed. That is what we are starting to see with the Brewers' Cup, because those wines that won are known specifically for winning a medal at the Indiana State Fair Indy International, and they're reported in wine and trade publications all over the world. I get those clips all the time. The Indiana State Fair is a premier competition. The Brewers' Cup is probably on a par with what happened with the wine competition at this stage of that event which had about a twenty-year head start on the Brewers' Cup. What will help is if the brewers themselves, particularly professionals, continue to market that. We have seen that microbreweries that have won awards here are putting it on their menus, they're making displays at the front of their establishment, and they are getting some recognition for that. That is what helps build credibility. It helps enhance your reputation and draws more people. I think that will continue to go on so if we continue to get more and more [entrants and entries] and they continue to spread the message and we get different winners and different celebrated beers from different parts of Indiana, the Midwest, and maybe further out throughout the country, it's just going to grow exactly as the wine competition did.

There are public dollars that go to support the Wine Grape Council, and there is a vested agricultural backing of that industry. We talk about wheat and barley not being very conducive in Indiana, but they sure can grow a lot of different kinds of grapes, and we are seeing more wineries developed as a result of this concerted effort by the Department of Agriculture. If we could grow the products that make beer, this competition would just soar.

It would be a great question for the Department of Agriculture as to whether growing hops would achieve parity with growing grapes in funding. The Indiana wineries will come to the wine tasting and sell cases of their wine at the event to people who are sampling at that party, which is separate from the competition. Right now the public is not a part of the Brewers' Cup. It would have to be separate from the Brewers' Cup. The Wine Competition is an elaborate event with the 3,000 wines that they judge. It's a three-day deal with judges from all over the world. Sure, why couldn't the Brewers' Cup grow into something like that, other than the fact you can't grow all the materials in Indiana and there isn't the subsidized support from the state?

I believe the Wine Competition began in the mid-1970s and turned into the Indiana International in the early 1990s. When Dr. Vine took it over, it grew exponentially. Dr. Richard Vine from Purdue and Purdue folks promote the competition, and of course they now house the Indiana Wine Grapes Council.

Over the years that I have been going to the wine event, these are professionals pouring, and they are very careful about the amount given to any one individual. Food is served, and people are partaking. They are there for the food as much as they are for the wine. It's clear there is some kind of written or unwritten specifics to be followed. I don't think there ever has been an issue of overindulgence. At the wine competition, they can get information about the different wineries, where they are located, what kinds of grapes are used. There is such a direct parallel between growing grapes and making wine, so if we did grow all the elements—more wheat, more barley, hops—that could certainly be part of the story that could be told here. The purpose of the Fair is to educate the public at large about agriculture in Indiana. Way back when, in the 1800s, when the Fair began, that's why people came, to find out who had what kind of machinery, who had what kind of technique, and when things needed to be planted, when they needed to be harvested in order to get the end result in peak condition. That's the whole purpose of the Fair. People came back year after year to find out what innovations had been made. Of course, they couldn't turn on the TV and find out or go to the internet and see where you can go for this information, so the Fair had a very, very specific purpose back in those early times, although as we have become less of an agrarian society, that is still a big part of what we do. Now, instead of people coming to the Fair so they can take that knowledge back to their farm or their home, they are taking it and using it more as general knowledge to be more educated consumers. But there still are a good number of rural families in particular that come and want to see the latest combines with GPS and all kinds of other technologies. So the purpose hasn't changed. It's just different from what it was 150 years ago.

There is no cash award for Brewers' Cup, only a trophy and/or a plaque.

The Brewers' Cup is an example of what can happen when people want to accomplish something. All it took was an idea by one or more people to present to the powers-that-be at the Fair. It got the competition off the ground, and the Brewers of Indiana Guild are taking it upon themselves to grow it and educate people and entice other people. The beauty of the Fair is that it reaches so many people. Hoosiers want to have a nice event or a nice product. If it's done well, if it's done right, then people are going to learn about craft beer. We are very fortunate to enjoy a reputation as one of North America's great agricultural fairs in particular and a great event overall. It's each individual event coming together to make that reputation. As a result the Fair itself is bigger than any one event. If it's working well, people are going to come to the Fair and learn about the Brewers' Cup, and Indiana craft beer will just grow over time. It's a perfect example of what the Fair is for. What's nice about it is that the Brewers' Cup Competition has grown and people have taken on a lot of responsibility in growing it.

Interview December 13, 2008, at 7703 Dartmouth Road, Indianapolis

Kahn's Fine Wine and Spirits
Cari Crowe

Kahn's Fine Wine & Spirits

5341 North Keystone Ave.
Indianapolis, IN 46220
317-251-9463
www.kahnsfinewines.com

CARI CROWE, BEER MANAGER (2008–2009)

I started working for Kahn's in March 2008 as a wine clerk and quickly moved up to being in charge of wine and liquor special orders. Then our beer manager, Cole Vargas, left to go back to school, so they asked me to fill in the position.

I've always been into fine wines, and from that I learned more about beer. I know my wines quite well and still enjoy it. But beer fit well with my personality, especially because I'm a woman. There aren't many women in beer sales. I enjoy the atmosphere. I've never brewed myself, but I've been exploring the process and the range of beers that are out there. You could probably drink a beer every day and never try everything. I find that I really like educating people and showing them there's more than just Sam Adams out there.

When someone walks into the store, I make them feel welcome. Some people come in there just to get a twelve-pack or a case of beer, but there are people who want to see what's new. Striking up a conversation has never been hard for me. I have a customer who knows I've had professional training and have beer knowledge, but he appreciates that I've translated that into speaking with him on his level. He doesn't know all the terms, so I feel my approach is a good way. I don't want to intimidate someone, but I still want to show them I know what I'm talking about.

Usually I ask questions, starting with broad styles and chipping away to specifics, asking whether they've gotten much into craft brewery tastings, if they've had Belgian or German. If they say they don't like beer, I will find one that they'll like. That definitely makes my job worthwhile.

Indiana craft beers sell themselves. The Leinenkugels and Sam Adams—the craftlike but mass-produced beers—I call them transitional beers or bridging beers because they help bring someone who is getting out of the macrobrew scene and into craft beer. Once they get past the macro, finding something that is made in their state, made in their hometown, it's so much easier to sell beer.

In our store, beer samplers usually don't work, but the Indiana beer sampler gives a nice

overview of beers from around the state. It's a great way for people to try things they've never had before and have some of their favorites they've had many times. Samplers sell themselves. The packaging is really nice. World Class Beverages has done a great job putting together their selections to point out the growing number of breweries in Indiana. When you can connect the public to the brewers, that personal connection makes it easy.

We did public tastings every Monday from 5:00 to 7:00 PM that we set up with representatives from the breweries or from our local distributors. Sometimes we've brought in brewers who want to talk about their beers. We get a great turnout for that. It's turned into a little community. They may not buy some-

thing, but they'll bring something to share, for other people to try—something from out of state that we can't get here or that they've homebrewed. It opens up a really nice conversation. I like being connected with the people who buy beer from me; I like being connected with brewers who make the beer I sell; I like being connected with all the reps. They're not just acquaintances; they're friends. I like to sit down and drink beer with them and talk about things other than beer, too. I like the people in the beer scene because they're people who are sensitive. They're not cutthroat. That's why I think I've found my niche in beer. Some people come in every week. I know them on a first-name basis. I know what they like, and I can give them a call and give them a head's up on something special coming out. My philosophy is to spread the wealth so a lot of people can get something special instead of just one or two people buying all of it. I'd rather make a lot of people somewhat happy than just a couple of people ecstatic.

Some things you do by advertising and some by word of mouth. But putting a face with a beer, putting a face with a brewery, gives it more of a personal interaction with the people who are creating. The macrobrew scene is impersonal and relies on advertising. I like our community of customers having a personal relationship with their beer. That is going to help elevate beer to the status those in the craft brew scene want it to be. We want it to be up there with wine. The wineries here in Indiana have a steady upward growth, and craft beer in Indiana is skyrocketing in popularity, especially breweries like Brugge, Three Floyds, and Upland. They want our beers. Our goal is to make our beers accepted by other people and prove that it's as important as wine. Through little things like creating that personal relationship, educating people that you can match beer with food just as you can with wine, you are going to elevate beer sales.

As far as my own aspirations, the doors are pretty open. Kahn's is known for training the future distributors, training the future in the industry. I can't tell you how many people have worked for Kahn's who have gone on to work for distributors and to create their own companies. I definitely want to train to be a beer judge, go through the beer judge certification program beyond being a beer manager at Kahn's, which is an undertaking unto itself. We have over 1,100 beers that I have to know about. I'd like to move into distribution and work for a brewery. If something comes along, I want to go for it.

I would like to see beer get the same level of recognition as wine. I want restaurants to have expansive beer menus. For me, beer is food. It can complement food just as well as wine can; it can be on its own.

I've always had wine or beer around me, so I was a responsible consumer in college. I think that a lot of times what happens is alcohol is so dehumanized or sensationalized by a family, by the media, and so kids want to drink it because it's a bad thing and it's exciting. In other countries, beer or wine is what you drink with meals. In Belgium, they make a beer lower in alcohol, 3 percent, for children. Same thing in Portugal, where they have a wine for children. So taking the sensationalism, taking the dehumanization away from it, being open to educate your children to what it is and not making it into this big thing will lead to more responsible usage. My dad would give me little sips of beer. I'm Catholic, so I tasted wine in church. No one made it out to be this big deal. I don't intend to shelter my own children from alcohol, nor do I intend on making them think it's such a wonderful thing that you want to be drinking all the time. I think this leads to more responsible usage.

Regarding philanthropy, Jim Arnold, the owner of Kahn's, supports Riley Hospital for Children, as do I. I was a Riley baby myself. Any opportunity I get to support them, give back to them, I do.

Fall 2009 Crowe joined Upland's marketing team.

Interview January 14, 2009, at NUVO Newsweekly

Cavalier Distributing Company
Mat Gerdenich

Cavalier Distributing

1650 Wales Ave.
Indianapolis, IN 46218
317-358-1970

MAT GERDENICH, OWNER

We cover the entire state of Indiana to distribute imports and U.S. microbrewery beers to stores, pubs, bars, and restaurants.

We moved into this space three and a half years ago; we went from 5,000 square feet to 16,000 square feet. This is the space BVL Distribution had. They were one of the first craft microbrew distributors. They sold to Monarch, and that's how World Class started. Ironically, we're right back in their space. We've been at it for six and a half years, so it's seven or eight years ago that BVL would have been in here.

IndianaBeer.com is the most efficient place to get information about Indiana beer.

The keg is the greenest package going. Everything about the keg should work for about thirty years. It's refillable and reusable. We pick them up at the brewery, deliver them to the bar, pub, or restaurant, and pick up and return the empties to the brewery. It's a good,

efficient system. All the breweries are moving to the most efficient system for bringing their beer to the customer. It's a matter of being cost-efficient and energy-efficient.

I have to clean out the draught systems every place I deliver, clean out the kegs, keep it all functional. There's actually certification for setting up and maintaining draught systems. The week before the Microbrewers Fest this year, I went up to Rockford, Illinois, to the MicroMatic warehouse and took the certified draught class and really learned a lot. MicroMatic makes the valve you tap into. It's got a long stainless steel tube that dips into the bottom of the keg. MicroMatic probably makes all of the keg valves and the couplers. The whole keg thing is something I had to learn.

Kegs are not universal. There are several systems, and a brewery has to balance out if its stock of kegs is compatible with the draught set up at bars and restaurants and pubs. We've had to make special rigging for our jockey boxes for beer festivals for Mad Anthony's kegs. We had to do something fast for the Phoenix Theatre Brew-Ha-Ha. Jon Simmons worked for us part-time when he was an assistant at Rock Bottom. Jon and I were talking about the problem and saying it would be nice to get a quick connect. So he went to the hardware store and came back with parts. That was a collaboration between Jon and me to get Mad Anthony's kegs to work.

We distribute Warbird and Mad Anthony, both out of Fort Wayne. It's interesting that Berghoff is the second oldest brewery in the United States, next to Yuengling, which is the oldest. Berghoff had a brewery in Fort Wayne that started in 1887. The State Street Grill in Fort Wayne has a nice painting that shows the four breweries that were in Fort Wayne at one time, and Berghoff was one of them.

When the consolidation was going on with BVL, all of the beer I really liked I couldn't get anymore, so I was kind of an angry consumer. I'd go to Kahn's and say, "What do you mean you can't get this beer anymore?" I didn't understand. I thought a bottle or a six-pack was to be on the shelf for me to buy whenever I felt like having it. Like 98 percent of the people out there, I didn't have a clue about all the people, all the energy, all the effort it took to get that six-pack or bottle of beer on the shelf. It's no different for wine or spirits or a regular grocery item for that matter. But all the beer I liked was disappearing from the shelf, and we were getting ready to go to Cincinnati for my wife's family, and I said, "I know what. I'll ask George. He'll know what's going on." George Fisher is my brother-in-law. He started Cavalier in Ohio. He's been at it for sixteen years. When I asked George, his answer was, "Man, if you have any interest in doing anything in Indy, come right in." We were looking pretty seriously at doing it, and at that time my wife was pregnant with our second daughter, and about midway through, we realized the baby had a major heart defect. It turns out she was born with a major heart and liver defect. We've lost track of how many surgeries she's had at the Riley Hospital for Children. So we realized, "This is not the time to start our own business and branch out on our own." So we put it on the back burner for a couple of years. When my daughter turned two, she started taking steps forward, and she started doing better, and the niche was still there to be filled, and so from a family standpoint it made more sense to do this now than two years earlier, so here we are today.

There was an Italian importer who summed up the industry very well: "When it comes to alcohol, the United States is not very united." Because of state laws, Cavalier Distributing in Indiana is an entity unto itself. Cavalier in Ohio is a single entity. We took the name for a working relationship to split pallets and trucking costs. There's also a company in Kentucky that belongs to my brother-in-law and my wife's uncle. We like to say we've got the Tristate area covered. Paperwise, we're three different companies, but we can help each other out. This helps keep costs down, keeps our inventory fresher.

Oddly enough, I got interested in craft beer in college. Normally in your college days you drink whatever is cheap and bad, and I have to admit I did plenty of that as well. My roommate my freshman year was a homebrewer. It was against the rules, but he'd sneak some of his homebrew into the dorm, and he made some really, really good homebrew. And that's how I ended up getting into craft beer. In the late '80s, the beer selection at Big Red Liquors was paltry compared with what it is now, but I'd save some money and I'd pick up some Belgian beer that was out there and would drink one of those. I got out of school in '87, and it seemed right around that time the Broad Ripple Brewpub opened up, so I've been going there since they opened and started getting a bigger appreciation for different styles. By that time I was pretty much hooked and was going to Kahn's buying what was on their shelves. I couldn't even buy all the beers they have at Kahn's right now. I'd like to say I've tried half of them, but it isn't even close to that. But back then I would have tried all that they had and I'd say, "There's nothing new for me to try." It gives you perspective as to how many more offerings there are available now in Indiana.

I've always wanted to do homebrewing, but never got around to it. I figure it's a good thing to do in retirement. Right now there's plenty to choose from.

I don't know how to really describe the growth in Indiana. It's kind of a vertical growth curve. I feel like I'm catching my tail and going along for the ride. Our first five years in business, gross sales doubled every year. This year we're at 30 percent growth. We haven't picked up that many new brands as in years past, but it's a real growth nevertheless.

I try to hire people who are passionate about the category of craft beer. The internet is a wonderful thing for learning and sharing. Kahn's does a really good job about staff knowledge. I'd go there, and we'd all try something new together, and I'd learn about it with them side-by-side. The variety boxes are a good way to learn. Gift boxes in December sell well because it's a great stocking stuffer. What do you give someone who already has everything? Well, if they're into good beer, that's a gift. Or if someone isn't into craft beer, giving a bottle of a good beer sends a subtle message. [Laughter]

The Microbrewers Fest is a great avenue for educating people about craft beer, but most people at this fest already know their stuff. They want to try the unique stuff or a different vintage of brews—stuff they've never tried before. But it's very busy, and you don't get a chance to really talk to people. But the FestiveAle to benefit cystic fibrosis, I'd say 75 percent of the people who come don't know much about beer. They are there to support the cause and to have a good time, and they are eager to learn. You can actually walk somebody down a flight of beers. This is a porter; this is a stout. It's a lot easier to explain the differences while they are tasting it.

There are two sides to benefit tastings. It's a great avenue to have people taste our products. You can't quantify it, but at the end of the day you hope it drives sales. If someone doesn't know that much about beer, take them to a beer festival that supports a good cause. It's a win-win situation. All the beer we bring is donated. At the Microbrewers Fest this year, we took about $6,000 worth of beer that comes out of the warehouse and it's like, "Man, that's a lot of beer." For a small distributing company, that's a huge investment, so I guess that's where our marketing budget is.

Going back to my own daughter, I have always wanted to have a special festival for Riley specifically to help their heart center. Kahn's does the Midwest Cabernet experience, which is a direct benefit to the heart center.

One of my great moments, and it's only touching one person at a time, but this kid comes up, it's his first beer coming into the festival, and he sees what I'm pouring, and he says, "That's my favorite beer." And I wouldn't give it to him, and he was mad. And I said, "I'm glad you like that beer, but you've obviously already had it. Look at all the other beers we have here. Which of these would you like to try?" He was getting angrier, and I said, "You're missing the point here." It was an American micro table, so we had eight different breweries, eight different styles. Well, he ended up tasting them all, and he said, "I really like these four. I don't much care for these four." He didn't make a face. I don't think there was anything he truly didn't like, but it was the beers on the darker side he didn't prefer. So I said, "You like hoppier beer. But don't give up on these. Your palate changes." He made it a point before the festival was over to come back and thank me. It's like the lightbulb went off.

It's really one person at a time.

Interview August 5, 2008, Cavalier Distributing

Afterword

Indiana's craft beer industry and *NUVO News-weekly* are celebrating their twentieth anniversaries in spring 2010, simultaneous with the release of this benchmark book. The first-person stories shared by the brewers and others connected with the craft category represent the same kind of passion for creating a product with enduring value that permeates the staff at NUVO. This book had its genesis with the first Microbrewers Roundtable on March 18, 2008, hosted by the Brewers of Indiana Guild, the Indiana State Fair, and *NUVO Newsweekly*. Since June 5, 2005, NUVO annually has produced a special Indiana craft beer issue, and since 2009 it has run a weekly Beer Buzz column on its food page, replacing sporadic weekly coverage.

Running throughout this collaboration has been the mission of both the Brewers of Indiana Guild and NUVO to inspire our patrons and readers individually and collectively toward responsible consumerism, civic engagement, and philanthropy. Both organizations aspire to enhance quality of life and the life of the mind. Handcrafted beer certainly preceded the printed newspaper, yet both originated to serve the immediate community with localized ingredients/issues and events, and while both are best served fresh, they equally have a tradition of lagering/archiving for the long view. Craft beer and newspapers are traditionally connected with consumer input and conversation. Together they represent our roots in Athenian democracy and in the earliest foundation of the United States as well as of the state of Indiana.

The stories in this book illustrate continuity, interconnectedness, and civic concern. They illuminate constant change grounded in a love of tradition. They involve us in all aspects of the craft beer industry. They inspire us with their dedication to restoring buildings, invigorating neighborhoods, and undertaking sustainable practices.

As you reach the close of this book, celebrate with me the legacy of home-based individuals doing what they love and loving what they do for the collective good.

Here's to craft brewed beer and hometown newspapers.

Kevin McKinney
Editor and Publisher
NUVO Newsweekly

Interviewees

David Baugher

Roger A. Baylor

Kwang Casey

Omar Castrellon

Greg Christmas

Dave Colt

Thomas D. Coster Jr.

Cari Crowe

Joan Easley

Jeff Eaton

Paul S. Edwards

Greg Emig

Aaron Evilsizor

Travis Fasano

Frank Felicé

Jon Fischer

Corey Fisher

John E. Frey III

Josh Gallof

Mat Gerdenich

Mark M. Havens

David Holmes

Adam Israel

Gerald Jackomis

Penn Jensen

Anita Johnson

Chris Johnson

Scott Johnson

Scott P. Kinney

Andrew L. Klotz

Charles Krcilek

Jon Lang

Liz Laughlin

Andrew Lewis

Carrie Lewis

Tony Macklin

Eileen Martin

Kevin Matalucci

James E. Matt Jr.

Steve Mazylewski

Jeff Mease

Ted Miller

Jon A. Myers

Brian Pickerell

Clay Robinson

Floyd Rosenbaum

Michael S. Rowe

Robert Sassano

Mark P. Schiess

Tom Schmidt

James Shembre

Belinda Short

Jon Simmons

Ronald E. Smith

Caleb Staton

Sam Strupeck

Blaine Stuckey

Jerry Sutherlin

Linda A. Swihart

John Templet

Daniel Valas

Thomas W. Walbank V

Micah Weichert

Index

Rita T. Kohn

Craft beer is Rita Kohn's beat at *NUVO Newsweekly,* where her weekly "Beer Buzz" (http://nuvo.net/dining/article/beer-buzz) appears along with her reviews of the arts. Her other books with Indiana University Press include *Always a People: Oral Histories of Contemporary Woodland Indians* and *Long Journey Home: Oral Histories of Contemporary Delaware Indians.* Kohn is co-producer of the Emmy award–winning WFYI Public Television documentary *Long Journey Home: The Delawares of Indiana.* Her stage plays have been produced nationwide.

Kris Arnold

Photographs by Kris Arnold appear in *NUVO Newsweekly's* print and web editions. Over the past four years he has created a photographic catalog of New Orleans on the anniversary of Hurricane Katrina. He currently is with the Indianapolis Museum of Art.

This book was designed by Jamison Cockerham and set in type by Tony Brewer at Indiana University Press and printed by Four Colour Imports. The sponsoring editor was Linda Oblack, the assistant sponsoring editor was Peter Froehlich, and the project editor was Brian Herrmann.

The text face is Arno Pro, designed by Robert Slimbach, and the display faces are Clarendon, designed by Robert Besley, and Script MT, designed by William Schraubstadter. All are issued by Adobe Systems.